THE THREE TRILLION DOLLAR WAR

ALSO BY LINDA J. BILMES

The People Factor (with W. Scott Gould)

ALSO BY JOSEPH E. STIGLITZ

Making Globalization Work
The Roaring Nineties
Globalization and Its Discontents

THE THREE TRILLION DOLLAR WAR

THE TRUE COST OF THE IRAQ CONFLICT

Joseph E. Stiglitz
and
Linda J. Bilmes

W. W. Norton & Company
New York London

Printed in the United States of America
First Edition

For information about special discounts for bulk purchases, please contact W. W. Norton Special Sales at specialsales@wwnorton.com or 800-233-4830

Manufacturing by RR Donnelley, Harrisonburg, VA
Production manager: Anna Oler

Library of Congress Cataloging-in-Publication Data
Stiglitz, Joseph E.
The three trillion dollar war : the true cost of the Iraq conflict / by Joseph E. Stiglitz and Linda J. Bilmes.
p. cm.
Includes bibliographical references and index.
ISBN 978-0-393-06701-9 (hardcover)
1. Iraq War, 2003—Finance—United States. 2. War—Economic aspects—United States. 3. War—Economic aspects—Iraq. I. Bilmes, Linda. II. Title.
DS79.76.S698 2008
956.7044'31—dc22 2007051400

W. W. Norton & Company, Inc.
500 Fifth Avenue, New York, N.Y. 10110
www.wwnorton.com

W. W. Norton & Company Ltd.
Castle House, 75/76 Wells Street, London W1T 3QT

2 3 4 5 6 7 8 9 0

This book is dedicated to all those who have died in Iraq and Afghanistan as well as to those still placing their lives at risk.

It is also dedicated to the returning veterans,

especially those who have become disabled.

We are thankful for their sacrifices;

they deserve all the care we can give.

Contents

Preface

BY NOW IT is clear that the U.S. invasion of Iraq was a terrible mistake. Nearly 4,000 U.S. troops have been killed, and more than 58,000 have been wounded, injured, or fallen seriously ill. A further 7,300 troops have been wounded or injured or fallen seriously ill in Afghanistan.[1] One hundred thousand U.S. soldiers have returned from the war suffering from serious mental health disorders, a significant fraction of which will be chronic afflictions.[2] Miserable though Saddam Hussein's regime was, life is actually worse for the Iraqi people now. The country's roads, schools, hospitals, homes, and museums have been destroyed and its citizens have less access to electricity and water than before the war.[3] Sectarian violence is rife. Iraq's chaos has made the country a magnet for terrorists of all stripes. The notion that invading Iraq would bring democracy and catalyze change in the Middle East now seems like a fantasy. When the full price of the war has been paid, trillions of dollars will have been added to our national debt. Invading Iraq has also driven up oil prices. In these and other ways, the war has weakened our economy.

Given the human suffering the war in Iraq has caused, it may seem callous to even think about the financial cost. Dry numbers will never capture the pain of those killed or maimed and scarred for life. But we believe that understanding the cost of war is essential.

The decision to go to war was based on a number of false premises. One asserted a link between Saddam Hussein and the terrible attacks of 9/11 on the World Trade Center and the Pentagon. Faulty intelligence led to claims that Iraq had weapons of mass destruction even though the inspectors of the International Atomic Energy Agency (IAEA) said there were none. Many argued that the war would be over quickly and that democracy would somehow bloom in Iraq. And, finally, there was the notion that the war would cost little and pay for itself.

In fact, the war has turned out to be hugely costly in both blood and treasure. We estimate that the total budgetary and economic cost to the United States will turn out to be around $3 trillion, with the cost to the rest of the world perhaps doubling that number again. In one sense, this book is about that $3 trillion—how America will be paying the bill for this war for decades to come, and why it is that the true costs are so much larger than the cost estimates originally provided by the Bush administration. But the book is also about much more than a single number. By examining the costs, we come to understand better the implications of the war, and perhaps learn how we can extricate ourselves from Iraq with the least amount of damage.

AMERICA HAS ALREADY paid a steep price for invading Iraq. The most visible burden is the toll on our fighting men and women. The economic burden is less readily apparent. Current expenditures, largely financed by borrowing, have been grossly underestimated, although even the vast sums we have spent have not been sufficient to achieve our objectives or protect our troops. Future costs, which will continue to escalate after we finally leave Iraq, have been deliberately glossed over.

These costs are certain to be huge and will continue for generations. That is the lesson of the 1991 Gulf War, a conflict that lasted for less than two months, with little ground fighting and 694,550 troops deployed to the Gulf. One hundred forty-eight U.S. soldiers were killed, and 467 injured in direct combat.[4] America's allies (primarily Saudi Arabia and Kuwait) paid for most of the combat operations of the first Gulf War. If you stop counting there, it seems the Gulf War was almost free.[5] But that fails to take into account the large number of veterans suffering from some form of disability from the war, so that today—more than sixteen years later—the United States still spends over $4.3 billion *each year* paying compensation, pension, and disability benefits to more than 200,000 veterans of the Gulf War.[6] We have already spent over $50 billion in Gulf War disability benefits. Even that number does not include the costs of ongoing veterans' medical care, of keeping U.S. forces stationed in Kuwait, of medical research into "Gulf War syndrome" illnesses,[7] and of all the government workers necessary to run these programs. Nor does it even scratch the surface of the broader economic consequences, for instance, from the loss of income for up to 100,000 soldiers exposed to chemicals associated with so-called Gulf War syndrome, 40,000 of whom have long-term disabilities.[8]

To arrive at the $3 trillion figure, we had to look beyond the government's bad budgeting and misleading accounting. It may sound strange to say it, but going to war is a big business. No modern firm would attempt to run its business without timely, accurate information provided by good accounting systems. Yet the accounting practices used by the government are so shoddy that they would land any public firm before the Securities and Exchange Commission for engaging in deceptive practices.

Just as bad accounting in the private sector misleads investors, so bad accounting in the government misleads ordinary citizens and contributes to major mistakes in the allocation of resources. When Army Spc. Thomas Wilson of the 278th Regimental Combat Team (a Tennessee National Guard unit then stationed in Kuwait) famously asked Defense Secretary Donald Rumsfeld, "Why do we soldiers have to dig through local landfills for pieces of scrap metal and compromised ballistic glass to up armor our vehicles?" Rumsfeld replied, "You go to war with the Army you have, not the Army you might want or wish to have at a later time."[9] In March 2003, "the Army we had" was desperately short of the resources—such as body armor and reinforced vehicles—necessary to fight a war of this kind and long on submarines and other heavy equipment designed to confront a Cold War–style enemy. At the very same time, officials of the International Atomic Energy Agency (the international agency charged with ensuring that Iraq did not have weapons of mass destruction) begged us to grant them another six months to complete their inspections work. Nevertheless, we were in such a hurry to invade Iraq that we ignored the IAEA and sent our young men and women to fight without even shielding them in proper body armor. Government accounting shows that we spent relatively little during the initial invasion of Iraq—but we are now faced with the long-term costs of caring for soldiers who were wounded during this period.[10]

Five years later, the United States is engaged in a national debate about how to exit the war. Few voices have openly supported the notion of a permanent occupation. The question appears to be not whether we leave, but when. This issue—which economists refer to as *intertemporal decision making*—is one which modern decision theories have a great deal to contribute. Although President George W. Bush has dismissed our earlier cost-of-war analysis, arguing that military policy would not be determined by accountants in green eyeshades, making informed choices about real-world options should clearly include cost as *one* of the factors to be taken into account. Our resources are not infinite. We must face the reality not only of how much we have already spent and committed to date, but also the implications of future choices. Decisions are always made with imperfect information, but modern economic techniques can help clarify the available information and enable us to make better decisions in these adverse circumstances.

Whether one thinks it was right or wrong to have gone to war, whether one thinks the war was conducted poorly or well, most Americans agree that it is our moral duty to provide adequate health care and disability payments for those who risk their lives for their country. Doing so will be costly, and the government must provide adequate funds.

Thus far, the administration has failed to plan adequately for returning Iraq war veterans and the scale of their injuries. There is insufficient funding for veterans' hospitals, a shortage of medical care in many cities—and long, tortuous delays in processing disability claims. Many of these claims are mishandled and our soldiers have to file appeals and fight yet another war when they come home—this time with the bureaucracy. In 2005, even as the war was in full swing, the Department of Veterans Affairs (VA) budget request for veterans' medical care was still based on projections done before the war had begun. In 2006, as the insurgency expanded, the VA's budget request was based on data from 2003. Not surprisingly, the VA ran out of money—forcing Congress to appropriate $3 billion in emergency funds just to keep the programs running for those two years.[11] In 2007, the president again asked for billions more in "emergency supplemental" funding so that military and veterans' hospitals would be able to handle the surge of returning troops with injuries.

But even with these emergency appropriations, we have not done right by our veterans. Returning servicemen and women have had to pay the price for the lack of preparedness, as evidenced by the scandal surrounding the Walter Reed Army Medical Center in Washington, D.C.[12] As we will see in chapter 3, Walter Reed is the tip of an iceberg of national disgrace. Wounded troops returning home are caught in a crossfire of bureaucratic confusion between the Defense Department and the Department of Veterans Affairs—resulting in shoddy outpatient facilities, endless red tape, and long delays in getting basic financial compensation. With almost 900,000 Americans still deployed to Iraq and Afghanistan operations,[13] it is important to rectify these mistakes so that veterans' future health and benefit programs are not hostages to political fortune—as they have been for the past five years.

What is true for our soldiers is also true of our military more generally: restoring it to health will be costly. There is widespread agreement that we should restore the U.S. military to its prewar strength and rebuild institutions such as the National Guard. The military has also announced plans to expand the size of the all-volunteer force by 2012. These projects will be expensive. The full costs are not being fully estimated thus far, let alone provided for in the defense budget.

The issue is not whether America can afford three trillion dollars. We can. With a typical American household income in 2006 just short of $70,000, we have far more than we need to get by.[14] Even if we threw 10 percent of that away, we would still be no worse off than we were in 1995—when we were a prosperous and well-off country. There is no risk that a trillion dollars or two or three will bankrupt the country. The relevant question is a rather different one: What could we have done with a trillion dollars or two or three? What have we had to sacrifice? What is, to use the economists' jargon, the opportunity cost?

At the beginning of the second Bush administration, the president talked about the seriousness of the country's Social Security crisis. But instead of paying for the war in Iraq, we could have fixed the Social Security problem for the next half century.[15]

Today, a Web site run by the National Priorities Project describes the current and direct military costs of the war.[16] A trillion dollars could have built 8 million additional housing units, could have hired some 15 million additional public school teachers for one year; could have paid for 120 million children to attend a year of Head Start; or insured 530 million children for health care for one year; or provided 43 million students with four-year scholarships at public universities. Now multiply those numbers by three.

There is also little doubt that had we spent one to two trillion dollars differently, we would actually be more secure. As we will explain in chapter 5, had we spent the money in investments in education, technology, and research, growth would have been higher, and we would have been in a far stronger position to meet future challenges. If some of the money spent on research were devoted to alternative energy technologies, or to providing further incentives for conservation, we would be less dependent on oil. The resultant lower oil prices would have obvious implications for the financing of some of the current threats to America's security.

For sums less than the direct expenditures on the war, we could have fulfilled our commitment to provide 0.7 percent of our gross domestic product to help developing countries—money that could have made an enormous difference to the well-being of billions today living in poverty. The United States gives some $5 billion a year to Africa, the poorest continent in the world: that amounts to less than ten days' fighting. Two trillion dollars would enable us to meet our commitments to the poorest countries for the next third of a century.

We could have had a Marshall Plan for the Middle East, or the developing countries, that might actually have succeeded in winning the hearts and minds of the people there. Even more modest ambitions could have been achieved for a fraction of what has already been spent on Iraq. The world has committed itself to eradicating illiteracy by 2015. Fully funding that campaign would cost some $8 billion a year—roughly two weeks of fighting the war.[17] We have even bungled our efforts to help Iraqis with reconstruction. In 2003, Congress approved $18.4 billion in reconstruction aid for the country—a sum that is three times per Iraqi what we spent for each European during the Marshall Plan. But instead of spending the money immediately to help fix the electricity, oil refineries, and schools of Iraq, the United States tied up most of the funds in endless bureaucratic squabbling between the Pentagon procurement office and Congress. A full year later, the security situation in Iraq had deteriorated and we had lost the hearts and minds of the people. Much of the money was refunneled into military activities or not spent at all.

We could even have spent the money on a tax cut for the average American. For middle-class Americans, recent years have not been so good: median income (that is, the income of the household, such that half of the households have a higher income and half a lower income) today is less than it was in 1999.[18] For the typical American household, the money spent on Iraq was important: had the taxpayer's taxes been reduced commensurately, or if the money had been spent on providing health care, it would have made a difference to hard-pressed middle-class families. There was another opportunity cost, no less telling: if even a fraction of the scarce military resources devoted to Iraq had been spent in Afghanistan, we might have done more to accomplish the mission we had set out there. As it is, we now have two quagmires.

What is clear is that there were a myriad of ways in which we could have spent the money better—leaving the country more secure, and more prosperous, and so better prepared to face future threats.

THIS BOOK IS based on a paper that we presented in January 2006, in which we conservatively estimated that the cost of the war would be between $1 and $2 trillion. Our goal was simple: to determine the true cost of the war. Regardless of whether one supported or opposed U.S. actions in the region, we believed that voters had a right to know the real cost of our policies.

For many readers, our numbers rang true. Americans had sensed that the war was costing them a great deal. Nor did the administration and its supporters make any real effort to dispute the numbers. There were a few technical critiques and in this book we have worked hard to respond to them.[19] Our critics focused on the fact that we did not take into account the benefits of the war.

For example, one war proponent argued that "the war will lead to large improvements in the economic well-being of most Iraqis relative to their prospects under the policy of containment [the previous policy]."[20]

Our intent, both in the original paper and in this book, is to focus on costs, because they can be measured with some accuracy. Of course, there are many important costs that cannot be accurately measured, and while these costs may be large, we do not include them in our $3 trillion tally. The benefits are more elusive, but it seems highly unlikely they will be significant. (Ridding the world of Saddam Hussein is undoubtedly a benefit, but it is impossible to quantify the value of his absence.) The quality of life in Iraq, measured by the lack of electricity, the high unemployment numbers, the mass exodus from the country, the huge numbers displaced within the country, the collapse of the middle class, and the soaring violence, suggests that, beyond the removal of Saddam Hussein, the Iraqi people have seen little good come of the war. Apart from America's oil and defense industries, it is hard to find any real winners.

We are both ardently opposed to the war and were against it from the start. Most of the problems were clear even before the war began. We feel comfortable that we are not writing about the mistakes and failures from the perspective of 20/20 hindsight. What is so sad about the failures of the Iraq debacle is that almost all the problems were predictable—and predicted.

As social scientists, we have both been involved in the study of the economics of the public sector and have tried to understand how governments work, the systematic ways in which they often fail, and what can be done to help governments better meet the needs of their citizens. We have both approached the problem not only from the perspective of academicians but also from the perspective of practitioners. For years, we served as political/technocratic appointments in the Clinton administration, trying to put into practice these ideas about how one can make government more efficient, more responsive, more accountable—and create better accounting systems to achieve those ends. We believe there is an important role for government in our society just as there is an important role for markets. Markets often fail to perform in the way desired; but the same is true for government. The failure in Iraq was not the result of a single mistake but the culmination of dozens of mistakes made over a period of years. Social scientists try to understand the systematic sources of these "failures" and look for reforms to reduce their likelihood and mitigate their consequences. For students of "government failure," the Iraq war is a case study.

Our awareness of our potential bias has influenced this study. We have, we believe, been *excessively* conservative. Even employing these conservative methodologies, we arrive at numbers that are mind-boggling—and this despite the fact that our quantitative estimates omit huge costs that could not be accurately measured.

Some would argue that we have not included the benefits of the war. We plead guilty to that charge. There was ample evidence *before* the invasion that the primary alleged benefit associated with going to war—destroying weapons of mass destruction—had no validity[21] and our belief has since been vindicated. There was ample evidence *before* the invasion that there was no link between al Qaeda and Iraq, but that the invasion risked creating more terrorists. That belief, too, has since been vindicated. There was ample evidence *before* the invasion that it would not lead to lower oil prices and more stable supplies; here again, our belief has since been vindicated. But even if benefits do unexpectedly appear, good decision making still requires that we have as accurate estimates of the costs as possible. This is what this book attempts to provide.

Acknowledgments

UNTANGLING THE COSTS of the war has not been easy, and it would not have been possible without the help of many.

The fact that so much of the data and information that *should* have been publicly available was not meant that some critical pieces of information have had to be obtained through the Freedom of Information Act (FOIA). We thank Paul Sullivan of Veterans for Common Sense, who helped us to understand the situation facing returning Iraq and Afghanistan war veterans, and who provided us with crucial data from the Defense Department and Department of Veterans Affairs obtained under the FOIA.

Robert Wescott was particularly helpful in reviewing the estimates of the macroeconomic costs. An earlier version of our analysis was presented at a joint session of the American Economic Association/Economists for Peace and Security in Boston in January 2005, and the discussion with other members of the panel—William Nordhaus, Bassam Yousif, and Steve Kosiak, and especially Alan Sinai—was particularly helpful. Robert Hormats shared his ideas about the cost of war and the problems posed by deficit financing. William Pfaff and Jamie Galbraith looked at parts of the manuscript. Research help was provided by Columbia University research assistants: Giselle Guzmán, Fang He, Izzet Yildiz, and Dan Choate. Thanks are owed to others at Columbia University: Jesse Berlin and Deborah Lizak. Thanks are especially owed to Jill Blackford, who helped in every aspect of the research and editing, and who worked heroically to bring the book together at the end. Some line editing was done by the very able Graham Watts, as well as Samantha Marshall and Amy Prince.

At Harvard, we especially wish to thank Brian Iammartino, who provided invaluable assistance in developing the cost model, and Harvard students Tony Park and doctoral candidate John Horton (himself a service-connected disabled Iraqi war veteran), for their contributions to the research. Thanks also to Michael Johnson and Jamie Georgia, two outstanding faculty assistants. We also thank Michael McGeary of the National Institute of Medicine for patiently explaining the disability compensation system to us, and for reviewing the detailed issue of compensation for amputations. We also wish to thank David Gorman and Joe Violante of Disabled American Veterans, David Sevier of the Commission on the Future of America's Veterans, and Paul Rieckhoff of Iraq and Afghanistan Veterans of America for helping us to understand the veterans' disability compensation system, the difficulty of transitioning from military to veteran status, and the plight of veterans returning from the current war. We also thank 2nd Lt. Matthew Fecteau, who has been serving in the U.S. Army in Iraq since 2006, for his generosity and courage, and for helping us to understand the day-to-day realities of life in the war zone. We appreciate the assistance of Nick Kitchen, a doctoral student at the London School of Economics who helped us to analyze the costs to Great Britain, Susan Anderson of the Massachusetts Bar Association, who explained to us how juries award compensation in cases of death and injury, and economist Matt Goldberg of the Congressional Budget Office, who took the time to review the CBO's methodology in detail with us.

We are indebted to a number of medical doctors who have helped us to understand traumatic brain injury and PTSD, including Dr. Charles Marmar and Dr. Karen Seal of the Veterans Hospital in San Francisco; Dr. Dan Lowenstein, professor of neurology at UCSF Medical School; Dr. Maureen Strafford of Cambridge, MA; and Dr. Gene Bolles, the former chief surgeon at Landstuhl Regional Medical Center in Germany.

At Norton, we want to thank our publisher Drake McFeely, as well as his colleague Kyle Frisina, and especially Brendan Curry, who was very helpful and patient throughout the editing process. At Penguin, we are again deeply indebted to Stuart Proffitt. Once again, the bulk of the editing was done by Anya Schiffrin, who patiently went through every draft of the book and helped at every stage of the writing. The idea of this book comes from her father, the publisher André Schiffrin, who also provided invaluable suggestions on how to shape it. A great deal of the credit for this book goes to Jonathan Hakim, who devoted countless hours to perfecting the cost model, helped to edit several chapters, and provided insight and guidance throughout. Finally, we pay tribute to the late Dr. Murray Bilmes, who served in the U.S. Army in the Pacific during World War II.

THE THREE TRILLION DOLLAR WAR

CHAPTER 1

Is It Really Three Trillion?

ON MARCH 19, 2003, the United States and its "coalition of the willing" invaded Iraq. The "shock and awe" attack was seen on televisions around the world, and as we watched the destruction, we wondered what would become of that country. It was not surprising that Saddam Hussein's forces were crushed almost immediately. The United States spends almost as much on weapons as the rest of the world together.[1] At the time, Iraq's economy was less than 1 percent of that of the United States. Ten years of futile war with Iran, during which hundreds of thousands of Iraqis had died,[2] had been followed by the Gulf War, in which another 75,000 to 105,000 soldiers died.[3] Then came over a decade of sanctions. It would have been truly shocking if America had not been able to overrun the Iraqi military quickly.

There was something unseemly in President Bush's gloating, little more than six weeks after the war started, in front of a "Mission Accomplished" banner on the decks of the USS *Abraham Lincoln*. Especially since the mission had not been accomplished. The mission was not to defeat the Iraqi army—that was a foreordained conclusion—but to create a viable democracy. For the neoconservative architects of the policy, Iraq was just the beginning. Their goal was to create a new democratic Middle East which would eventually achieve a lasting peace between Israel and Palestine. That mission too was not accomplished, and today the dream of a stable, free, democratic Iraq seems as far away as ever.

On March 19, 2008, the United States will have been in Iraq for five years—longer than the three years and eight months we were involved in World War II; the two years and two months in World War I; the three years and one month in Korea; and even the four years Americans fought each other in the Civil War. And yet, there has been little progress in Iraq during these five years. Not only has Iraq itself descended into internecine conflict, but the rest of the region has become more unstable. Hatred of the United States is palpable in the Middle East and has spread around the world. According to the Pew Global Attitudes Project, in many countries, including some longtime allies, the United States is viewed as the greatest threat to global peace—even greater than Iran and North Korea,[4] the two countries that President Bush elevated, along with Iraq, to membership of the "axis of evil."

Within Iraq, U.S. forces are viewed as occupiers rather than liberators, with polls showing that 70 percent of Iraqis want the United States to leave.[5] Iraq's GDP is just recovering to where it was before the war; [6] at least one out of four is unemployed. The lack of electricity has become the symbol of how badly the reconstruction has gone. It not only provides a quantitative indicator of failure, but means that there is no air conditioning, no refrigeration. In the sweltering heat, tempers boil and food spoils. In Baghdad, electricity is available for about half the number of hours daily that it was before the war. There is controversy regarding the exact number of violent Iraqi deaths to date, variously estimated from 100,000 to more than 150,000; combined with higher rates of death from other causes, "excess" deaths may number 700,000 or more. The higher figures are based on standard statistical techniques.[7]

The middle class, so essential to the functioning of a democratic society, has been destroyed—a point made forcefully even by the man America chose to be the country's first post-occupation prime minister, Ayad Allawi.[8] Some 2 million Iraqi refugees are scattered throughout the world. These are in addition to some 2 million Iraqis who have been uprooted within their own country.[9] Most of those fleeing have gone to Jordan and Syria, but somewhat more than 26,000 Iraqis have come to Sweden seeking asylum or family reunification through 2006, with another 20,000 expected in 2007. Sweden, a country far smaller than the United States, has accepted more refugees than the 1608 the United States had taken in by October 2007.[10] Had America taken in the same number of refugees, relative to its population, it would have accepted nearly 900,000.

Underestimating the Cost of War

THE BUSH ADMINISTRATION was wrong about the benefits of the war and it was wrong about the costs of the war. The president and his advisers expected a quick, inexpensive conflict. Instead, we have a war that is costing more than anyone could have imagined. The cost of direct U.S. military operations—not even including long-term costs such as taking care of wounded veterans—already exceeds the cost of the twelve-year war in Vietnam and is more than double the cost of the Korean War. And, even in the best case scenario, these costs are projected to be almost ten times the cost of the first Gulf War, almost a third more than the cost of the Vietnam War, and twice that of World War I.[11] The only war in our history which cost more was World War II, when 16.3 million U.S. troops fought in a campaign lasting four years, at a total cost (in 2007 dollars, after adjusting for inflation) of about $5 trillion.[12] With virtually the entire armed forces committed to fighting the Germans and Japanese, the cost per troop (in today's dollars) was less than $100,000 in 2007 dollars. By contrast, the Iraq war is costing (*directly*) upward of $400,000 per troop.[13]

The chronic underestimation of costs has continued throughout the war. In January 2007, the administration estimated that it would cost $5.6 billion to deploy an additional 21,000 troops for the proposed "surge" in troop levels. But this estimate referred only to the cost of deploying the combat troops themselves for four months. According to the non-partisan Congressional Budget Office (CBO), the surge would also require deployment of 15,000–28,000 combat support troops, a mobilization that would raise the cost to at least $11 billion (for four months), rising to $27–$49 billion if the "surge" continued for twelve to twenty-four months.[14] Even this expanded estimate did not take into account the long-term health and disability costs for veterans and the cost of replacing the equipment that these additional troops would use. Nor did it factor in other costs of the surge that the CBO pointed out in a separate report, including the reduced availability of U.S. troops for other potential conflicts for a period well beyond the actual deployment.[15]

Most Americans have yet to feel these costs. The price in blood has been paid by our voluntary military and by hired contractors.

The price in treasure has, in a sense, been financed entirely by borrowing. Taxes have not been raised to pay for it—in fact, taxes on the rich have actually fallen. Deficit spending gives the illusion that the laws of economics can be repealed, that we can have both guns and butter. But of course the laws are not repealed. The costs of the war are real even if they have been deferred, possibly to another generation. But before we examine those costs, let's look back at what the administration said as we went to war.

Early Estimates of War Costs

ON THE EVE of war, there were discussions of the likely costs. Larry Lindsey, President Bush's economic adviser and head of the National Economic Council, suggested that they might reach $200 billion.[16] But this estimate was dismissed as "baloney" by the Defense Secretary, Donald Rumsfeld.[17] His deputy, Paul Wolfowitz, suggested that postwar reconstruction could pay for itself through increased oil revenues.[18] Office of Management and Budget director Mitch Daniels and Secretary Rumsfeld estimated the costs in the range of $50–$60 billion, a portion of which they believed would be financed by other countries. (Adjusting for inflation, in 2007 dollars, they were projecting costs of between $57 and $69 billion).[19]

The tone of the entire administration was cavalier, as if the sums involved were minimal. When Ted Koppel of ABC interviewed Andrew Natsios, the widely respected administrator of the Agency for International Development, on *Nightline* in April 2003, Natsios insisted that Iraq could be rebuilt for $1.7 billion.

TED KOPPEL: All right . . . when you talk about 1.7, you're not suggesting that the rebuilding of Iraq is gonna be done for $1.7 billion?

ANDREW NATSIOS: Well, in terms of the American taxpayers contribution, I do, this is it for the U.S. The rest of the rebuilding of Iraq will be done by other countries who have already made pledges, Britain, Germany, Norway, Japan, Canada, and Iraqi oil revenues, eventually in several years, when it's up and running and there's a new government that's been democratically elected, will finish the job with their own revenues. They're going to get in $20 billion a year in oil revenues. But the American part of this will be $1.7 billion. We have no plans for any further-on funding for this. . . .

TED KOPPEL: I want to be sure that I understood you correctly. You're saying the, the top cost for the U.S. taxpayer will be $1.7 billion. No more than that?

ANDREW NATSIOS: For the reconstruction. And then there's $700 million in the supplemental budget for humanitarian relief, which we don't competitively bid 'cause it's charities that get that money.

TED KOPPEL: I understand. But as far as reconstruction goes, the American taxpayer will not be hit for more than $1.7 billion no matter how long the process takes?

ANDREW NATSIOS: That is our plan and that is our intention. And these figures, outlandish figures I've seen, I have to say, there's a little bit of hoopla involved in this.[20]

Even Lindsey, after noting that the war could cost $200 billion, went on to say, "The successful prosecution of the war would be good for the economy."[21]

In retrospect, Lindsey grossly underestimated both the costs of the war itself and the costs to the economy. Assuming that Congress approves the rest of the $200 billion war supplemental requested for fiscal year 2008, as this book goes to press Congress will have appropriated a total of over $845 billion for military operations, reconstruction, embassy costs, enhanced security at U.S. bases, and foreign aid programs in Iraq and Afghanistan.[22]

As the fifth year of the war draws to a close, operating costs (spending on the war itself, what you might call "running expenses") for 2008 are projected to exceed $12.5 billion a month for Iraq alone, up from $4.4 billion in 2003, and with Afghanistan, the total is $16 billion a month. Sixteen billion dollars is equal to the annual budget of the United Nations, or of all but thirteen of the U.S. states. Even so, it does not include the $500 billion we already spend per year on the *regular* expenses of the Defense Department. Nor does it include other hidden expenditures, such as intelligence gathering,[23] or funds mixed in with the budgets of other departments.

Moreover, as we discuss below (and more fully in chapter 4), these purely budgetary costs—huge though they are—represent only a portion of the overall cost of the war.

While the focus of this book is on the Iraq war, in practice, there are many difficulties in separating out the actual budgetary amounts spent in Iraq and Afghanistan and on related operations.[24] Although the president's budget for fiscal year 2008 does show separate requests for Iraq and Afghanistan, the Defense Department provides little detailed information on costs. War and baseline funds are mixed in the same accounts.[25] Nor does the Department of

Veterans Affairs make a distinction between the two operations in its cost estimates. The Congressional Budget Office (CBO) does not separate funding for Iraq from Afghanistan in its scenarios for future funding. The breakdown we use is based on work done by the Congressional Research Service (CRS), which draws on "a variety of sources and methods to estimate the distribution of war-related funds appropriated for Defense, Foreign Affairs, and Veterans medical costs."[26]

Factors Driving Up Spending

THE MAJOR FACTORS driving up war costs go beyond the number of troops deployed or the operating pace or "optempo" of the war. Since 2004, the average number of military personnel deployed to the region in a given period has grown by 15 percent—but the costs have rocketed by 130 percent. Similarly, the intensity of operations is estimated to have risen by 65 percent during the period—half the rate of cost increases.[27]

Three major factors are behind these ballooning costs. One, of course, is the rising cost of personnel—both U.S. servicemen and women and military contractors. Even though the average number of service members deployed has risen only slightly, the cost *per troop* has increased considerably. Recruitment, combat pay, hardship benefits, and reenlistment bonuses have all been jacked up (reenlistment bonuses can reach $150,000). The Army has relied to an unprecedented extent on Reservists and the National Guard, who must be paid a full salary plus combat pay and other benefits once on active duty rather than a stipend for one weekend per month.[28] While we allocate the costs of Reserves and National

Guard between Iraq and Afghanistan largely to the extent that they were deployed and injured in the different theaters, in a sense, the vast majority of these costs should be attributed to Iraq. Had we not gone to war in Iraq, we would have been able to rely on our standing military to a much larger extent. Just the 82,800 to 142,000 active duty troops stationed in Iraq between May 2003 and January 2005, had they been assigned to Afghanistan, would have obviated most of the need to call up the Reserves and National Guard. If we include the thousands of troops that helped support them, the need would have been even less.[29] On the benefit side, there may be a debate on the extent to which the Iraq war's diversion of attention from Afghanistan has contributed to the failures there; but on the cost side, there is no question: It was the Iraq war, following on the Afghanistan war, which put the stresses on the military that have driven up costs in so many ways.

The growing use of contractors in Iraq and Afghanistan doing everything from cooking and cleaning to servicing weapons systems and protecting U.S. diplomats has increased operational expenses far more than if we had relied solely on the Army. A 2006 survey by the Department of Defense's Central Command showed that the United States is employing more than 100,000 private contractors; this number represents a tenfold increase over the use of contractors during the Gulf War in 1991.[30] Given our failure to increase the size of the military, the United States cannot operate without them. For the most part, these people work side by side with U.S. troops and share the risks and hardship. An estimated 1,000 contractors have been killed since 2003.

The invasion of Iraq opened up new opportunities for private military security firms. The State Department alone spent more than $4 billion on security guards in 2007—up from $1 billion three years ago. Blackwater Security got an initial toehold in 2003 with a $27 million no-bid contract to guard L. Paul Bremer III, the administrator of the Coalition Provisional Authority (the U.S. occupational authority in Baghdad). That contract was expanded to $100 million a year later. By 2007, it held a $1.2 billion contract for Iraq and employed 845 private security contractors.[31]

In 2007, private security guards working for companies such as Blackwater and Dyncorp were earning up to $1,222 a day; this amounts to $445,000 a year.[32] By contrast, an Army sergeant was earning $140 to $190 a day in pay and benefits, a total of $51,100 to $69,350 a year.[33]

Worse, the military has been competing against itself: the high pay for the contractors is one of the factors forcing the Army to offer ever higher bonuses for reenlisting. Soldiers, as their tour of duty comes to an end, can go to work for contractors at much higher wages. Despite huge increases in reenlistment pay, the military is losing some of its most experienced personnel to the private contracting firms.

Many have questioned the wisdom of such reliance on private contractors instead of strengthening the core military force, but not just because of the higher costs. Not only were these contractors more expensive than troops; they were not subject to military discipline or supervision.[34] Of course, most contractors are hardworking, honest people, performing under difficult conditions. But the brutality of a few has become legendary and has inflamed the conflict.[35]

The use of contractors is, in essence, a partial privatization of the armed forces. Yet there are good reasons why countries do not privatize their military. It makes sense for governments to privatize steel mills; or even to privatize natural monopolies like electricity or gas, provided adequate regulatory frameworks are implemented to make sure that these monopolies do not use their market power to overcharge consumers. It does not make sense to privatize the military. Proponents of privatization often argue that it encourages customer responsiveness. Steel companies can enhance their profits by offering products that are more to the liking of their customers, of higher quality and greater reliability. For the most part, those who interact with military contractors do not do so voluntarily; there is no market where they can choose to be interrogated by a contractor from the United States, or by some other provider. Indeed, the incentives are perverse. The incentives of the contractor are to minimize his costs, and those incentives do not take into account the nation's broad range of public objectives.

The extensive use of contractors raised still another problem: the potential for profiteering and corruption is high.[36] Allegations of overpayments to Halliburton, the defense contractor formerly headed by Vice President Dick Cheney, are well known, but this is the tip of the iceberg.

These problems in turn reflect more fundamental deficiencies in the contracting arrangements, both in how they are awarded in the first place, and how they are supervised after they have been awarded.

The irregularities in the award system are not just an accident. As a matter of good government policy—to encourage competition and to get the best deal possible for taxpayers—most contracts should be tendered through competitive bidding. But the Bush administration has often chosen to short-circuit this process by using "sole source bidding," claiming that there is a need to act expeditiously, without waiting for the competitive process to work. Even worse, many of these contracts are "cost-plus" contracts—the contractor gets reimbursed for everything he spends, and gets a profit margin on top (providing perverse incentives—the more that is spent, the greater the profit). An argument for sole sourcing can be made at the beginning of an unexpected war. Giving out a multiyear contract, as was done for Halliburton, went well beyond what was necessary.

A damning example is the fate of the huge sum of $18.4 billion in reconstruction funding—for the rebuilding of civilian projects in Iraq such as schools, hospitals, electrical grids, and roads—that Congress approved in the summer of 2003. President Bush had fought hard for the money, telling a reluctant Congress that restoring basic services was essential to the U.S. strategy.[37] Congress wanted to make sure that the money went directly to firms that could help create jobs in Iraq. After much debate, it enacted the reconstruction bill on condition that the contracts must be awarded through competitive bids, unless the Secretary of Defense (or Secretary of State in the case of a State Department contract) certified in writing that sole sourcing was required. This created a standoff between Secretary Rumsfeld—who wanted to award the contracts to the usual big defense contractor firms without competition, but refused to send a letter to the committee chairman—and the Congress. The result was that one year later, only $1 billion had been spent. As we shall see, most of the money was later siphoned off into military activities or never spent at all.

Bad contracting procedures were followed by inadequate supervision—which, for obvious reasons, can be particularly costly in cost-plus contracts. There simply were not enough personnel to provide adequate oversight. The State Department has only seventeen people in its contract compliance department to oversee $4 billion worth of contractors. The Department of Defense (DOD) is in even worse shape, having failed to invest in its acquisition and procurement workforce for many years. Between 1998 and 2004 the DOD's total spending on contracting increased by 105 percent, while the number of people it employed to award and supervise contracts declined by 25 percent.[38]

No wonder then that reports of contracting irregularities are so numerous, including $10 billion in questionable bills reported by the Defense Contract Audit Agency.[39] Another $8.8 billion from the Development Fund for Iraq disappeared under the lax financial controls of the Coalition Provisional Authority.[40]

In America, corruption takes on a more nuanced form than it does elsewhere. Payoffs typically do not take the form of direct bribes, but of campaign contributions to both parties. From 1998 to 2003, Halliburton's contributions to the Republican Party totaled $1,146,248, and $55,650 went to the Democratic Party. Halliburton received at least $19.3 billion in lucrative single-source contracts.[41]

Excess costs to the government are reflected in excess profits to the defense contractors, who have been (along with the oil companies) the only real winners in this war. Halliburton's stock price has increased—by 229 percent since the war began, exceeding even the gains by other defense firms, such as General Dynamics (134 percent), Raytheon (117 percent), Lockheed Martin (105 percent), and Northrop Grumman (78 percent).[42]

The rising price of fuel is a second reason that costs have increased so much. A modern army runs not just on its stomach but also on fuel oil. The world price of oil has risen from around $25 per barrel when the war started to close to $100 as this book goes to press. The price of fuel delivered to Iraq has risen even faster, driven by heavy transport costs from long and dangerous supply lines.

The third, and perhaps most significant, reason for the spiraling costs of war is the growing need to pay for a general "reset" of equipment and weaponry as the stock of military equipment wears out and the length of the campaign forces the Pentagon to make equipment purchases that it initially chose to ignore.[43] A glaring example is the mine-resistant ambush-protected (MRAP) armored vehicles, which have a V-shaped hull that puts the crew more than three feet off the ground and are designed to withstand the underbelly bombs that cripple the lower-riding Humvees. The Marines discovered the superiority of MRAPs in 2003 and started making urgent requests for them in early 2005. It was not until 2006, when Secretary of Defense Robert M. Gates took over, that the Pentagon made the decision to replace its fleet of 18,000 Humvees with the better technology. Meanwhile, improvised explosive devices (IEDs) have accounted for more than 1,500 U.S. fatalities.

In addition, monthly costs have risen due to the cost of training and equipping Afghan and Iraqi security forces. We have spent more than $30 billion on training indigenous forces in both countries since 2004, a cost that was not anticipated in the original estimates of the war.[44]

Fundamentally, costs have accelerated in Iraq because resources were skimped at the start of the war and the campaign has gone badly. Had the Defense Department heeded former Secretary of State Colin Powell's doctrine of "overwhelming force," it would have used more troops and spent more money at the outset, but the insurgency might have rapidly been brought under control and the war brought to an earlier conclusion. Now, after five years of fighting and an estimated 19,000 Iraqi insurgents dead, there are more insurgents than at the outset, and more enemies of the United States throughout the Middle East.[45]

Costs Not Counted

THE TOTAL COST of the war is higher than the official number used by the administration because there are so many costs that it does not count. For example, government officials frequently talk about the lives of our soldiers as priceless. But from a cost perspective, these "priceless" lives show up on the Pentagon ledger simply as $500,000—the amount paid out to survivors in death benefits and life insurance. After the war began, these were increased from $12,240 to $100,000 (death benefit) and from $250,000 to $400,000 (life insurance).[46] Even these increased amounts are a fraction of what the survivors might have received had these individuals lost their lives in a senseless automobile accident. In areas such as health and safety regulation, the government values a life of a young man at the peak of his future earnings capacity in excess of $7 million—far greater than the amount the military pays in death benefits.[47] Using this figure, the cost of the nearly 4,000 American troops killed in Iraq adds up to some $28 billion. The costs to society are obviously far larger than the numbers which show up on the government's budget.

Another example of hidden costs is the understating of U.S. military casualties. The Defense Department's casualty statistics focus on casualties that result from hostile (combat) action—as determined by the military. Yet if a soldier is injured or dies in a nighttime vehicle accident, this is officially dubbed "non combat related"—even though it may be too unsafe for soldiers to travel during daytime. In fact, the Pentagon keeps two sets of books. The first is the official casualty list posted on the DOD Web site. The second, hard-to-find set of data is available only on a different Web site and can be obtained under the Freedom of Information Act. This data shows that the total number of soldiers who have been wounded, injured, or suffered from disease is double the number wounded in combat.[48] Some will argue that a percentage of these non-combat injuries might have happened even if the soldiers were not in Iraq. Our new research, which we describe in chapters 2 and 3, shows that the majority of these injuries and illnesses can be tied directly to service in the war.

Of course, while we focus on the economic costs of the thousands of American lives lost or ruined by the war, it is impossible to calculate the human costs paid by the soldiers, their families, and their communities. We can calculate the disability pay, and the loss to the workforce, of the soldiers who return from the war with post-traumatic stress disorder; it is far harder to calculate the cost of the family stress, broken marriages, and the despair of those who have lost hearing, vision, or limbs.[49]

There is a further reason for pessimism concerning the eventual costs of the war—to both the veterans and their families. As this book went to press, the *Journal of the American Medical Association* reported a new study on mental health problems evidenced months after demobilization. The authors point out that earlier studies showed "soldiers were more likely to indicate mental health distress several months after return than upon their immediate return."[50] A second screening, administered three to six months after return, showed 20.3 percent of active and 42.4 percent of reserve component soldiers as requiring mental health treatment.[51]

A Faulty System of Accounting

THE WAY THAT the U.S. government does its accounting further obscures the true costs of the war. The standard method that the government uses to keep its books is based on "cash" accounting. This logs what is actually spent today but ignores future obligations, including, in the case of war, such factors as future health care and disability costs. Cash accounting makes things look cheaper at the moment—for example, not purchasing expensive vehicles to protect soldiers from improved explosive devices—but hides the long-term costs of medical care if an IED explodes and injures someone.

The problems with cash accounting are so serious that all businesses in America larger than a corner grocery store are required by law to use "accrual" accounting—a system that shows future costs as they are incurred, not when they are actually spent down the road. The discrepancy between cash and accrual accounting is always a concern. But the size of the future costs in this war makes the underreporting especially severe. Taking these accrued future obligations into consideration accounts for much of the difference between our tally and the official tally.

Other bad accounting practices allow the Department of Defense to hide expenditures on the Iraq war within its ordinary budget. The Department of Defense swallows over $500 billion of tax dollars a year (not including the war) but fails dismally to account for where the money goes. In 2007—for the tenth year running—the department flunked its financial audit, with auditors citing material weaknesses in virtually every area. The department's own Inspector General recently told the Senate Homeland Security Committee that

> The Department [of Defense] faces financial management problems that are long standing, pervasive, and deeply rooted in virtually all operations. Those financial

> management problems continue to impede the Department's ability to provide reliable, timely and useful financial and managerial data to support operating, budgeting and policy decisions. . . . The weaknesses that affect the auditability of the financial statements also impact DOD programs and operations and contribute to waste, mismanagement and inefficient use of resources.[52]

The lack of financial control makes it difficult to account for the costs of conducting the war in Iraq. As the Government Accountability Office put it: "Neither DOD nor the Congress reliably knows how much the war is costing and how appropriated funds are being used or have historical data useful in considering future funding needs."[53]

Between 2002 and 2008, the military budget not including the appropriations for Iraq and Afghanistan has increased by more than $600 billion cumulatively. This is significantly faster than the rate by which defense spending has risen over the past forty years. It cannot be attributed entirely to ordinary increases in personnel, procurement, and inflation. We estimate that at least one fourth of this incremental (or "excess") increase has been devoted in one way or another to fighting the wars in Iraq and Afghanistan—more than $150 billion in DOD spending over the past five years.

But it is not just in the Defense Department budget that Iraq war costs are hidden. They appear in the budgets (now and for the future) of Social Security, the Labor Department, and HUD (the Department of Housing and Urban Development). Yet as large as the budgetary impact of the Iraq war is on the federal government, many costs are displaced elsewhere. When Iraq war expenditures are pushed out of the public sector, the cost has not gone away. For example, failing to provide adequate budgetary support for the VA has obliged many veterans in need of medical care to purchase it privately. While this reduces *government* spending, there are no real savings for the country. So, too, the costs of taking care of veterans and their families impose a significant burden on state governments which is not reflected in federal government statistics. That is why, in estimating the overall costs of the war on America, we have to look beyond the impacts on the federal budget, a task to which we turn in chapters 4 to 6.

Subverting the Budget Process

THE ADMINISTRATION'S APPROACH to funding the war has been flawed from the start. A central part of our democracy entails congressional oversight and approval of all spending. Appropriations are supposed to originate in the Congress; all anticipated expenses are supposed to be budgeted. It is understandable that, at the beginning of the war, expenditures could not have been anticipated, and that funding would be through emergency appropriations—which is supposed to be reserved for needs that are "unforeseen, unpredictable, and unanticipated." It is understandable that the president requested the initial funds for the invasion of Afghanistan in this way.[54]

But it is difficult to understand why, five years into the war, we are still funding it in largely the same manner. The pattern of asking for money in dribs and drabs, constantly revising the total costs—always upwards—has continued. In May 2007, the Pentagon estimated that it would need $141.7 billion for (fiscal) 2008 to continue to wage the wars effectively. By September, Secretary of Defense Gates reestimated the costs of our continuing engagement, increasing the number to nearly $190 billion; and when President Bush finally submitted his budget request for 2008 for the war, the number was several billion higher.

The use of "emergency" funds to pay for nearly all of five years of war makes a mockery of the budget process. "Emergency" funding is not subject to the standard caps on spending that Congress is required to observe. In addition, it may be submitted with a much lower standard of budget justification on the assumption that it is for genuine emergencies—like Hurricane Katrina—where the utmost speed is needed to get the funding to the field.

The emergency process denies the highly professional budget staff of both political parties—the budget committees, the authorizing committees, and the appropriations committees—the opportunity to review the numbers thoroughly. The emergency "supplemental" war requests were often kept secret until the last possible minute. This effectively has denied not just Congress but even the administration's own analysts in the Office of Management and Budget the opportunity to consider the numbers carefully. Given this lack of transparency, it should not be surprising that at the same time that we have seen widespread waste and profiteering in payments to contractors, we have also seen a lack of timely requests for vital equipment and continuing shortfalls in such critical areas as veterans' health care.

Every serious government oversight organization has criticized this way of paying for the war, citing instances of double-counting of obligations, mismatches between budgeted and actual expenditures, questionable figures, and lack of information about basic factors that affect costs such as troop strength and military reset needs.[55] The bipartisan Iraq Study Group, led by former Republican Secretary of State James A. Baker III and former Democratic congressman Lee Hamilton, called the administration's budget requests "confusing . . . making it difficult for both the general public and members of Congress to . . . answer what should be a simple question: How much money is the President requesting for the war in Iraq?"[56]

The Congressional Research Service has called the DOD's budget explanations of the cost of operations in Iraq and Afghanistan "limited, incomplete, and sometimes inconsistent." The nonpartisan Congressional Budget Office has also complained that "because appropriations for wars are mixed with DOD's baseline budget, information about 'what has actually been spent' or outlays is not available. That information is important for estimating the cost of alternate future scenarios and also for showing the effect of war costs on the federal deficit."[57]

Perhaps the most damning indictment of DOD war accounting comes from David Walker, the widely respected, non-partisan Comptroller General. He has testified that the lack of cost data and supporting documentation "make it difficult to reliably know how much the war is costing."[58]

WHILE UNDERMINING THE normal democratic processes of accountability, the emergency funding method did have some distinct advantages for the administration. First, it has in practice enabled the administration to muddy the cost of the war, perhaps in hope that by trickling in different requests, no one would notice the soaring total costs. Second, it helped reinforce the administration's public posture that progress was being made in the field and that the war would soon be "won." Moreover, the weak congressional oversight over the emergency funding had, from the administration's perspective, some further rewards: the supplementals provide a tempting pot of money that enables the Defense Department to fund a variety of non-war projects with minimal congressional scrutiny. On top of this, the administration could collude with Congress by turning a blind eye to an avalanche of "pork barrel" spending measures that had nothing to do with the war but that were tacked on to the emergency appropriations bills.

The congressional budgetary process is there for good reason. Resources are scarce. Money spent in one place could have been spent in another. Careful scrutiny allows democratic accountability and helps weed out waste, fraud, and corruption. Had our government been forced to subject its war requests to that process, the costs would have been more transparent, the trade-offs open to view, and the need to increase taxes or cut spending to contain the deficit clear.

The Framework

FROM THE UNHEALTHY brew of emergency funding, multiple sets of books, and chronic underestimates of the resources required to prosecute the war, we have attempted to identify how much we have been spending—and how much we will, in the end, likely have to spend.

The figure we arrive at is more than $3 trillion. Our calculations are based on conservative assumptions. They are conceptually simple, even if occasionally technically complicated. We have based all of our estimates and assumptions on government sources—the Congressional Budget Office (CBO), the Government Accountability Office (GAO), the Department of Defense (DOD), the State Department, the Department of Veterans Affairs (VA)—and on other published government reports.

We have also used data from respected independent sources such as the National Institute of Medicine, the *New England Journal of Medicine*, the National Brain Injury Association, the Veterans Disability Benefits Commission, and the Report of the President's Commission on Care for America's Returning Wounded Warriors (the Dole-Shalala Commission), as well as on data secured for us under the Freedom of Information Act by veterans' organizations. Before getting into the details of the calculations, it is worth understanding the framework, which we have divided into ten steps.

Step 1. *Total relevant appropriations/expenditures to date for military operations.* This is the simplest step, adding up all the various amounts that have been appropriated for the war. We have counted all war-related appropriations from fiscal year 2001 through December 25, 2007. (We have assumed that the rest of the proposed FY 2008 Supplemental will be enacted in step 4.) This includes funds in both supplementals and regular appropriation acts for DOD, State Department, USAID, and medical costs for the Department of Veterans Affairs. These funds cover military operations, base security, reconstruction, foreign aid, embassy costs, and veterans' health care[59] for the three operations that comprise the "Global War on Terror" (GWOT), the Pentagon's name for operations in and around Iraq and Afghanistan. These include Operation Iraqi Freedom (OIF),

Operation Enduring Freedom (OEF—Afghanistan), and Operation Noble Eagle (ONE), which encompasses base construction and embassy security, among other things.

Step 2. *Add "operational expenditures" and savings hidden elsewhere in the defense budget.* As noted earlier, the Defense Department has provided incomplete and often inconsistent information on how it is allocating funds between regular and war accounts. We attempt to estimate how much of the huge increase in defense expenditures during the past five years is attributable to Iraq and Afghanistan, and how much, in other ways, of Iraq war expenditures is hidden elsewhere in the defense budget. (It is at this step that we also attempt to account for any defense savings from going to war.)

Step 3. *Correct for inflation and the "time value" of money.* A dollar today is different from a dollar five years ago. And this will be even more true when we come to explore future expenditures, which we look at through 2017. Inflation means that past dollars are worth more than present dollars, and future dollars are worth less; and even without inflation, the fact that money can be put in a bank and earn interest means that one would rather pay out a dollar ten years from now than pay a dollar today. (This is called the "time value" of money.) The federal government can borrow money: as this book goes to press, the government borrows at 4.5 percent, and the inflation rate is just over 3 percent, so that the real interest rate is around 1.5 percent (the real interest rate takes account of the fact that, because of inflation, the value of the dollars the government pays back in a year are less than the value of the dollars it borrows today; the real interest rate is just the difference between the interest rate and the inflation rate). In fact, 1.5 percent is approximately the real interest rate which has prevailed over the past half century, and so that is the number we use in our calculations. In this book, we translate all expenditures into equivalent 2007 dollars.[60] This means that past expenditures get counted more (than if we just add up the "current" dollars), but future expenditures get counted less.

These first three steps give us what is called "the present discounted value" of operational expenditures to date—that is, the value in 2007 dollars of what we have spent. *But the meter is still ticking.*

Step 4. *Add future operational expenditures (both direct expenditures and those hidden elsewhere in the budget).* The operating cost of the conflict in future years will depend on several factors, including the number of troops and contractors we continue to deploy in the region, the level of combat engagement, and the rate at which we continue to use up, repair, and replace weapons and equipment. Even if the new president acted expeditiously and ordered a quick but orderly departure, it would almost surely require twelve months—taking us through the end of 2009. The more likely scenario is that there will be debate and discussion, consultations and deliberation, all of which will take time, and that in the end, the rundown of our troops will be more gradual. Any realistic assessment of the cost of the war needs to consider what we will have to pay for U.S. military operations over the next few years, as well as the cost of bringing troops and equipment home and maintaining a smaller deployment or peacekeeping force into the future. We base our estimates on official scenarios, which are explained in detail in chapter 2. When corrected for inflation and the time value of money, this gives us the total expected present discounted operational costs, that is, the total operational costs of the war, in 2007 dollars.

Step 5. *Add future (and current) costs of disability and health care for returning veterans.* One of our largest long-term financial obligations is the cost of providing disability compensation and medical care to service members who have fought in the war. To date, more than 1.6 million U.S. troops have been deployed, all of whom will be eligible for VA medical care for at least two years. Some 39 percent of veterans of the first Gulf War have received disability compensation. We expect that, judging from the number of claims that have been filed already, at least the same proportion will be entitled to receive disability pensions as a result of the current conflict. These costs can be considered "promissory notes" of the war—accrued liabilities that *must* be paid. We have included these liabilities in our assessment, just as any corporation is required to list its long-term liabilities (such as pension obligations) on its balance sheet.

Step 6. *Add future costs of restoring the military to its prewar strength, replenishing spent armaments, repairing equipment whose maintenance has been deferred.* We have already counted the operating costs of repairing and replacing ammunition, vehicle parts, and equipment being used up and replaced right away. But we have not been repairing or replacing equipment as fast as it is being worn out. There is a significant long-term additional cost in replacing and upgrading equipment worn out or destroyed by the war effort, a process known as "reset." In the current conflict, many vehicles are operating at ten times the peacetime rate—but we are not replacing them as rapidly as they are being used up. As a result, the Army's equipment arsenal is under strain. We have estimated the costs of restoring the military to its prewar strength, including all forces and the National Guard. Additionally, the Pentagon has announced plans to significantly increase the size of the U.S. Army by 2012, so that America can maintain its capacity to respond to crises outside of Iraq. We have therefore attributed to Iraq the cost of this incremental rise in forces for the period of time when we have troops deployed in Iraq.

Step 7. *Add budgetary costs to other parts of government.* The war has imposed costs across the government—not just at the Defense Department. Some of these costs are related to providing benefits to veterans: severely wounded veterans are eligible for a variety of additional programs, including Social Security disability compensation, subsidized loans, and other benefits.

The war affects the federal budget in other ways, some of which are hard to calculate: it has led to soaring energy costs, and, we argue in chapter 5, the economy is weaker than it otherwise would have been. This means that tax revenues are lower.

Together, steps 5, 6, and 7 allow us to calculate the *total budgetary cost of the war to the federal government, ignoring interest.*

Step 8. *Add interest.* The United States has borrowed most of the funds used to wage the war. We will have to repay this debt *with interest.* There are three amounts to consider: interest we have already paid on money we have already borrowed; interest we will have to pay in the future on what has already been borrowed; and interest payments on future borrowings. Since 2003, interest payments have accounted for less than 8 percent of the national budget—mostly as a result of the low deficits and balanced budgets of the Clinton era. The high borrowing to pay for the war will push interest up to more than 10 percent of the federal budget by 2011. We provide a conservative estimate of this interest, but we are careful to separate out this cost, because many economists argue that these interest payments should not be blamed on the war itself, but on the particular method used to pay for it. We pick up some of these costs in another way, when we examine the *opportunity costs*—what the economy would have looked like had we spent the money in another way.

The last two steps focus on converting budgetary costs into economic costs.

Step 9. *Estimate the cost to the economy.* For instance, we go beyond the budgetary costs resulting from the thousands of deaths and injuries from the war, recognizing that death benefits do not adequately measure the loss in output and that disability payments underestimate what these individuals would have earned had they been able to earn a normal living. There are a number of other *social and economic costs* that exceed the budgetary costs; these, while they may be large, are harder to quantify. They include the lost economic contribution of family members who have to leave the workforce to care for disabled veterans, as well as costs to state and local governments and other parts of society.

Step 10. *Estimate the macroeconomic impact.* The war has led to higher oil prices and larger deficits that crowded out private investments, and diverted government expenditures from schools, roads, research, and other areas that would have stimulated the economy more in the short run and produced stronger economic growth in the long run. Higher oil prices too have weakened the American economy—even if a few industries, especially the oil companies, have done well. In this step, we provide conservative estimates of the war's macroeconomic impact.[61]

Most economists would not count both interest and economic costs, because there is an element of double counting. Thus, we estimate that the total cost of the war ranges from $2.7 trillion in strictly budgetary costs to $5 trillion in total economic costs. We also considered a "best case" scenario in which the United States would withdraw all its combat troops by 2012 and fewer veterans would need medical care and disability pay. Even under this extremely optimistic scenario, the total economic cost of the war exceeds $2 trillion. Under the circumstances, a $3 trillion figure for the total cost strikes us as judicious, and in all likelihood errs on the low side. Needless to say, this number represents the cost *only to the United States*. It does not reflect the enormous cost to the rest of the world, or to Iraq.

Table 1.1. *The Growing Costs of the War*

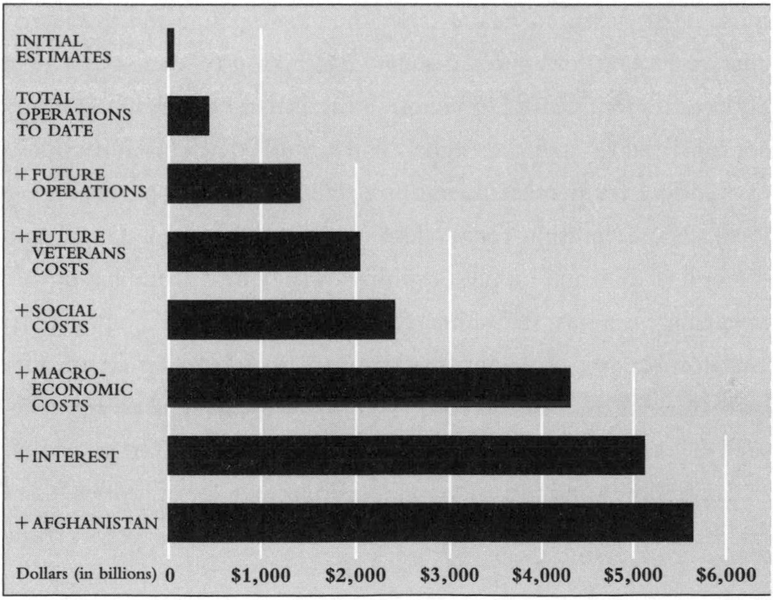

CHAPTER 2

The Costs to the Nation's Budget

THE UPFRONT COST of the wars in Iraq and Afghanistan, the amount Congress has appropriated and the military has spent or is about to spend, now exceeds $800 billion. That number—the one most often discussed in the news media—includes the president's current request for approximately $200 billion to wage the war in 2008, plus more than $645 billion in funds that Congress has already appropriated for Iraq and Afghanistan since 2001.[1] This money covers funding for combat operations, transporting troops, deploying, feeding, and housing them, deployment of National Guard and Reserves,[2] food and supplies, training of Iraqi forces, purchasing and repairing weapons and other equipment, munitions, supplementary combat pay, providing medical care to troops on active duty and returning veterans,[3] reconstruction,[4] and payments to countries such as Jordan, Pakistan, and Turkey for their logistical help.

Six hundred and forty-five billion dollars is a lot of money—and $845 billion is even more. Of this amount, three quarters, or some

$634 billion, is for Iraq, ten times the Bush administration's early estimates for the Iraq war, and more than the amount we spend on Medicare and Medicaid combined each year.[5] However, it considerably understates the amount that we predict the war will cost—a budgetary cost, excluding interest, on the federal government alone that we realistically believe is likely to reach $2.7 trillion. How do we arrive at such a large number?

We have estimated the true budgetary costs to the United States based on two possible scenarios.[6] The first is what we consider to be the "best case" scenario—the most optimistic scenario we can envisage in terms of the speed of U.S. withdrawal, the level of casualties, and the needs of veterans. We feel it is excessively optimistic—the *minimum* possible cost that the conflict will incur.

Our second scenario, which we call the "realistic-moderate" scenario is based on a longer timeframe for deployment of active duty troops, a higher demand for medical needs and disability claims for service members returning from the war, and a more comprehensive tally of costs to the government and the country. In this scenario we have also included incremental defense spending and other, hidden expenditures that, while they may not be labeled "war costs," are clearly the result of the conflict.[7]

However, even our "realistic-moderate" scenario is conservative, and understates the true costs. There are many costs we have not included, such as the full cost of disability compensation payments made to our veterans so far. Neither scenario provides any contingency for increased American troops to offset those that may be pulled out of Iraq by our Coalition partners.[8] In our calculations, we simply assume that the military effort makes do with this decreased support. Our realistic-moderate scenario includes an estimate of *past* war costs hidden inside the Defense Budget but ignores such costs going forward, other than the "reset" costs, even though we believe that these expenditures are likely to be large.

The budgetary costs of the conflict can be divided into four categories. First, there is the money we have already spent to conduct the wars in Iraq and Afghanistan (net of the amount of money we have saved in the process). Second, there are future costs—the future costs of waging the Iraq war and the costs we will have to pay even after the war is over. These include the cost of continuing military operations; the cost of providing medical care and disability compensation to veterans; the increased disability payments through Social Security; the cost of replacing military equipment, weaponry, and inventory, and restoring the armed forces to their prewar strength; and the cost of bringing troops and equipment home at the end of the conflict. Third, there are "hidden" costs that are related to the war, such as increases in the core defense budget (e.g., the higher cost of recruiting new soldiers) and the cost of expanding the size of the military. Finally, there are the interest costs on all the money we have borrowed to fight the war.

Costs of War to Date

THE UNITED STATES has now spent $645 billion on the wars in Iraq and Afghanistan. The operating costs, or monthly "burn rate," in these wars have been rising steadily since 2003—from $4.4 billion to $8 billion to $12 billion to an estimated $16 billion in 2008. To think of it another way, roughly every American household is spending $138 per month on the *current operating costs* of the wars, with a little more than $100 per month going to Iraq alone.

Future Costs of War

EVEN IF BOTH wars end tomorrow, our financial obligations will not. U.S. taxpayers owe billions of dollars to veterans who have become eligible for mandatory disability compensation, plus medical care and benefits. We also face a formidable and expensive challenge in rebuilding our military: replacing worn-out equipment, restoring the forces (including the National Guard) to combat readiness, and investing in more protective vehicles and weaponry. This will take years. Another major cost involves the funds required to bring the troops and equipment home.

But until we leave, there is the ongoing cost of combat operations and deploying troops in the field—the funds required to continue fighting the war. The projected amount depends on what we assume about the size of the force, the length of time they remain deployed in the theater, and the kind of mission they are engaged in.

In our "best case" scenario, we have estimated that the number of U.S. troops in Iraq and Afghanistan will decline to 180,000 (the pre-"surge" level) in 2008, then fall to 75,000 by 2010. By 2012, this will drop to a non-combat force of 55,000 servicemen and women.[9] This is a truly "best case" assumption, in view of the fact that the United States still keeps 80,000 troops in the Korean theater, and still had over 20,000 U.S. troops in Kuwait ten years after the end of the first Gulf War.

In our cost projections, we have included the nearly $200 billion that President Bush has requested for operations in fiscal year 2008,[10] as well as funding for operations from 2009 to 2017. We estimate that both the costs per troop and the overall operational costs will decline by 50 percent as the force shifts to a non-combat role. These future expenditures would add $521 billion in today's dollars (of which $382 is for Iraq) to our tally of operational war costs. However, we have based this figure on the highly optimistic assumption that we will be able to reduce not only our own costs but also our reliance on expensive contractors by half. If we replace demobilized support troops with private contractor services, it is unlikely that our monthly costs would decline this rapidly.

In the "best case" scenario, we project that the number of unique troops deployed to the conflict by 2017 will total 1.8 million.[11] It is this total number of deployed troops, which is critical in determining future veterans' medical and disability costs, that we will turn to shortly.

Our second scenario we believe is far more realistic. The administration has constantly painted a rosy picture: success is just around the corner. The American people deserve to know what the costs will be, not just in the best case. Still, we do not want to be accused of depicting an excessively pessimistic scenario, or of exaggerating costs; accordingly, even what we call the "realistic-moderate" scenario employs assumptions that are, almost assuredly, too conservative. It assumes that troop levels will decline more slowly as we approach 75,000 in 2012. This scenario is based on the recent deployment estimates by the Congressional Budget Office, which in turn is based on their discussions with the Defense Department. We also assume that these troops will continue to serve a primarily military function, including offensive operations against al Qaeda, working alongside Iraqi and Afghan forces, and maintaining security in violent neighborhoods. The number of troops required under this scenario will total 2.1 million by 2017. The continuation of combat operations means that the cost of deploying U.S. troops in this scenario will remain at $400,000 per capita, and that the fixed costs (such as maintaining bases) do not decline with troop levels.[12] Under this scenario, we expect total future operating costs (those explicitly attributed to the wars) to exceed $913 billion by 2017, of which $669 billion is for Iraq.

Veterans of the Iraq and Afghanistan wars who are wounded, injured, or become ill while on active duty are eligible to claim disability pay and benefits under a complex formula administered by the Department of Veterans Affairs (VA), which also provides health care to veterans through its vast network of hospitals and clinics. The VA provides additional benefits depending on the individual veteran's situation, including specially adapted housing grants, vocational rehabilitation, veterans' life insurance, and dependency and indemnity compensation paid to deceased veterans' surviving spouses and children. We will take a closer look at the VA's work with returning soldiers, and the costs associated with it, in the next chapter.

In both the "best case" and the "realistic-moderate" scenarios, we have projected the likely costs for providing medical treatment to returning veterans and paying them the disability compensation and other benefits they have earned. We have based this projection on the actual claims rate to date from Iraq and Afghanistan veterans. (However, many of those serving second and third deployments have not yet been discharged, and as we explain later, the likely disability rate among these may be considerably higher.) We have also used the 1991 Gulf War as a benchmark because current veterans are evaluated for benefits based on the same eligibility criteria that were used to decide whether Gulf War veterans qualified for benefits.

The history of soldiers who returned from the first Gulf War suggests that the costs of providing medical care and disability to our veterans will be high—very high. Though combat operations lasted for only a few weeks and left 147 dead and 235 wounded, 45 percent of the 700,000 Gulf War veterans have filed disability compensation claims, of which 88 percent have been approved. This costs the United States $4.3 billion in annual disability benefits.[13] Close to half have been treated in the VA medical system.[14]

The Iraq and Afghanistan conflicts have continued for five years, with the average serviceman or woman deployed for fifteen months and about one third serving second or third deployments. Most troops have served in grueling conditions. Each deployment increases the veteran's exposure to firefights and thereby increases the risks of disability *more* than proportionately.[15] Unlike previous wars, it is not only the combat troops who are at high risk for death and injury. Many "support troops"—those driving vehicles, performing medical evacuations, refueling aircraft—are also in danger. And there has been a greater involvement of Reservists and the National Guard—typically thirty-five-year-olds with families who can claim supplementary benefits. Women make up 14 percent of the troops. For all these reasons, we believe a projection based on comparison with the first Gulf War is extremely conservative: the number of troops who qualify for benefits in this new theater may be much higher; and more important, the current veterans will require more extensive medical care. Returning Iraq / Afghanistan veterans file claims for an average of five disabling conditions, compared with three for their Gulf War counterparts. Nearly 37 percent of soldiers who have returned from Iraq and Afghanistan have already sought medical treatment at VA hospitals and clinics (see Table 2.1). And current trends show that Iraq and Afghanistan veterans are even more likely to file disability compensation claims than the Gulf War veterans, and even more likely to have those claims approved.

Table 2.1. *More Iraq and Afghanistan Veterans Seek VA Health Care Each Year, FY 2003–2008*

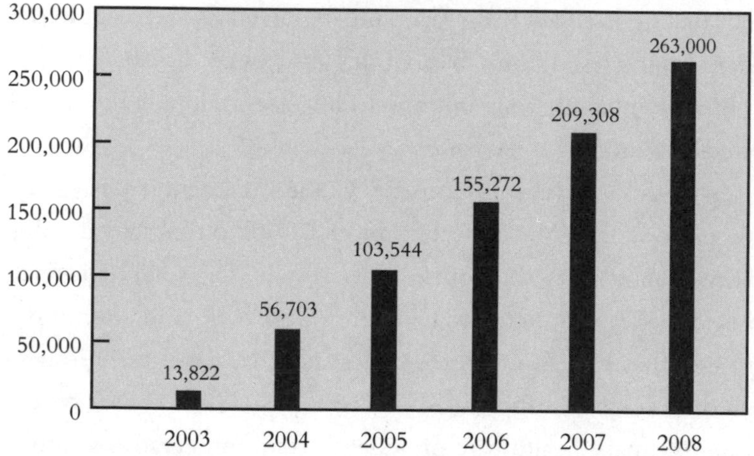

Source: U.S. House of Representatives Budget Committee, based on U.S. Department of Veterans Affairs.

Our "best case" scenario assumes that veterans' disability claims show a similar profile to those of Gulf War veterans—that is, 45 percent eventually claim some level of disability and 88 percent of those claims are at least partially granted. This would mean that 712,800 of our troops will eventually claim benefits. We estimate that the average payment to a disabled Iraq or Afghanistan war veteran will be the same as the average to a disabled Gulf War veteran

($542 per month) and that veterans' benefits will receive annual cost-of-living adjustments at the same rate as Social Security.[16] We project that injuries in the theater of operations will continue to occur at the current rate until 2011, when the force converts to a non-combat role. At that point we reduce the injury rate and all other operating costs by 50 percent.

For estimating the future cost of medical care, we project that 48 percent of current veterans will eventually seek treatment from the VA. Of these, we assume that 60 percent will seek short-term treatment (lasting less than five years) and 40 percent will remain in the system for the rest of their lives. Both scenarios predict that medical health care inflation will continue to increase at double the rate of general inflation, as it has for decades.

Under this set of assumptions, the U.S. government will pay $121 billion for veterans' health care[17] and $277 billion in veterans' disability benefits, over the course of their lives. The total long-term costs to the VA will therefore be $398 billion. Remember this is the best case that we can imagine—it assumes that fewer than 20 percent of all Iraq and Afghanistan war veterans will use the VA system as their primary health care provider (a very conservative assumption) and that only 39 percent of Iraq and Afghanistan veterans will eventually qualify for any disability compensation at all.

Our "realistic-moderate" scenario assumes that the conflict involves a total of 2.1 million servicemen and women and an active U.S. military presence in the region through 2017. In this scenario, assuming that the rate of death and injuries per soldier continues unchanged, we predict that 850,000 troops will file disability claims. Here, using a set of more realistic expectations for disability compensation adjustment, and projecting average monthly payments at the current average for all disabled veterans ($592), we estimate that the long-term cost of providing disability compensation will be $388 billion.[18]

In this scenario, we estimate that half of the veterans who use the VA medical system will remain in the system permanently (one quarter of all troops); and we project future costs of treatment based on the current average cost of treating each veteran in the system. Under these assumptions, we estimate that the cost of providing lifetime medical benefits to veterans will be $285 billion. This would bring the long-term cost to the U.S. taxpayer to $683 billion—close to what we have spent to prosecute the war in the first five years.

Social Security disability compensation to veterans of the conflict is another major cost of the war. Unlike veterans' disability pensions, the criteria for Social Security are very clear: any veteran who cannot work or hold down a job is eligible. The compensation benefit is currently about $1,000 per month. Veterans who have a 50 percent or more service-connected disability under the VA's guidelines (for physical handicaps or mental health conditions such as post-traumatic stress disorder) will likely meet the Social Security criteria. Many of the 45,000 Americans who were injured seriously enough that they had to be medically airlifted out of the combat theaters will qualify. So will one third of the almost 52,000 troops diagnosed with PTSD.[19] Individually, these amounts might seem small; but when added up over the four decades these individuals may receive payments, we estimate the totals will be in the range of $25–$44 billion.

Just as the Iraq war has taken a heavy human toll on the troops sent to fight there, the sand, heat, and harsh terrain are taking a heavy toll on equipment. We are using up basic equipment and weaponry much more rapidly than we can replace them. In fact, studies estimate that we are churning through equipment at six to ten times the normal, peacetime rate.[20] To date, the Army and Marines have rotated some 40–50 percent of their equipment through Iraq and Afghanistan. The Marine Corps has estimated that 40 percent of its ground equipment and 20 percent of its air assets are being used to support current operations.[21] Even in 2005, the GAO reported that "readiness" ratings for the twenty key equipment items showed a distinct decline since 1999. This group included tanks, armored fighting vehicles, trucks, helicopters, and combat aircraft.[22] In addition, the military has used up "prepositioned" stocks of fuel and supplies, drawn replacements from newly deploying units (leaving them short of equipment), and depleted much of the equipment brought by the National Guard.[23]

The armed services have also made a policy choice to keep equipment in the war zone and to rely almost exclusively on "in-theater" repair capabilities. As a result, much of the equipment has not undergone higher-quality depot maintenance since the start of operations. The quality of maintenance work inside the theater has many shortcomings, including substandard performance by contractors and insufficient personnel. A recent GAO report found that less than 7 percent of the major equipment in "sustainment" stock in the theater was fully mission-capable—even though this equipment is supposedly replacement for items damaged in combat. The GAO has also discovered that some U.S.-based units which are short on equipment and training time are also deferring depot maintenance. (GAO, "Preliminary Observations on Equipment Reset Challenges and Issues for the Army and Marine Corps," GAO-06-604T, March 2006.)

This approach, like other aspects of the administration's policy, will not only end up costing taxpayers; it will also mean that there will be a period during which our forces will not be as prepared as they should be. Indeed, from the perspective of the military, this lack of readiness is the major cost. As the defense analyst Carl Conetta wrote in 2006:

> Maintenance deferral has the character of borrowing on the future; eventually, the bill will come due. Equipment failures will accumulate. And equipment in larger quantity will have to be sent off to depots—or be replaced. While this more-thorough process of "resetting" the force is underway, units will have to make do with less or with lower quality equipment. For this reason, the postwar reset will constitute a refractory period—a period of diminished readiness. The Army will retain over 280,000 pieces of major equipment in Iraq until the end of the mission. . . . Decreased equipment readiness is not the only cost that will persist into the postwar period. There will be financial costs as well.[24]

The high level of casualties over half a decade has undermined the "human capital" of the armed forces; and further problems have been created by the difficulties in recruitment, forcing the military to enlist those it would never have accepted before the war. We will have to invest heavily in these troops to restore their prewar levels of strength, fitness, and readiness.

There are varying estimates of the cost and the length of time it will take to restore our military to its full strength. Cost estimates have ranged from $10 to $15 billion per year for the remainder of the conflict, and a minimum of two or three years beyond that just for the Army; and $2 to $3 billion for the Marines. Some defense analysts argue that it could take anywhere from ten to twenty years to reset. The Reserve forces, the National Guard, the Air Force, the

Navy, and other services will all require reset investments as well.[25] Assuming that we require $13 billion per year to rebuild Army forces and equipment, $2.5 per year for the Marines, and $1.0 billion for the Guard, Navy, and Reserves, and attributing 10 percent of the Air Force reset costs to the current conflicts, we estimate that over a period of fifteen years the military will require $250–$375 billion to rebuild the entire armed services.[26]

Deferring the maintenance of military equipment and the replacement of equipment until after the Iraq war is bad policy. But it has several political advantages. It lowers the current cost of the war and allows some of the costs to be shifted into the general defense budget. An example of this is the situation facing the Air Force fleet, which is older than ever and wearing out faster because of heavy use in Iraq and Afghanistan. The Air Force now spends 87 percent more on maintenance for its fleet of warplanes than it did ten years ago—due to the larger number of missions, the harsh flying conditions in Iraq, and the aging of the planes (twenty-four years old as compared with twenty-one in 2001).[27] The Air Force is seeking to purchase new aircraft to lower the age of its fleet—at a cost of some $400 billion over the next two decades. But this long-term cost is disguised as ordinary military replenishment.

The cost of eventually bringing troops and equipment home is another big bill that will eventually have to be paid. This involves demobilizing troops, transporting them home, providing them with transition services from active duty to veteran status, and transporting equipment, weapons, and munitions. There are 2,000 Abrams tanks and Stryker and Bradley fighting vehicles; 43,000 other vehicles, including more than 18,000 Humvees; more than 700 aircraft; and more than 140,000 metric tons of equipment and supplies, all of which will need to be repaired, transported, stored, and redistributed when they get back to the United States. We estimate that demobilization will cost over $20 billion (assuming that the normal costs of rotating troops will be covered by regular war appropriations).

"Hidden" War Costs in Defense Spending

U.S. APPROPRIATIONS LAW provides that funding for wars should be separated from regular defense appropriations. Wars cost extra: the money we are spending on Iraq and Afghanistan is *in addition to* the regular defense budget. America's total spending on defense vastly exceeds what we are spending on the wars. In 2007, for example, the United States spent $526 billion on defense items in addition to the $173 billion it spent on the Iraq and Afghanistan conflicts. However, in practice there is much overlap. The regular salaries of U.S. troops in Iraq are paid out of the regular defense budget. Extra pay, such as combat pay and hardship allowance, is paid for by extra war appropriations.

Defense spending has been rising rapidly as a share of GDP—from 3 percent in 2001 to 4.2 percent in FY 2008. However, this is not a historic peak or anything close to it. More troubling is that defense spending has been growing as a percentage of discretionary funding (money that is not required to be spent on entitlements like Social Security), from 48 percent in 2000 to 51 percent today. That means that our defense needs are gobbling up a larger share of taxpayers' money than ever before.

One of the ways that the administration has hidden the true cost of the Iraq and Afghanistan conflicts is by hiding war expenditures inside this burgeoning "normal" defense budget. The Pentagon's budget has increased by more than $600 billion, cumulatively, since we invaded

Iraq.[28] It is difficult to determine just how much ordinary funding is being siphoned off into the war effort (or vice versa).[29] As we saw in chapter 1, Pentagon financial accounting is so poor and lacking in transparency that the department has never even come close to earning a clean financial opinion. DOD's independent auditors cited material weaknesses[30] in the department's financial management systems, fund balances, inventory, operating materials and supplies, plant property and equipment, contractor-acquired material, environmental liabilities, accounting entries, and accounts payable—in other words, everywhere. The auditors referred to the department's accounts as "misleading," "deficient," and "inadequate."[31]

The fact that "ordinary" defense expenditures are being used for the war can be seen most directly in the Pentagon's monthly budgetary "sweep," in which any underspending on continuing programs is not carried forward but immediately reallocated to war spending. As another example, the Pentagon is also making a huge investment to expand the Special Operations Forces—in order to train more soldiers who can operate in difficult ground conditions like Iraq and Afghanistan.

Nonetheless, in our best case scenario, we have granted the DOD the benefit of the doubt and assumed that none of this excess $600 billion is related to Iraq and Afghanistan; we assume, in other words, that the Pentagon has been able to separate out its war expenditures funding needs so that all war spending has been classified as such.

However, in our realistic-moderate scenario, we count one quarter of this additional defense spending toward the war effort. We do this to take into account the many areas in which the war has indirectly made the Pentagon's "base" costs much bigger, such as intelligence funding, recruiting, and compensation.

Recruitment efforts offer a glimpse of the Iraq war's impact on overall defense spending rates. DOD has had to pay much higher sums to recruit and retain soldiers. The Pentagon has boosted regular military pay by 28 percent, doubled special pay, and added "concurrent" receipt of military and veterans' retirement benefits—much of this funded through the regular appropriations. And as trained soldiers become casualties, new soldiers have to be trained to replace them. Not surprisingly, given opposition to the war and scary casualty numbers, the military has struggled to meet its recruiting and retention targets for troops and officers. During 2005, the U.S. Army was below its recruitment goal for most of the year and eventually lowered its targets in order to achieve them.[32] In an effort to boost recruitment, the Pentagon raised the maximum enlistment age from thirty-five to forty-two, and progressively relaxed standards for appearance and behavior. In 2006, it began allowing more convicted felons to join the Army.[33] In 2007, the Army met its recruiting target, but only 73 percent of those enlisted were high school graduates—far short of the Pentagon's 90 percent goal. Recruiting among blacks and women has fallen precipitously. The number of "category 4" recruits—those who score lowest on aptitude tests—has risen. The erosion of standards may even lower the morale and effectiveness of the Army and make the long-term task of rebuilding the military more difficult and costly than ever.[34]

The Army National Guard, Army Reserves, and Marine Reserves also have experienced recruiting shortfalls. Applications to West Point and the U.S. Naval Academy have fallen 10–20 percent from their prewar levels. The Army is already predicting a shortage of 3,000 line officers in 2007, despite giving faster promotions (from captain to major), bonuses, and other perks.[35] The director of officer personnel management for the Army's Human Resources Command, Colonel George Lochwood, has estimated that the Army has only half the senior captains it needs.[36]

The military has responded by hiring thousands of additional recruiters, increasing its national advertising campaigns, and offering sign-up bonuses of up to $40,000 for new recruits. It also offers more generous educational, retirement, and disability benefits, provides "fast-track" routes to citizenship for Hispanic recruits and their families, and has increased benefits to families of soldiers. Experienced troops, who might otherwise leave the military for lucrative positions with private contractors, are now offered reenlistment bonuses of up to $150,000. In fiscal year 2007, after falling behind its May and June targets, the Army adopted a "Quick Ship" bonus plan whereby young people are paid a bonus up front if they report to basic training within thirty days of signing up. All of the armed forces are dedicating more time and effort to studying personnel needs and attrition problems. The cost for the military per recruit has increased from $14,500 in 2003 to a projected $18,842 in 2008.[37] These increased costs to the taxpayer are due largely to the unpopularity of the Iraq war, but many are concealed in the regular defense budget.

The military has finally admitted that fighting the war in Iraq without increasing the size of the armed forces has an impact on our defense capabilities elsewhere—a decision the respected military analyst Michael O'Hanlon calls "long overdue. . . . At the latest, it should have been made as soon as it became obvious in mid-2003 that the post-Saddam Iraq stabilization mission would be difficult and long."[38] It now intends to increase the total size of the armed forces by 92,000 by 2012—which will place an even greater strain on recruiting and retention efforts and force the United States to spend more to maintain the all-volunteer force.[39] To date, the president has requested $5 billion for this purpose in his request for supplemental war funding, and has asked for another $12 billion in the regular defense budget. CBO has estimated that the full request will total another $147 billion in the period through 2009–17. While the increased costs ought to be viewed as part of the war, the military will record most of it as increases in the "base" of defense spending. We have included $16 billion per year for this expansion in our realistic-moderate scenario.[40]

The costs of this war are so high that we hesitate to even mention "small" amounts of only a few billion. Yet there are numerous expenditures that do not get counted among the costs. For example, despite the overall lack of planning that has characterized this war, in the months prior to March 2003 the Pentagon spent $2.5 billion of its regular appropriation on planning for the invasion. It is easy to forget that in many other contexts, $2.5 billion would be a substantial amount of money.[41]

In this book, we focus on the *incremental costs of the war,* to the budget and to the Defense Department. Some have argued that fighting the Iraq war may have saved us some money. One of the biggest challenges economists face when trying to estimate costs is what's known in the jargon as the "counterfactual." What would have happened had we not gone to war? A commonly accepted perspective asserts that we would have continued the status quo, including enforcing the no-fly zones (restrictions we imposed on Iraq after the Gulf War, that it not fly over certain parts of the country). In this view, then, there was a slight savings in going to war: we no longer had to enforce the no-fly zones. In our calculations we subtract from the war the estimated cost of $10 billion per year to the Pentagon of policing the no-fly zones.[42] The question is, however, where did these savings go? They clearly did not go to cuts in Defense Department expenditures. The most plausible explanation is that the money went toward increased expenditures in Iraq, implying again that we have underestimated the true costs.

Costs to Other Branches of Government

ALTHOUGH THE BRUNT of war costs will be borne by the departments of Defense, State, Veterans Affairs, and Social Security, the Iraq conflict will also impose costs on other government departments. These include the Department of Labor (insurance and worker's compensation for contractors), the Department of Housing and Urban Development (housing loans to veterans), the Department of Agriculture, and the Small Business Administration (subsidized farm and business loans), and the increase in fuel costs for the entire government. While they may be significant, we do not include any of these budgetary impacts in our tally of the war's costs.

For example, a little known but mounting expense for the government is the insurance and worker's compensation we pay for private contractors operating in Iraq, through a program administered by the Department of Labor. The Defense Base Act of 1941 requires all U.S. government contractors and subcontractors to obtain worker's compensation insurance for civilian employees who work on U.S.-funded projects overseas. The insurance covers medical expenses, time lost from work, and disability and death benefits. It covers all U.S.-financed contractors, whether an American engineer or an Iraqi truck driver.[43] This means that every U.S. company must insure each of its employees against the risk of being killed or hurt. Because the insurance itself is prohibitively expensive during wartime (thus discouraging companies from bidding on these jobs), the U.S. government pays the premiums to insurance companies for the contractors. But in spite of this fact, if the contractors are killed or injured in an "act of war" (whether or not the injury or death occurred during work hours), the U.S. taxpayer is also responsible for paying disability, medical, and death benefits.[44]

Contracting is at record levels, with over 100,000 contractors operating in Iraq; and with so many contractors, not surprisingly, the expenses mount. Two costs are incurred by the government: the cost of insurance premiums and the cost of payouts. It is difficult to estimate how much the government spends on insurance premiums, because no agency regulates the premiums, and no one tracks the overall costs. Insurance premiums are estimated to cost between 10–21 percent of salaries. That means that the U.S. government would pay $10,000 to $21,000 in insurance for a private security guard earning $100,000 annually. Weekly pay ranges from $60 for Iraqi translators and laborers, to $1,800 for truck drivers, to as much as $6,000 for private security guards employed by companies like Blackwater Security. But even assuming we paid only 15 percent of a weekly wage of $1,000, for 100,000 contractors this adds another $780 million to the government's annual costs.

Death benefits to survivors and worker's compensation payments are long-term annual costs, payable for many years with automatic cost-of-living adjustments. Contractors have suffered high rates of death and injury in Iraq. The nature of the conflict is that support troops and support staff (translators, truck drivers, repairmen, and construction workers) have offered a "soft" target for insurgent attacks.[45] To date, it is estimated that 1,001 U.S. contractors have been killed and more than 12,000 wounded. Calculating only from this limited sample, and assuming that only half of the dead and wounded file claims, we can estimate that the long-term cost of providing these benefits may exceed $3 billion.[46]

The next chapter focuses on the medical costs that returning veterans will impose on the VA. But there are a host of other medical costs, hard to quantify, that will be borne by other parts of the government. For example, many returning veterans will have low incomes—partly because of their disabilities—that qualify their families for Medicaid and SSI, the supplementary income program under Social Security. Veterans who reach sixty-five will be eligible for Medicare. It is likely that many returning veterans will have higher medical costs as a result of their service—another example of where America will be paying for the costs of the Iraq and Afghanistan wars decades after they are over.[47]

There are two other categories of costs to the budget—neither of which is insignificant: the war has raised the costs of oil and energy for everyone, including the government; and the war has hurt our macroeconomy, and when the macroeconomy is weaker, so too are tax collections. With revenues lower and expenses higher, deficits are larger. In chapter 5, we estimate the reduction in GDP; from that, we can estimate the loss in tax revenues. Under the very "best case" scenario, limiting ourselves to the seven years 2003 to 2009, the loss is only $11 billion; more reasonable estimates put the tax loss at between $128 billion and $368 billion; but to err on the conservative side, we simply ignore these revenue losses.

Increased energy costs to the Department of Defense can be thought of as being implicitly included in the war expenditures; but there have been significant burdens to other departments of government. The non-defense agencies of the federal government consume over $4 billion in energy each year, with significant energy costs in the Department of Energy, the U.S. Postal Service, the VA (in hospitals, for example), NASA, Transportation, and the General Services Administration.[48] As the price of oil has climbed from $25 to nearly $100 dollars per barrel, these agencies have had to absorb these costs without receiving offsetting increases in their budgets. We have included $400 million per year of these extra energy costs as part of the budgetary impact of the war.[49] In the case of some agencies, expenditures have not increased to offset the higher energy costs. These agencies have been forced to cut back on their programs, which is another dimension of the costs of war.

Cost of Borrowing and Paying Interest on the Debt

AT THE ONSET of the Iraq war, the U.S. goverment was already running a deficit. Given that no new taxes have been levied (indeed, taxes, especially for upper-income Americans, were lowered shortly after we went to war), and non-defense expenditures have continued to grow, it is not unreasonable to assume, for purposes of *budgeting*,[50] that all of the funding for the war to date has been borrowed, adding to the already existing federal budget debt. We have already added, in our realistic-moderate scenario, almost $1 trillion to our national debt of $9 trillion to pay for the war so far.[51]

All this money will need to be repaid—with interest. Three categories of payments will eventually be due: interest we have already paid on the money we already borrowed; what we still owe on what we borrowed; and what we will have to borrow to pay for future war operations, including the interest we will have to pay on any future borrowings. In the first category, we have already spent $100 billion, of which some $75 billion is just for Iraq.

Some have argued that we should not include interest payments *as a cost of war.* The Bush administration chose to finance the war in this way and opted to cut taxes and not to cut other sources of expenditure. Presumably, it could have paid for the war some other way and thus avoided having to make interest payments on funds used to fight the war. A similar argument could be made for many other aspects of the cost of the Iraq war: some of the injuries described earlier are not necessarily the inherent consequences of the war itself, but of how the war has been conducted. The war—how it was fought and how it was financed—can be thought of as a package; it is the budgetary implications of this package that we are attempting to assess here.

Another way of seeing the consequences of the war—and the way we have financed it—is the following. Every year, we have been borrowing a couple hundred billion dollars to fight the war; even as—or if—the war ramps down, payments for disability and health care for returning veterans will be ramping up. Like borrowing to buy a car, the interest payments often rival the cost of the car itself; so too for war: interest on what we borrowed and interest on what we have to borrow to pay the interest on what we owe mount. We estimate in our realistic-moderate scenario that these interest payments, just by 2017, will amount to $1 trillion (the present discounted value of which, in 2007 dollars, is over $800 billion for Iraq and Afghanistan together). The next administration will face these bills, combined with the challenge of the nation's other needs, long postponed—a crumbling infrastructure, insufficient to meet the needs of America's growth, a health care system that fails to deliver for a substantial fraction of the population, and an education system whose deficiencies are long recognized; even if it should raise new taxes, the war and its aftermath will mean that the nation's debt will be much larger than it otherwise would have been: by 2017, in our realistic-moderate scenario, by $3.6 trillion (equivalent to $2.8 trillion in 2007 dollars), and even then, most of the bills for health care and disability payments will still not be due.

There is a simple message of this book, one that needs to be repeated over and over again: there is no free lunch, and there are no free wars. In one way or another, we will pay these bills. Conservatives emphasize the costs of raising taxes—there is a "deadweight loss," a loss in efficiency, in output, from the diminished incentives from the higher taxes. If we decide to someday pay these debts, then the cost to the economy may well be far more than the trillions of dollars of increased indebtedness. We need to include the *extra* cost of the burden of taxation to pay off the debt, a burden that the Bush administration has pushed onto our children. If we decide to continue to postpone paying off these debts and simply pay the interest due, taxes will be higher, year after year, forever—with all the consequent costs. If we decide to let the debts mount, as we borrow more and more money from abroad, we as a nation will be poorer; and for all our borrowing, some of the debt will come at the expense of domestic investment, either private or public, again at great expense to future growth. We will pay a price for the war, but we will also pay a price for trying to pretend that there was no cost and postponing these costs on to the future. These extra "bills due" could easily increase the costs of the war by 50 percent or more. The cumulative interest bill is a reminder of such economic realities.

In one way or another, we will be paying for these costs, today, next year, and over the coming decades—in higher taxes, in public and private investments that will have to be curtailed, in social programs that will have to be cut back. There is no free lunch—one cannot fight a war, especially a war as long and as costly as this war, without paying the price. .

COMBINING PAST AND future required expenditures, health and disability costs for veterans, and the expenditures hidden in the Defense Department budget, we estimate total expenditures for Iraq alone to be from $1.3 to $2 trillion—not counting interest payments. If we include the full costs of the two conflicts, the costs range from $1.7 billion in the best case scenario to $2.7 trillion in our realistic-moderate one. When we add the present discounted value of interest through 2017 alone, the total comes to $1.75 trillion for the best case scenario and $2.65 trillion for the more realistic one. When we add the two conflicts together, the total, with interest, comes to $2.3 trillion for the best case scenario and a whopping $3.5 trillion in the more realistic case. And as a reminder, even the "realistic" estimate is conservative.

But these are just the budgetary costs. They do not include the costs to the economy—the full economic costs of those who have been killed or injured, the cost inflicted by the soaring oil prices, the weaker future growth as a result of investment "crowded out" by the soaring deficit.

Table 2.2. *The Running Total: Budgetary Costs of the Iraq War*

Cost in billions	Best case	Realistic-Moderate
Total Operations to Date *(Spent to Date—2001–2007)*	$473	$473
Future Operations *(Future Operations only)*	$382	$669
Future Veterans' Costs *(Veterans Medical + Veterans Disability + Veterans Social Security)*	$371	$630
Other Military Costs/Adjustments *(Hidden Defense + Future Defense Reset + Demobilization, Less No-Fly Zone Savings)*	$66	$267
Total *(without interest)*	**$1,292**	**$2,039**
	Plus Interest	
Interest Costs *(Interest paid to date + Future interest on current debt + Future interest on future borrowing)*	$462	$616
TOTAL *(with interest)*	**$1,754**	**$2,655**

Table 2.3. *The Running Total: Budgetary Costs of the Afghanistan War**

Cost in billions	Best Case	Realistic-Moderate
Total Operations to Date *(Spent to Date—2001–2007)*	$173	$173
Future Operations *(Future Operations only)*	$139	$244
Future Veterans' Costs *(Veterans Medical + Veterans Disability + Veterans Social Security)*	$51	$87
Other Military Costs/Adjustments *(Hidden Defense + Future Defense Reset + Demobilization)*	$66	$137
Total *(without interest)*	**$429**	**$641**
	Plus Interest	
Interest Costs *(Interest paid to date + Future interest on current debt + Future interest on future borrowing)*	$151	$200
TOTAL *(with interest)*	**$580**	**$841**

*Includes Operation Enduring Freedom (Afghanistan) and some costs for Operation Noble Eagle (enhanced base security in Iraq and Afghanistan). Some costs for U.S. participation in NATO-led operations in Afghanistan may not be included.

Table 2.4. *The Running Total: Budgetary Costs of the Iraq and Afghanistan Wars*

Cost in billions	Best Case	Realistic-Moderate
Total Operations to Date *(Spent to Date—2001–2007)*	$646	$646
Future Operations *(Future Operations only)*	$521	$913
Future Veterans' Costs *(Veterans Medical + Veterans Disability + Veterans Social Security)*	$422	$717
Other Military Costs/Adjustments *(Hidden Defense + Future Defense Reset + Demobilization, Less No-Fly Zone Savings)*	$132	$404
Total *(without interest)*	**$1,721**	**$2,680**
	Plus Interest	
Interest Costs *(Interest paid to date + Future interest on current debt + Future interest on future borrowing)*	$613	$816
TOTAL *(with interest)*	**$2,334**	**$3,496**

Those who have paid the highest price are the men and women who have been fighting in Iraq and Afghanistan. The payments that they will receive for their disabilities and medical costs come nowhere near measuring the toll of the war. But these budgetary costs provide, at least, a starting point—to which we turn in the next chapter.

CHAPTER 3

The True Cost of Caring for Our Veterans

THE IRAQ WAR has placed an unremitting burden on our troops in the field. More than half of those who serve are under twenty-four; some are barely out of high school. Many have been required to remain on active combat duty far longer than their original commitment. Of the total number so far sent to Iraq, some 36 percent have been drawn from the National Guard and Reserves—men and women who typically have to leave husbands, wives, jobs, and small children at home.[1] While on duty there is no place to get away from the incessant fighting and the constant threat of death.

This group of men and women also contains an unprecedented number who have been wounded or injured and survived.[2] The Vietnam and Korean wars saw 2.6 and 2.8 injuries per fatality, respectively. World War I and World War II had 1.8 and 1.6 wounded servicemen per death, respectively. In Iraq and Afghanistan, the ratio is more than 7 to 1—by far the largest in U.S. history. If we include non-combat injuries, the ratio soars to 15 wounded for each fatality.[3]

In round numbers, this means that by the end of November 2007, some 67,000 U.S. troops had suffered wounds, injuries, or disease in Iraq and Afghanistan. True, some of these non-battlefield injuries would have been incurred even if the individuals had been on peacetime duty. But the American taxpayer will still have to pay the cost of their disability compensation and medical care, regardless of how they were injured. We have estimated that at least 45,000 of the injuries and diseases are directly attributable to the current conflict, based on an analysis of casualties during the five years before and the five years subsequent to the invasion of Iraq. This includes a 50 percent increase in the rate of injuries that occur outside of combat (such as vehicle crashes, aircraft accidents, and other non-battle injuries).[4]

By August 2007, two thirds of those who were medically evacuated from Iraq were victims of disease.[5] Thriving on the troops' crowded and sometimes unsanitary living conditions, microbial pathogens have caused diarrheal illnesses and acute upper-respiratory infections in Iraq and Afghanistan, similar to diseases seen during the first Gulf War. A number of military personnel have suffered various insect-borne diseases (leishmaniasis, a potentially fatal bloodborne disease transmitted by the bite of a sandfly, has afflicted thousands of U.S. troops), as well as nosocomial infections, brucellosis, chicken pox, meningococcal disease, and Q fever.[6] Smaller numbers of servicemen and women have had serious adverse reactions to the anthrax vaccine, antimalaria Lariam pills, and other mandatory medications.

Finding these numbers has not been as easy as it should, because the Defense Department is highly secretive about the true number of casualties. While it reports deaths of servicemen and women from both combat and non-combat operations, the DOD's official casualty record lists only those wounded in combat. The department maintains a *separate, hard-to-find* tally of troops wounded during "non-combat" operations, a figure that includes those injured during vehicle and helicopter crashes and training accidents, as well as those who succumb to a disease or physical or mental illness during deployment that is serious enough to require medical evacuation to Europe. (Even this tally does not include troops with non-battle injuries who are not airlifted out.) The military has considerable discretion in defining any injuries as combat-related—and some incentive to label them non-combat because it does not want to credit the enemy with a success. Thus, helicopter crashes that take place at night may not be included (even though it is unsafe to travel during the day) unless it is known with certainty that the craft was shot down by enemy fire. We found this list almost accidentally when the Department of Veterans Affairs published a complete casualty tally on its "Fact Sheet: America's Wars" in September 2006, which was linked to the full DOD source of data for all combat and non-combat casualties. Since Bilmes published her initial paper in January 2007, the DOD has insisted that the VA use only the *combat* casualty figures reported on DOD's main Web site, and the military's newly reorganized second site makes it difficult to locate and interpret the full casualty report. Despite these efforts at obfuscation, veterans' organizations have successfully used the Freedom of Information Act to obtain access to the full set of data and to circulate it to Congress and to the public.[7]

The enormous jump in survival rates we mentioned earlier is a tribute to advances in battlefield medicine, but it has budgetary consequences which the government has consistently failed to anticipate. All veterans, regardless of how their injuries were inflicted, are eligible for disability pensions and other benefits (including medical treatment, long-term health care, pensions, educational grants, housing assistance, reintegration assistance, and counseling). There are large costs, both for providing such benefits and for administering the programs. And underfunding can have serious consequences for the veterans—and even raise long-term costs. Currently, for instance, a combination of understaffing, poorly designed systems, and administrative incompetence has meant that there are frequently glitches in moving veterans off the DOD payroll and onto the VA payroll to obtain disability benefits. Not only do the increased needs of new veterans mean that sometimes they do not get the care they need; often they get served only by crowding out older veterans, who must wait longer—or may never get the care they need.[8]

This chapter examines the U.S. government's capacity to pay disability compensation, provide high-quality medical care, and offer other essential benefits to veterans of the conflicts in Iraq and Afghanistan. The population of veterans we focus on in this chapter is the 751,000 soldiers who have already served in Iraq and Afghanistan and been discharged. Future cost projections are based on continuing demand from these veterans and projected demand from troops still deployed. (By contrast, chapter 4 examines the total social costs of a small subset of this population—the troops who have sustained serious physical injuries or severe mental illness.)

Most of the sources we employ in our analysis, including the VA's data, do not differentiate between veterans returning from Iraq or Afghanistan or adjacent locations such as Kuwait. One third of those serving in the Iraq war have been deployed two or more times and many of them have served both in Iraq and Afghanistan, and / or other locations.[9] Of course, for the purposes of estimating the long-term cost to the government of caring for veterans, it does not matter where they served. However, the overwhelming majority of the deaths and injuries have been in Iraq—90 percent of those listed as wounded on the Pentagon's casualty reports.[10] We therefore attribute 90 percent of the cost of medical care and disability compensation to the Iraq conflict.

This chapter focuses on the budgetary costs to the United States of providing health care and disability to returning veterans. As the United States continues to place an emphasis on developing the Iraqi military to replace the American presence, it is worth asking what the cost to that country will be of providing medical care and any kind of long-term benefits to Iraqis who are fighting in this war. They will clearly be large—already more than 7,620 Iraqi soldiers have been killed, and many tens of thousands of Iraqi soldiers have been wounded (in chapter 6 we address the costs to Iraq and other countries).

Injuries Incurred by U.S. Soldiers in Iraq

AT HOME, WE are witnessing an unprecedented human cost among the veterans who return from Iraq and Afghanistan. More than 263,000 have been treated at veterans' medical facilities for a variety of conditions. More than 100,000 have been treated for mental health conditions, and 52,000 have been diagnosed with post-traumatic stress disorder (PTSD).[11] Another 185,000 have sought counseling and readjustment services at walk-in "vet centers."[12] By December 2007, 224,000 returning soldiers had applied for disability benefits. Most of these veterans are providing evidence of multiple health problems. The average claim cites five separate disabling medical conditions (e.g., loss of hearing, skin disease, vision impairment, back pain, and mental health trauma). The least fortunate among our veterans have suffered unimaginable horrors, such as brain trauma, amputations, burns, blindness, and spinal damage. Some have multiple injuries, a condition physicians refer to as "polytrauma." One in four returning veterans has applied for compensation for more than eight separate disabling conditions.[13]

Currently, improvised explosive devices, booby-trapped mines, and other types of roadside bombs generate two-thirds of all traumatic combat injuries.[14] The blasts create rapid pressure shifts, or blast waves, that can cause direct brain injuries such as concussion, contusion (injury in which the skin is not broken), and cerebral infarcts (areas of tissue that die as a result of a loss of blood supply). The blast waves also can blow fragments of metal or other matter into people's bodies and heads. Today's troops wear Kevlar body armor and helmets, which reduce the frequency of penetrating head injuries but do not prevent the "closed" brain injuries produced by blasts. These injuries can result in a diagnosis of "traumatic brain injury" or TBI.

TBI is one of the distinctive injuries of this war, because unlike previous conflicts where the mortality rate from such injuries was 75 percent or higher, the majority of these troops can now be saved.[15] Forward surgical teams pack open wounds on the battlefield and the wounded are evacuated to Landstuhl Air Force Base in Germany within twenty-four hours. Veterans who come to VA hospitals for medical treatment say they have been exposed to anywhere from six to twenty-five bomb blasts during their combat experience.

TBI is classified as mild, moderate, or severe according to the length of time the patient has lost consciousness and the duration of amnesia following the injury. Moderate and mild patients may suffer symptoms that include cognitive deficits, behavioral problems, dizziness, headache, perforated eardrums, vision and neurological problems. These injuries are different from the kind of concussion or "bruise on the brain" that can heal. Recent studies have shown that TBI inflicted by bombs can lead to permanent damage at the cellular level, even among mild and moderate victims.[16] Severe patients can suffer permanent damage that will result in a "persistent vegetative state." Up to one quarter of soldiers with blast-related injuries die.[17]

Dr. Gene Bolles, a Vietnam veteran with over thirty years of surgical experience, was chief of neurosurgery at the Landstuhl Regional Medical Center in Germany for two years. In a recent interview he had this to say about his experience:

> What I saw there . . . constantly in our intensive care units were these very badly injured young men and women with often only one extremity [left], severe burns, blinded—just severely, severely, injured people. I've had soldiers breaking down in tears becoming very emotional as they would tell me some of the things they were seeing and what bothered them. I've heard so much of that come from the soldiers it's taken a while for me to have a good night's sleep. These were the severest injuries I've seen in my career.[18]

Trapped in Limbo

WHEN OUR SERVICEMEN and women who have suffered mental and physical injuries finally do come home, they face a host of challenges as they try to find timely medical treatment and obtain disability benefits. Returning troops have been caught in a kind of limbo between the Department of Defense, which is responsible for the active duty military (including medical care at military facilities), and the Department of Veterans Affairs (VA), which manages medical treatment and disability compensation for service members who have been discharged. The VA is divided into the Veterans Benefits Administration (VBA), which determines eligibility for, and administers a wide range of, disability-related programs; and the Veterans Health Administration (VHA), which is responsible for the VA's hospitals, clinics, and other medical facilities. Despite numerous government studies, task forces, and declarations of intent, the two departments have failed to provide a "seamless" transition for disabled soldiers.

The transition problems entered the public consciousness after the widely reported fiasco at Walter Reed Army Medical Center outpatient facilities, where soldiers awaiting military discharge were kept in squalid conditions. Despite the fact that the hospital was operating at capacity and had experienced an influx of thousands of wounded troops returning from Iraq, the Pentagon had ordered a hold-down on costs and expenses (dubbed "efficiency wedges") at Walter Reed, because it was slated for eventual closure.[19] A nine-member bipartisan commission appointed by Secretary Robert Gates after the conditions came to light issued a blistering report on the situation, saying that the Pentagon had shown "virtually incomprehensible" inattention to maintenance and "an almost palpable disdain" for caring for our veterans.[20]

The root of the problem at Walter Reed, however, is the awkward, duplicative system by which wounded servicemen and women transition from military to veteran status. Had the patients at the Walter Reed outpatient center transferred into VA facilities, they would have lost all their military benefits and had no income to live on until they could qualify for veterans' benefits—which could take months or even years. Hundreds of outpatient clinics around the country have veterans trapped in similar circumstances. As Deputy Defense Secretary Gordon England told the Senate Armed Services Committee, "a problem with the transition from DOD to VA is that the disability ratings process is 'one size fits all,' the same basic procedures are followed inside the Department and during the transition to the VA for all individuals. The 11% of cases that are those wounded or severely wounded in war are funneled through *exactly the same system* as the other 89%—the career service members transitioning to retirement."[21]

Throughout the process, the burden of securing medical validation and getting the paperwork completed, including a 23-page application, falls primarily to the veteran (unlike systems in Australia, New Zealand, and the U.K., where the government effectively accepts the veteran's claim prima facie). DOD often fails to provide the statistical documentation necessary to move veterans from its payroll and medical care systems into the VA payroll and medical systems. The result is that veterans often need to undergo a second round of medical diagnostic tests in order to qualify for VA disability benefits and medical care.

And many veterans are simply overwhelmed by the volume and complexity of paperwork they need to complete. As Republican congressman Tom Davis III of Virginia put it: "You could put all the wounded soldiers in the Ritz-Carlton and it wouldn't fix the personnel, management and recordkeeping problems that keep them languishing in outpatient limbo for months while paperwork from 11 disjointed systems gets shuffled and lost."[22]

Even some soldiers with serious injuries lose this second battle with the bureaucracy. An e-mail that Linda Bilmes received on February 6, 2007, provides just one example:

Dear Prof. Bilmes,

I saw you on Democracy Now [TV show] on Feb 6, 2007. I have sent many letters and talked to Senate offices. We seem to be getting no where. My Nephew, Patrick Feges, was severely wounded in Iraq, Nov 2004. He had a visit from President Bush at Walter Reed Hospital, Purple Heart from Gov. Perry, but has to this date received NO benefits. He has been working with the VA, but letter after letter does not solve the problems. President Bush can use any numbers describing the wounded or the cost, but nothing is going to solve this problem, if no one is paying attention. Or cares.

Thank you
Kathleen Creasbaum, Patrick's Aunt

Patrick Feges of Sugarland, Texas, had been walking to the mess hall in Ramadi, in Iraq, when a mortar exploded. The blast severed a major artery and destroyed his stomach. Age nineteen at the time, he was listed in "very critical" condition, treated in four hospitals in three countries over five weeks, and finally received life-saving surgery at Walter Reed. Patrick recovered, although he lost mobility in his ankles and knees, suffered abdominal pain, and could not stand up for long periods. His injuries meant he had to abandon his plan to become a mechanic, but he decided to attend culinary school using the education and compensation benefits he was entitled to receive from the VA. After nineteen months, he still had not received a single penny in benefits and was living at home with his mother, who had taken a second job at night to help support him and his four siblings. (Patrick later received all of his education and retroactive disability compensation, but only after we provided his information to veterans' advocates Paul Sullivan and Steve Robinson, who intervened with the VA and told Patrick's story to *Newsweek* magazine.)[23]

Despite the media focus on the plight of soldiers like Patrick Feges, a presidential commission, a further commission ordered by Secretary of Defense Gates, and numerous congressional hearings, veterans still face long delays in obtaining disability benefits.

In the remainder of this chapter, we estimate the cost of providing the two primary types of assistance that we provide to our veterans: disability compensation and medical care.

Disability Compensation

THERE ARE 24 million living veterans in America, of whom roughly 3.5 million (and their survivors) receive disability benefits. Overall, in 2005 the United States was paying $34.5 billion in annual disability entitlement pay to veterans from previous wars, including 211,729 from the first Gulf War, 916,220 from Vietnam, 161,512 from Korea, 356,190 from World War II, and 3 from World War I. In addition, the U.S. military pays $1 billion annually in disability retirement benefits.[24]

Each of the more than 1.6 million troops deployed in Afghanistan and Iraq (and the hundreds of thousands more who are expected to serve before the conflicts are over) are potentially eligible to claim disability compensation from the Veterans Benefits Administration. Disability compensation is money paid to veterans with "service-connected disabilities"—meaning that the disability was the result of an illness, disease, or injury incurred or aggravated while the person was on active military service. Veterans are not required to seek employment nor are any other conditions attached to the program.[25]

Compensation is granted according to the degree of disability, measured on a scale from 0 percent to 100 percent, in increments of 10 percent.[26] Annual benefits range from $1,380 per year for a 10 percent disability rating to about $45,000 for those completely disabled.[27] The average benefit is $8,890, although this varies considerably. Vietnam veterans, for instance, average $11,670.[28] Veterans who are at least 30 percent "service-connected"[29] can qualify for additional benefits such as vocational rehabilitation, housing renovations, transportation, dependent support, home care, and prosthetics. Once deemed eligible, the veteran receives the compensation payment as a mandatory entitlement for life. Should he die, his survivors become eligible for benefits.

There is no time limit on when a veteran can claim disability benefits. The majority of claims are made within the first few years after returning, but many disabilities do not surface until later in life. Veterans are permitted to reopen a claim or file for increases. The VA is still handling hundreds of thousands of new claims from Vietnam-era veterans for post-traumatic stress disorder and cancers linked to Agent Orange exposure.

The process for ascertaining whether a veteran is suffering from a disability, and at what percentage level, is complicated and lengthy. First, the serviceman or woman has to navigate through the disability evaluation process within the military. This begins with a "medical evaluation board" (MEB) assessment, which takes place at a military treatment facility where a doctor identifies a condition that may interfere with a person's ability to perform his or her duties. If the person is deemed to be unfit for duty, he or she is then referred to a "physical evaluation board" (PEB), which decides if the illness or injury causing the unfitness is linked to military service. Depending on the particular circumstances, a serviceman or woman may then qualify for disability retirement benefits or a lump-sum disability severance payment.[30]

A veteran must then apply to one of fifty-seven regional offices of the Veterans Benefits Administration (VBA), where a claims adjudicator evaluates service-connected impairments and assigns a disability rating. The veteran needs to provide evidence of military service records, medical examinations, and treatment from VA, DOD, and private medical facilities. For veterans with multiple disabilities, the adjudicator assigns a composite rating. If a veteran disagrees with the regional office's decision, he or she can file an appeal to the VA's Board of Veterans Appeals. Typically, a veteran applies for disability in more than one category, for example, a mental health condition as well as a skin disorder. In such cases, VBA can decide to approve only part of the claim—which often results in an appeal. If the veteran is still dissatisfied, he or she can further appeal it to two even higher levels in the U.S. federal courts.[31] One in every eight claims is appealed.

The process for approving claims has been the subject of numerous complaints and Government Accountability Office studies and investigations. Even in 2000, before the war, the GAO identified long-standing problems, including large backlogs of pending claims, lengthy processing times for initial claims, high rates of error in processing claims, and inconsistency across regional offices.[32] In a 2005 study, the GAO found that the time to complete a veteran's claim varied from 99 days at the Salt Lake City office to 237 days in Honolulu.[33] In a 2006 study, GAO found that 12 percent of claims were inaccurate.[34]

The Veterans Benefits Administration has a huge backlog of pending claims, including thousands from the Vietnam era and before. In 2000, the VBA had a backlog of 228,000 pending initial compensation claims, of which 57,000 had been waiting for more than six months.[35] At the end of 2007, due in part to the surge in claims from newly injured veterans, the VBA's backlog was over 400,000 new claims, with 110,000 pending for more than six months.[36] The total number of claims, either new or in the process of being adjudicated, exceeds 600,000. The VA has announced that it expects to receive another 1.6 million claims over the next two years.

The VBA now takes an average of six months to process an original claim, and an average of nearly two years to process an appeal.[37] By contrast, the private sector health care/financial services industry processes over 25 billion claims a year, with 98 percent processed within sixty days of receiving the claim, *including* the time required for claims that are disputed.[38] Perhaps the most distressing implication of the six-month-long bottleneck in the VA claims process is that it deprives veterans of benefits at the precise moment when—particularly for those in a state of mental distress—they are most at risk of suicide, falling into substance abuse, divorce, losing their job, or becoming homeless.

Some soldiers can use the "Benefits Delivery at Discharge" program to avoid a long spell without benefits. This program allows soldiers to process their claims up to six months prior to discharge, so they can begin receiving benefits as soon as they leave the military. However, the prevalence of extended deployments, the number of second and third deployments, the use of "stop-loss" orders,[39] and the resulting unpredictability about when a soldier will be discharged have made it much more difficult to use this program; furthermore, it has not been not available to those in the National Guard.[40]

The transition from DOD to VA medical facilities is more complicated for seriously wounded veterans. A wounded veteran may receive initial treatment at Walter Reed Army Medical Center before being transferred to a VA facility. The incompatibility between the DOD and the VA paperwork and tracking systems means that these veterans can have a hard time securing the maximum disability benefits at discharge. This tracking and paperwork disconnect not only creates unnecessary problems in moving veterans through the system, but also makes it more difficult to analyze the data on military injuries in medical and other studies.

The Pentagon's poor accounting system causes yet more problems for veterans. GAO investigators have found that the DOD pursued hundreds of battle-injured soldiers for payment of non-existent military debts. In one instance, an Army Reserve staff sergeant who lost his right leg below the knee was forced to spend eighteen months disputing an erroneously recorded debt of $2,231. This blot on his credit record prevented him from obtaining a mortgage. Another staff sergeant who suffered massive brain damage and PTSD had his pay stopped and utilities turned off when the military erroneously recorded a debt of $12,000 because it neglected to record his separation from the military. In a third case, an Army staff sergeant paralyzed from the waist down received no net pay for the last four months he was in the Army, in payment of a non-existent $15,000 debt. This happened in January 2005; it was not until February 2006 that the sergeant was finally repaid the money. Yet another case stemmed from a soldier who was erroneously listed as absent without leave while she was actually being treated for inoperable shrapnel in her knee. Ironically, these fake debts are often registered because the soldier loses personal equipment (such as body armor and night-vision goggles) after being seriously wounded and evacuated from Iraq. Hundreds of injured soldiers may be in this situation.[41]

Given the problems that exist now in the system, it is imperative that we consider the demand for benefits that will arise from future veterans of the conflicts in Iraq and Afghanistan. It is difficult to predict the exact number who will claim for some amount of disability, but we know that already 31 percent of the soldiers who have returned have filed claims. We expect that percentage to rise.

The first Gulf War provides a basis for comparison. Certainly, soldiers from the Iraq and Afghanistan wars will qualify for disability based on the same criteria that are used to evaluate first Gulf War veterans.[42] Some 45 percent of the veterans of that conflict filed disability claims; 88 percent of their claims were approved at least in part.[43] The United States currently pays about $4.3 billion annually in disability payments to veterans of the first Gulf War.[44] Some have argued that the claims from that war have been unusually high because those soldiers suffered such high exposure to chemical toxins. But in both Iraq wars, a number of veterans were exposed to depleted uranium used in antitank rounds fired by U.S. M1 tanks and U.S. A-10 attack aircraft. And service members in both Iraq and Afghanistan have been deployed for months on end, involved in severe ground warfare and heavy exposure to urban combat.[45] VA psychiatrist Jonathan Shay, winner of a 2007 MacArthur Fellowship for his work among combat veterans, points out that "the mental health toll of the Iraq war is more comparable to Vietnam—except that the soldiers today face a different technological and conceptual environment, and of course the survival rate is much higher."[46]

In addition, there is a lag between mental health conditions being diagnosed and the veterans' ability to file a disability claim for them. To date, the VA has diagnosed 52,000 cases of PTSD, but only 19,000 claims have been filed for it. GAO has reported that it takes one year, on average, for PTSD claims to be filed. It is likely that the number of such claims will grow rapidly from now on. We therefore believe that the number of disability claims from the current conflict is likely to be at least as high as the claims from the first Gulf War, if not higher.

Of the 1.6 million U.S. servicemen and women so far deployed in the Iraq/Afghanistan conflicts, 751,000 had been discharged by December 2007. All are potentially eligible for disability benefits, and by December 2007, 224,000 veterans had applied. Through mid-summer 2007, 90 percent of those applying for disability were approved.[47]

The estimated costs of providing disability benefits to veterans are immense. To recap, in our conservative scenario, we reached an estimate of $299 billion for disability benefits; in our moderate scenario, the figure was $372 billion. These figures exclude some veterans' benefits such as private, state, and local health care, disability, and employment benefits for returning veterans. They also exclude the costs associated with veterans' family members, including compensation and education benefits for surviving spouses and children.

We have assumed in our best case scenario that, on average, compensation will equal that of claimants from the first Gulf War: $6,506. This is a conservative assumption because in the first Gulf War, each veteran claimed for an average of three disabling conditions, whereas this new group of veterans claims for an average of five conditions.[48] Furthermore, we already know that the actual rate of serious injuries is much higher than in the first Gulf War.

The realistic-moderate scenario assumes that the average payment per claims is the actual average for new claimants in 2005, which is $7,109.[49] This may still be conservative, considering that Vietnam veterans receive an average of over $11,000 and many analysts consider the injuries in this war to be more similar to Vietnam.

Increasing Workload

OF COURSE, THE issue is not simply cost but also efficiency in providing benefits to disabled veterans. The Iraq and Afghanistan

Table 3.1 *Projected Increase in Disability Claims in "Best Case" Scenario*

DISCHARGED TO DATE	2007	2008	2009
Cumulative Discharged to Date	751,000	751,000	751,000
Benefits Claim Rate	27.3%	28.5%	29.7%
Beneficiaries - Discharged to Date	204,873	214,125	223,377
Benefit Rate	$6,502	$6,697	$6,898
Total Costs of Benefits ($b)	$1.3	$1.4	$1.5
FUTURE DISCHARGES	**2007**	**2008**	**2009**
Cumulative Future Discharges	0	104,900	209,800
Benefits Claim Rate	19.4%	21.4%	23.4%
Beneficiaries - Discharged to Date	0	22,432	49,110
Benefit Rate	$6,502	$6,697	$6,898
Total Cost of Benefits ($b)	$0.0	$0.2	$0.3
GRAND TOTAL			
Net Disability Claims	204,873	236,557	272,487
Cost/Claim	$6,502	$6,697	$6,898
Grand Total ($b)	$1.3	$1.6	$1.9

war veterans are filing claims of unusually high complexity. To date, the backlog of pending claims from these recent war veterans is 40,000, but the vast majority of servicemen and women have yet to file. That the Veterans Benefits Administration is sympathetic to the plight of disabled veterans should not obscure the fact that the system is already under tremendous strain. If only one fifth of the returning veterans who are eligible claim in a given year, and the total claims reach a rate even comparable to the first Gulf War, the best case scenario for the VA is that the number filing over the next ten years could easily rise to more than 700,000, with almost 75,000 new applicants in a single year (see Table 3.1).[50]

2010	2011	2012	2013	2014	2015	2016	2017
751,000	751,000	751,000	751,000	751,000	751,000	751,000	751,000
31.0%	32.2%	33.4%	34.7%	35.9%	37.1%	38.4%	39.6%
232,630	241,882	251,134	260,387	269,639	278,891	288,144	297,396
$7,105	$7,318	$7,538	$7,764	$7,997	$8,237	$8,484	$8,738
$1.7	$1.8	$1.9	$2.0	$2.2	$2.3	$2.4	$2.6

2010	2011	2012	2013	2014	2015	2016	2017
314,700	419,600	524,500	629,400	734,300	839,200	944,100	1,049,000
25.4%	27.5%	29.5%	31.5%	33.5%	35.6%	37.6%	39.6%
80,035	115,205	154,205	198,286	246,196	298,352	354,755	415,404
$7,105	$7,318	$7,538	$7,764	$7,997	$8,237	$8,484	$8,738
$0.6	$0.8	$1.2	$1.5	$2.0	$2.5	$3.0	$3.6

312,664	357,087	405,757	458,673	515,835	577,244	642,899	712,800
$7,105	$7,318	$7,538	$7,764	$7,997	$8,237	$8,484	$8,738
$2.2	$2.6	$3.1	$3.6	$4.1	$4.8	$5.5	$6.2

The VBA has more than 9,000 claims specialists, who are required to assist the claimant in obtaining evidence, in accordance with hundreds of arcane regulations, procedures, and guidelines. They must also rate the claims, establish claims files, authorize payments, conduct in-person and telephone interviews, process appeals, and generate various notification documents. They decide the effective date that the veteran is entitled to receive the benefit, since claims are granted retroactively. In other words, these employees play a critical role in whether a veteran can secure his or her benefits.

But currently, the agency faces an enormous staffing problem. According to the VA, new employees need two to three years of experience and training to become fully productive. In May 2007, 40 percent of the claims staff had been employed for less than three years; 20 percent had been there for less than one year.[51] Many experienced staffers have been diverted from processing claims in order to train new hires. Moreover, several VBA regional offices still use antiquated IT systems that make it difficult for the specialists to do their job efficiently—forcing them to use unreliable old fax machines to obtain vital documentation from veterans and medical providers.

Proposals to fix this problem that are currently in Congress include funding for 500–1,000 additional administrative staff members to process the claims backlog. But this alone will not reduce the long waiting times that veterans face. At best, a few hundred inexperienced new staffers (assuming they can all be hired quickly) may produce a marginal improvement in claims-processing time, during a period in which the agency faces a huge influx of complex claims. Indeed, it is conceivable that the task of training and integrating a large number of inexperienced people will in the short term actually lengthen processing times, decrease accuracy, and increase the level of appeals. The problem is further compounded by the fact that many experienced VBA personnel will be retiring over the next five years.[52]

Medical Care for Veterans

THE VA ALSO provides medical care to more than 5 million veterans each year through the Veterans Health Administration. This includes outpatient health care, as well as dental, eye, and mental health care, hospital inpatient and outpatient services at 158 hospitals, 800 community clinics, 136 nursing homes, 209 veterans' centers, and other facilities nationwide. Medical care is free to all veterans for the first two years after they return from active duty; thereafter, the VA imposes co-payments on certain categories of veterans, with the amounts related to the level of disability and the income of the veteran.[53] It is likely that Congress will increase the number of years of free care from two to four or five, a move we strongly support.

The VA has long prided itself on the excellence of care that it offers. In particular, VA hospitals and clinics are known to perform a heroic job in areas like rehabilitation. The medical staff are experienced in working with veterans and provide a sympathetic and supportive environment for the disabled. The VA also plays a major role in educating medical students: 107 of the 126 medical schools in the United States are formally affiliated with a veterans' hospital, and these hospitals train 20,000 medical students and 30,000 residents each year.[54]

Given this sterling reputation, the demand for VA medical treatment now far outstrips supply. In 2003, former VA Secretary

Anthony Principi announced the decision to ration care based on need and income level. He suspended enrollment of the lowest priority group of veterans ("Priority Group 8"), those who were above a certain income level and not disabled, and increased co-payments and other fees for other groups. This has placed VA health care out of reach for at least 400,000 veterans since then.

Soldiers and other troops returning from Iraq and Afghanistan now face long waiting lists—especially in certain specialties—and in some cases simply absence of care. To date, 35 percent of the 751,000 eligible discharged veterans from Iraq and Afghanistan have sought treatment at VA health facilities. This figure comprises less than 5 percent of the total patient visits, but it will grow. According to the VA, "As in other cohorts of military veterans, the percentage of [Iraq and Afghanistan] veterans receiving medical care from the VA and the percentage of veterans with any type of diagnosis will tend to increase over time as these veterans continue to enroll for VA health care and to develop new health problems."[55]

The war in Iraq has been noteworthy for the types of physical injuries sustained, especially traumatic brain injuries, but the largest unmet demand is in mental health care.[56] The strain of extended deployments, the stop-loss policy, stressful ground warfare, and the uncertainty surrounding discharge and leave have all taken their toll. Some 38 percent of the veterans treated so far—an unprecedented number—have been diagnosed with a mental health condition. These include post-traumatic stress disorder, acute depression, and substance abuse. According to Paul Sullivan, "The signature wounds from the current wars will be (1) traumatic brain injury, (2) post-traumatic stress disorder, (3) amputations and (4) spinal cord injuries, and PTSD will be the most controversial and most expensive."[57]

Mental health disorders are extremely costly, both because they require long-term treatment and because those who suffer from them have a greater tendency to develop physical medical problems. Long-term studies of Vietnam veterans have also shown that PTSD leads to worse physical health throughout a veteran's life.[58] According to the Veterans Disability Benefits Commission, PTSD sufferers had the worst overall health scores in the veteran population, and one in three veterans diagnosed with PTSD was permanently incapable of working, classified as "individually unemployable." The National Institute of Medicine found that while PTSD accounts for 8.7 percent of total disability claims, it represents 20.5 percent of compensation benefit payments.[59]

PTSD is highly prevalent as a result of multiple rotations into combat, the widespread use of IEDs, and the absence of a defined "front line" in battle. Troops who have returned from Iraq and Afghanistan also talk about the moral ambiguity of seeing combatants dressed as civilians, of not knowing who is friend or foe. Studies have found a strong correlation between the length of time a soldier serves in a war zone and the likelihood of developing PTSD.[60] For this reason, we can expect that servicemen and women on their second and third deployment are at high risk. Most of those serving second and third deployments have not yet returned. Moreover, psychiatrists point out that a good many PTSD symptoms—confusion; vertigo; being easily startled; numbness; difficulty in sleeping, concentrating, and communicating—can also be symptoms of traumatic brain injury, and so there is some difficulty and overlap in the diagnoses.

Compared to veterans of earlier conflicts, Iraq and Afghanistan war veterans are far more likely to seek help for mental health distress, in part because of awareness campaigns run by veterans' organizations and an outreach campaign conducted by the VA itself.

There is no reliable data on the length of waiting lists for returning veterans, but even the VA concedes that they are so long as to have the effect of denying treatment to a number of mental health patients. In *Psychiatric News* for May 2006, Frances Murphy, M.D., then Under Secretary for Health Policy Coordination at the VA, stated that mental health and substance abuse care are simply not accessible at some VA facilities. When the services are available, Dr. Murphy added that in some locations "waiting lists render that care virtually inaccessible."[61]

Veterans' groups have filed a national class action lawsuit against the Department of Veterans Affairs on behalf of veterans and their families seeking or receiving death benefits or disability compensation for PTSD. The plaintiffs estimate that the class includes between 320,000 and 800,000 veterans, a figure they arrive at by multiplying the number of troops deployed by their estimated incidence of PTSD (20–50 percent). The plaintiffs are not seeking financial compensation; rather, they want the VA to acknowledge a number of policy failures. "This isn't a case about isolated problems or the type of normal delays and administrative hassles we all occasionally experience with bureaucracies," says Gordon P. Erspamer, the lawyer representing the veterans on a pro bono basis. "This case is founded on the virtual meltdown of the VA's capacity to care for men and women who served their country bravely and honorably, were severely injured, and are now being treated like second-class citizens. The delays caused by the VA have created impenetrable barriers to relief for thousands of impaired veterans."[62]

The administration has followed the same pattern of underfunding for veterans returning from the war that it has followed in financing the war itself. In fiscal year 2006, the VA had to request $2 billion in emergency funding, which included $677 million to cover an unexpected 2 percent increase in the number of patients (half of whom were Iraq and Afghanistan veterans); $600 million to correct its inaccurate estimate of long-term care costs; and $400 million to cover an unexpected 1.2 percent increase in the costs per patient due to medical inflation. In the previous fiscal year, the VA requested an additional $1 billion in emergency funding, of which one quarter was for unexpected needs related to the current conflict and the remainder was to cover an overall underestimation of patient costs, workload, waiting lists, and dependent care.[63] The pattern of underfunding noted in 2005, where needs were projected on the basis of data from 2002, before the war in Iraq began, has repeated itself every year of the war. The VA has told Congress that it can cope with the surge in demand, despite overwhelming evidence to the contrary.[64] For FY 2008, the Congress is demanding an additional $3 billion in emergency funding (above the president's request) for the VA health care system to cope with the rising demand.

As the demand for medical care increases, the already overwhelmed Department of Veterans Affairs may be unable to meet it, particularly in rural areas where the organization has found it difficult to recruit medical staff. Brain trauma units and mental health facilities are experiencing staff shortages, and the VA also needs to expand systems such as triage nursing to help maximize the effective use of scarce medical resources. The quality of medical care is likely to continue to be high for those veterans treated in the new polytrauma centers, but the current state of service means that not all facilities can offer such high quality in a timely fashion.

The budget shortfalls and the testimony of experts like Dr. Murphy suggest that veterans returning from Iraq and Afghanistan, particularly those with mental health conditions, may not be able to obtain the health care they need. These veterans are at high risk of unemployment, homelessness, family violence, crime, alcoholism, and drug abuse, all of which impose an additional human and financial burden on the nation. When the VA does not provide these services, costs are shifted to others; local and state governments provide many of the social services that veterans require, but some are already under tremendous strain and may not be able to cope.

As we discussed in chapter 2, in our best case scenario, we have estimated that the annual cost of providing care to the 48 percent of current veterans who will eventually seek treatment from the VA is $3,500, based on reports that the current cost to the VA of treating veterans of the Iraq and Afghanistan wars is about this amount.[65] However, this is almost certainly too low, because the current average bill includes initial visits required to validate a condition (that a veteran needs just to qualify for disability compensation). The cost of those visits is much lower than the cost of treatment. To recap from chapter 2: this scenario assumes that 1.8 million U.S. troops are eventually deployed, and that troop levels fall to 55,000 non-combat soldiers in 2012. Injury rates and other costs are reduced by 50 percent from this point onward. Under this set of assumptions, the U.S. government will pay out $121 billion for veterans' health care, $277 billion in veterans' disability benefits, and $25 billion in Social Security disability compensation over the course of their lives. The total long-term costs to the federal government will therefore be $422 billion.

In the realistic-moderate scenario, we use the current *average annual cost* to the VA of treating all veterans in the system, which is $5,765.[66] This scenario assumes that the conflict involves a total of 2.1 million servicemen and women and an active U.S. military presence in the region through 2017. Assuming that the rate of death and injuries per soldier continues at current rates, we estimate that 50 percent of those who enroll in the VA health care (one quarter of all disabled veterans) will continue to use the VA as their lifetime health care provider. Under this set of assumptions, the cost of providing lifetime medical costs to veterans will be $285 billion, $388 in disability benefits, and $44 billion in Social Security compensation, bringing the total long-term cost to the U.S. government to $717 billion.

We have already emphasized that the VA is not the only part of the federal government that will face incremental costs as a result of the injuries and disabilities stemming from the Iraq and Afghanistan wars. For instance, many of the injured will be unable to get jobs providing family health care benefits; Medicaid will pick up at least part of the tab. The single, largest number that can easily be quantified is Social Security disability benefits. The combined cost of health care, VA disability, and Social Security disability for our

Table 3.2. *Total Medical, Disability, and Social Security Disability Costs for Veterans*

Veterans' Cost (in U.S. $billions)	Best Case	Realistic-Moderate
Iraq Medical	106.4	250.1
Iraq Disability	242.9	341.2
Iraq Social Security	21.7	38.4
Iraq Total	**371**	**629.7**
Afghanistan/Medical	14.7	34.7
Afghanistan/Disability	33.7	47.3
Afghanistan/Social Security	3.0	5.3
Afghanistan/Total	**51.4**	**87.3**
TOTAL COSTS	**422**	**717**

moderate scenario comes to nearly three quarters of a trillion dollars; in the best case scenario, it is still almost half a trillion dollars.

We should reemphasize that these scenarios are very conservative in several of their key assumptions, for instance, in assuming that only half the returning veterans will eventually seek any medical treatment at all from the VA. Many returning veterans do not have any alternative source of health care, and until this country provides a system of universal care, the VA system will be the only available option. We have also made a leap of faith in assuming that the VA can hire the additional medical personnel required to provide the requisite health care without raising salaries.

We have seen how returning veterans now face a bureaucratic nightmare, including long backlogs in processing claims. But we have also seen that much larger demands will almost surely be imposed on the system. Without a major overhaul of the current system, veterans are virtually guaranteed bigger claims backlogs, longer waiting lists, and a possible diminished quality of medical care. The hundreds of thousands of new veterans who seek medical care and disability compensation in the next few years will overwhelm the system in terms of scheduling, diagnostic testing, claims evaluation, and access to specialists in such areas as traumatic brain injury. Veterans with mental health conditions are most likely to be at risk because of the lack of manpower and the inability of those scheduling appointments to distinguish between higher- and lower-risk conditions.

Nor have we included the cost of increased administrative and medical staff that will be needed to meet the huge demand. There is a tendency in some circles to view such civil servants as part of a bloated bureaucracy. But no agency, public or private, can administer programs of the size we are discussing without incurring substantial administrative costs. The necessary expansion of the VA staff to handle these obligations—between a half and three quarters of a trillion dollars—will themselves reach into the billions, perhaps tens of billions of dollars. Such "overhead" or "transactions" costs typically exceed 10 percent or more of the benefits disbursed, even in well-run private programs—suggesting that the requisite incremental administrative spending may indeed by substantial.[67]

The budgetary costs on which we have focused here are only part of the overall costs of war. Just as there has been no preparation for delivering the promised benefits to our veterans, there has also been no preparation for paying the cost of another major entitlement program. Formally, the VA's disability benefits are a "mandatory" benefit—they are not subject to the annual appropriations process. Such expenditures are traditionally labeled as "entitlements." By contrast, the VA's medical budget is discretionary, that is, lawmakers appropriate funds on an annual basis. But the country has a moral obligation to provide returning veterans with the medical benefits that have been promised, and it is hard to conceive of the nation walking away from such a commitment. In our analysis, we have projected costs and assumed that Congress will provide the requisite funding. (There are slight differences in our estimates of these medical costs over the period 2007–17 and that of the CBO [in our best case scenario, our estimate is $16.6 billion; that of the CBO is $7–$9 billion]. The major difference lies in the large *lifetime* costs—going well beyond the next ten years—which CBO's methodology ignores.)

In any of the scenarios, the funding needs for veterans' benefits comprise an additional major entitlement program along with Medicare and Social Security. President Bush has frequently spoken out about the funding gap for Social Security. The magnitude of that gap depends on assumptions about wage growth, migration, and life expectancy; but in most scenarios, the consequences of the funding gap are not imminent. By contrast, the Iraq war has created, since 2003, a new, large, and growing entitlement funding gap.

This additional entitlement for veterans' medical care will place additional strain on the discretionary budget—which is the source of funding for the veterans' medical system. History suggests that after a war, the public often loses interest in taking care of its veterans. Veterans are likely to lose out again unless we can secure the monies for taking care of them in trust funds.

Veteran's disability benefits and medical care are two of the most significant long-term costs of the Iraq war. The war—in all of its dimensions—has budgetary costs, but it also has broad social and economic costs. This is especially true of the human toll, which has been borne by our troops. This chapter has focused exclusively on the budgetary costs of caring for veterans. It does not take into account the value of lives lost or decimated by grievous injury. Nor does it take into account the economic impact of the large number of veterans living with disabilities who cannot engage in full economic activities. These economic and social costs may be far greater than the budgetary costs faced by the federal government; they are the subject of the next chapter.

CHAPTER 4

Costs of War That the Government Doesn't Pay

PREVIOUS CHAPTERS FOCUSED on the budgetary costs of the war—the dollar costs to the U.S. Treasury and, ultimately, to the American taxpayer. These costs are staggering—between $1.7 and $2.7 trillion, even without counting interest costs. But this is still not the complete picture. It ignores the substantial "social" costs of the war—those costs that aren't captured in the federal government budget but that nevertheless represent a real burden on society. We estimate that these social costs add at least $300 billion to $400 billion to the total war bill—before we even count in the macroeconomic costs that are the subject of the next chapter.

Some of the major costs, including the loss of productive capacity of the young Americans killed or seriously wounded in Iraq, can be quantified; but there are a number of other social costs that are not easily quantified but that nonetheless constitute a significant portion of the hidden costs of the war.

Social and economic costs differ from budgetary costs in several ways. First, they include costs borne by those other than the government, such as veterans, their families, or the communities where they live. An example of this is when a family member is forced to quit (or change) jobs in order to be a caretaker for a disabled veteran. Consider, for example, a veteran with severe physical or brain injuries who is 100 percent disabled. He will receive about $45,000 from the Department of Veterans Affairs and perhaps an additional $12,000 in Social Security disability pay. He will receive health care and some additional benefits. But all of this adds up to a fraction of what it costs to look after a young man (or woman) who needs help getting dressed, eating, washing, and performing other daily activities, as well as constant medical attention, twenty-four hours every day, seven days per week. Someone else—perhaps a wife, husband, parent, or volunteer in the community—is bearing the real cost of providing this care.

If veterans' hospitals cannot hire enough mental health professionals to treat the epidemic of PTSD, the burden is further shifted onto the veterans and families. They are the ones who bear the cost of waiting in a queue for long hours, facing month-long delays to get a doctor's appointment, and traveling hundreds of miles to seek medical attention.[1]

Social costs may also differ from budgetary costs when prices paid by the government do not reflect full market value, or where there is a broader short- or long-term impact on the economy as a whole. The formula for calculating veterans' disability compensation is supposed to approximate the earnings that a veteran would have obtained had he or she not become disabled. But a recent in-depth analysis by the Veterans Disability Benefits Commission[2] showed that the dollar amounts paid to younger veterans and to those with severe mental disabilities do not come anywhere close to matching what they could have earned.[3] In addition, the U.S. government's disability stipend doesn't compensate for the pain and suffering of the veteran and his family, or the impairment in quality of life. These costs are very real—but hard to quantify.

The Economic Value of the Loss of Life

ONE OF THE major *economic costs* is the loss of the productive capacity of young Americans who have been killed or seriously wounded in Iraq. We have estimated these costs, which we refer to as "social costs," for soldiers who have been killed, wounded, or injured. The government's budgetary cost for a soldier who is killed, for instance, is relatively small. Although no one doubts that the military mourns the loss of its men and women, the official military payout when one dies amounts to only $500,000. This is in the form of a $100,000 "death gratuity," and $400,000 in life insurance paid to the family survivors.

The amount is a small fraction of the value used in even the narrowest economic estimates of the value of a lost life, what a person might have earned had he/she been able to fulfill his/her normal life expectancy. One way to think about the economic value of a life lost is to recognize that the compensation an individual would have received had he been injured or killed in an ordinary automobile accident or an accident in the private workplace would have been far higher than what soldiers receive. Juries, for instance, frequently award much higher amounts in wrongful death lawsuits; recent awards have reached as high as $269 million.[4] In 2005, a jury awarded $8.5 million to a train conductor who sustained mild traumatic brain injury following a train wreck. The conductor suffered what appeared to be a mild concussion and was treated and released from the hospital. Soon after his release, he began to experience headaches. He returned to the hospital, underwent an MRI, and was sent home after it showed nothing unusual. After a period of weeks, his family reported that he was exhibiting odd behavior and drinking too much. Eventually, the MRI scans were re-examined and they showed small brain hemorrhages, a sign of closed brain injury. The conductor could no longer work; he was awarded $8.5 million in compensation.[5]

For troops returning from Iraq and Afghanistan with mild traumatic brain injuries, this kind of story is all too familiar. Very frequently, the families notice behavioral changes and the veteran cannot hold down a job. People with traumatic brain injury also have a higher rate of using health care facilities and experiencing medical problems such as cognitive impairment and motor dysfunction. Once individuals with TBI return to the community, they typically face increased costs caused by their more frequent use of outpatient medical services. Because people with TBI have cognitive impairments in memory, attention, and what scientists call executive functioning, they may have difficulty adhering to medication regimens, keeping appointments, and following other parts of their treatment plan.[6] Even where TBI is diagnosed correctly, the maximum compensation the government provides is less than $60,000 per year in combined veterans' and Social Security disability benefits. This is a fraction of the amount brain injury experts estimate for the typical lifetime costs for a person surviving a severe TBI, which exceeds $4 million.[7]

Economists have developed a systematic procedure for valuing a life lost, called the "value of statistical life" (VSL) which the government uses, for instance, in determining whether the cost of some government regulation (e.g., for automobile safety or protecting the environment) is worth the value of lives saved. To take one example, if someone is killed in an environmental disaster, the Environmental Protection Agency estimates that the loss from that death is $7.2 million.[8] In many cases, those killed in Iraq were young men and women in peak physical condition, at the beginning of their working lives.[9] The true economic loss from their deaths could be much higher.

This method is also widely used by insurance companies and other private sector concerns, for instance, in determining the appropriate compensation for a "wrongful death." While there are a wide range of VSL values in use, even by different government agencies, the $7.2 million number chosen for the value of an American who is killed in an environmental or workplace accident is near the center of the range, and is the number that we use in this study.[10] Furthermore, all of the numbers are much larger than the $500,000 our servicemen and women receive, which is the amount we counted in our earlier budgetary costs.

Using a VSL of $7.2 million, the economic cost of the more than 4,300 American deaths in Iraq and Afghanistan to date already exceeds $30 billion, far greater than the budgetary cost of $2.15 billion. Even this estimate does not take into account any indirect costs—such as the impact on morale or the heightened risk of PTSD among comrades of the fallen soldier who may have witnessed the death.

We should also apply the VSL to the estimated 1,000 U.S. contractors who have died in the region, many of whom were highly skilled specialists, working on reconstruction projects such as fixing the electricity grid and oil facilities. In valuing their deaths, we again have not counted the impact on the success of the project in Iraq, or the fact that their high casualty rate has made it more difficult and expensive for Western contractors to hire replacements to perform these jobs.

If we include U.S. military contractors, and the likely additional fatalities from the conflict in the future—even in the best case scenario—the social costs of the Iraq war's fatalities rise to greater than $50 billion in 2007 dollars. And while it seems harsh to convert these deaths into cold financial numbers, at the same time it is important to recognize that our economy and our society will suffer as a result of the fatalities in this war.

The Economic Cost of the Seriously Injured

THE WOUNDED TOO contribute significantly to the cost of the war, both in a budgetary sense (in the form of lifetime disability payments, housing assistance, living assistance, and other benefits) and in an economic sense.

To date, there have been more than 65,000 "non-mortal casualties," among U.S. servicemen and women deployed to Iraq and Afghanistan, nearly half of them in combat. Some 14,000 of these troops were seriously wounded and unable to serve after their injuries. The injuries include wounds from shells, explosions, gunfire, mortar, land mines, grenades, and firearms, as well as infections resulting in such conditions as brain and spinal injuries, blindness, facial deformity, multiple broken bones, nerve damage, cardiac and internal organ damage, and mental breakdown. The total number also includes 35,000 servicemen and women who were injured in other ways while serving (truck accidents, construction accidents, training accidents, friendly fire, and so on) or who succumbed to illness or disease and required medical evacuation.

Thousands more veterans incur various injuries and illnesses while on active duty but are not medically evacuated. These numbers are reflected in the more than *quarter of a million* returning soldiers who have already been treated at a veterans' medical facility. Eighty percent of these veterans have applied for disability benefits, which means that over 200,000 men and women who fought in Iraq or Afghanistan have been left with a physical or mental impairment. But this is just the troops that have already returned. Before the war is over—and in its aftermath—the numbers are likely to more than double.

Assigning a dollar value to these injuries is complicated. The standard approach that economists use is to ask: How much would the person have paid *not* to have this happen? This is called the "value of statistical injury." One might callously take the view that someone who volunteers to join the armed forces recognizes the implicit risk of death or injury in that decision.[11] But applying this logic to casualties from the Iraq war does not work quite that cleanly. The majority of troops who are serving in Iraq and Afghanistan did not fully understand the risk. One third of them have been drawn from the National Guard or are Reservists who could not have imagined that they would be deployed overseas for long periods of time. Even within the regular Army, Air Force, Navy, and Marines, few could have reasonably expected that they would face deployments of fifteen months (instead of the usual twelve), shortened home leave, second, third, and even fourth deployments, mandatory extensions, and other measures that have made some of their service less than voluntary.

We have estimated the economic loss to the wounded based on

the severity of their injuries. We assigned economic values to soldiers who have suffered brain injury, amputation, blindness, other types of severe injuries (burns, spinal, and major organs); injuries that require medical evacuation (excluding those counted above); and post-traumatic stress disorder. We estimate that those soldiers with grievous injuries, who can no longer be employed, suffer an *economic* loss as great as someone who has been killed, because their labor output will essentially be lost to the economy. Therefore, we should assign them a VSL of $7.2 million, similar to the one we used to calculate the value of statistical life. Those with serious service-connected injuries, but with less than full disability, are (as we noted), evaluated by the VA in determining disability benefits as to their "percentage disability." We apply those percentages in assessing the overall economic costs of disability.[12]

Whereas in the previous chapter we focused on the cost to the government of caring for all veterans from Iraq and Afghanistan, the social costs described in this chapter focus more narrowly on the economic loss from those who have been killed, wounded, injured, or severely mentally impaired. Some analysts have questioned whether non-battlefield casualties should be attributed to the war. Clearly, they are a budgetary cost to the government—VA hospitals do not reject a wounded soldier because his helicopter crashed on takeoff (as opposed to being shot down in combat). But it is also true that accidental injuries occur during peacetime operations. The question is whether the Iraq war has produced *incrementally* more non-hostile casualties than would be expected for troops in peacetime operations. To answer this question, we compared the rate of accidental ground casualties among active duty troops for the five years prior to the war with the rates since 2003. We found that the rate of non-combat deaths for troops deployed in Iraq in the period 2003–07 has been *more than double* the rate for the five years prior to 2001.[13] A similar pattern can be observed for accidental injuries.

Experts attribute this increase to the fact that, even more than in previous wars, the support troops deployed in Iraq are in harm's way. As Dr. David Segal, director of the Center for Research on Military Organization at the University of Maryland, explains: "In past conflicts, there were tremendous differences in exposure to psychological trauma between combat troops and support troops. Now it doesn't matter. Now people in logistics and other support functions are seeing more combat than in past wars. Basically once you put boots on the ground in Iraq, you're in a combat zone."[14]

The Economic Cost of Mental Health Disability

ANOTHER SIGNIFICANT ECONOMIC cost arises from war-related mental health disabilities. Leading veterans' advocates say that mental health disorders will be the top medical problem facing veterans of the Iraq and Afghanistan conflict.[15] The numbers to date confirm this; already, more than one in seven returning veterans has been treated for mental health issues by the VA. Suicide rates in the Army for the past two years have been 17.3 soldiers per 100,000 and 19.9 per 100,000, respectively, the highest levels in sixteen years.[16] In past years, the rate has averaged 11.6 per 100,000. One quarter of these servicemen and women took their own lives while serving in Iraq or Afghanistan.

Not surprisingly, those who are deployed longer or face repeated deployments face the greatest risk of mental health problems.[17] One recent study by the Defense Department, confirming previous studies, found that soldiers deployed longer than six months, or who had been deployed multiple times, were more likely to screen positive for a mental health issue. This is partly because the longer they serve, the more likely it is that a soldier will face the death or disfigurement of a comrade. The study reported that two thirds of soldiers and Marines showing signs of a mental health problem knew someone who had been seriously injured or killed. And the study showed that deployment length in itself was directly linked to morale issues in the Army.[18]

Veterans are entitled to disability pay if they suffer from mental illness; but the Veterans Disability Benefits Commission discovered that the amount such veterans receive understated their economic loss by a wide margin. For example, VA benefits covered only 69 percent of the income that a thirty-five-year-old veteran with a mental health disability could have expected to earn had he been healthy. For veterans who are rated 100 percent mentally disabled, the commission found that the lifetime earnings disparity—the difference between what the veterans could have earned and the disability compensation they were paid—was as high as $3.6 million.[19]

The commission also found that veterans with severe mental health disorders had the poorest overall ratings on health and quality of life. Among those suffering from PTSD, one out of every three was not capable of working at all ("individually unemployable"). In addition, long-term mental health disorders led to poor physical health. As the commission points out: "Physical disability did not lead to lower mental health in general. However mental disability did appear to lead to lower physical health in general."[20] This confirms the findings of Dr. Charles Marmar, chief psychiatrist at the Veterans Hospital in San Francisco, who has led a thirty-year longitudinal study of Vietnam veterans. His study found that

PTSD patients suffered diminished well-being, physical limitations, compromised health status, permanent unemployment, days spent in bed, and episodes of violence.[21]

The Cost of Quality-of-Life Impairment

THE DISABILITY COMMISSION provides a sense of the kind of serious impairment to their lives that veterans experience: 57 percent of all veterans with any kind of disability suffer "severe or very severe" bodily pain. This finding is all the more extraordinary because the data includes veterans who are rated only 10 percent disabled. Nearly half of the veterans surveyed took daily pain medication, and one quarter required help in routine activities such as bathing, dressing, and preparing meals. Overall, 53 percent of the veterans reported that their disability had "a great effect" on their lives. Three quarters agreed with the statement: "Living with my service-connected disability bothers me every day."[22]

The impairment to quality of life was strongest among veterans with mental health disorders. While this is hard to quantify, studies have attempted to do so. For example, 99 percent had a worse health status, overall, than would have been expected in their age bracket. They also scored extremely poorly on overall life satisfaction. The overall satisfaction with life, even for those rated as 10 percent disabled, is only 61 percent; for those rated 50–90 percent mentally disabled, the measure hovers around 30 percent.[23]

The VA does not currently pay *explicit* compensation for quality-of-life impairments. With compensation often not even covering the loss of earnings, there is obviously nothing left for those impairments. However a number of other countries, including the

United Kingdom, Canada, Australia, and New Zealand, pay specific compensation for the loss of quality of life. Maximum lump-sum in these countries ranges from $220,459 in Australia to more than $500,000 in Britain.[24]

The Disability Commission and the Dole-Shalala Commission viewed the failure to compensate for lost quality of life with concern. Based on their recommendations, and those of the National Institute of Medicine, the Bush administration has recently proposed overhauling the disability rating system to include a new quality-of-life payment that would compensate for limits in day-to-day activities that result from a veteran's disability. This would be in addition to the standard monthly payment that is supposed to compensate for loss in earnings capacity. In our analysis of the budgeting impact of the war, we have not included the economic value of these impairments—implying, once again, that our estimates are too conservative—but clearly, if these recommendations are adopted, it will significantly increase the budgetary costs.

The Strain on Veterans' Families

THE U.S. GOVERNMENT'S disability stipend doesn't compensate for the pain and suffering of the veteran's family, or the impairment in their quality of life. These costs are very real, but many of them are again hard to quantify.

Repeated tours of duty have imposed an enormous emotional, social, and economic strain on the individuals serving and on their families. Here is how Paul Rieckhoff, director of Iraq and Afghanistan Veterans of America, describes the situation:

> Right now, when a service member is critically wounded, friends and family members put their lives on hold to be at their loved one's bedside during the weeks and months of recuperation. Annette McLeod is one such family member. When her husband, Specialist Wendell McLeod, was injured while serving in Iraq, she rushed from her Chesterfield, South Carolina, home to be with him at Walter Reed in Washington, DC. Caring for her husband, who sustained multiple injuries to the back and head, became her full time job. After three months at Walter Reed, the human resources department at the factory where she had worked for 20 years told her she had exhausted her time off. She was forced to give up her job and all of her benefits.

The McLeods' story encompasses two additional costs of the war: the cost to the families of having to sacrifice their income and even their jobs, which we have quantified; and the cost of the emotional strain on the families, which is impossible to value.

Current law offers caregivers few employment protections, so they not infrequently lose their jobs and suffer financial consequences. The Dole-Shalala Commission estimated that in 20 percent of families of veterans who were wounded, injured, or otherwise incapacitated (e.g., with mental illness), someone has been forced to leave his or her employment in order to become a full-time caretaker.[25] Many other families have had to hire a caretaker. We estimate that about half of families have made some significant adjustments in their lives in order to accommodate the returning veteran.

There is an economic cost to the families having to make these sacrifices. We believe this will impose an economic cost in excess of $50 billion, even in the best case scenario. This assumes that 20 percent of veterans with serious injuries (including TBI, amputation of limbs, blindness, deafness, severe burns) and 30 percent of those with severe PTSD will require that a family member give up their current work, or hire a full-time caretaker, in order to become a primary caregiver to the veteran.

Many families will also incur significant expenses in providing health care for returning veterans, both immediately after their return and over the long term—beyond the amounts paid for by the government. Veterans with serious brain injuries, polytrauma, blindness, deafness, severe burns, and amputations will require additional medical attention for the rest of their lives.[26]

While these troops are receiving medical treatment from the Defense Department, most of the costs will be paid for by the Department's TRICARE system.[27] This will cover the veteran's hospitalization and care in a military hospital (e.g., in Walter Reed). But even then, the veterans and their families, many of whom lack supplemental private health insurance or disability insurance, will be obligated to absorb any costs that are not covered. This places an especially heavy financial burden on families with low incomes. For example, Professor Uwe Reinhardt of Princeton University told the Senate Veterans Affairs Committee how he went to visit his son, a Marine captain who was wounded in Afghanistan. "When we went to Landstuhl [military hospital in Germany] to visit our son, I asked myself, 'How easy is it actually for people from the lower economic strata to fly to Landstuhl?' My wife and I just jumped on the plane and flew there and stayed in a hotel. Those visits are crucial to the healing. So it is a real problem."[28]

After a wounded serviceman or woman leaves the military, the family will need to help him or her secure extensive documentation and evidence in order to enter the veterans' medical system. During the transition from military to veteran status, it is usually the family that ends up paying the veteran's living costs and health care.

These costs can be considerable, although once again they are difficult to quantify. The government pays for standard treatments, rehabilitation, physiotherapy, prosthetic devices, and some medication. It will not cover most of the costs for supplementary nursing and in-home care, for standard alternative therapies, and for some newer prescription medications and treatments. All told, we believe that the excess medical costs to the veterans and their families will be significant, but for this study, we have not quantified the costs. It is worth stressing that some injuries, such as serious traumatic brain injury, require millions of dollars of care throughout the veteran's life.

Estimating the Major Social Costs

WE ESTIMATE HERE the true social costs of the Iraq and Afghanistan conflicts that are in excess of the budgetary costs, that is, that are in excess of what the government pays. For each death, we attribute a VSL of $7.2 million per life, minus the $500,000 the government pays out for each soldier killed. For serious injuries, we calculate the value of economic loss due to injury, less the amount paid in disability compensation.[29] Taking into account the value of lives lost, the value of economic loss due to serious injury and mental impairment, and the social costs for families that have had to give up their jobs or hire caretakers for the wounded, and subtracting out government transfer payments to disabled veterans, we still find that the economic cost of the Iraq war adds $262 billion to the total costs *beyond the budgetary expenditures* under the best case scenario, and $367 billion in the realistic-moderate scenario. Including Afghanistan and related operations, the cost ranges from $295 to $415 billion.

Our best case scenario includes only the direct combat injuries who did not return to duty and half the serious non-combat injuries (in order to approximate the number of incremental casualties—the number that is in addition to those that would have occurred in a peacetime army).[30] We have assumed that this 50 percent ratio of incremental injury extended to other forms of disability, so we have only included 50 percent of serious PTSD sufferers[31] and 50 percent of other serious non-battle injuries, such as blindness, serious vision impairness, deafness, and traumatic brain injury.

However, we have serious reservations about this approach. Considering that 263,000 troops have already been treated by the VA, and 52,000 diagnosed with PTSD (which does not arise at all during peacetime), it seems highly arbitrary to reduce the number of non-battle disabilities by half. In addition, in peacetime, the casualty rate among Reservists and the National Guard would have been very small, since few of them would have been deployed at all.

Accordingly, our realistic-moderate scenario takes all serious casualties into account when calculating social costs. This includes all serious injuries incurred in hostile and non-hostile conditions: all troops who require medical evacuations plus one third of all PTSD patients, as well as a smaller allowance for the economic loss attributable to all other servicemen or women who were wounded sufficiently seriously to be evacuated from the theater for medical treatment.

In both scenarios, we have assumed that servicemen and women who were wounded during the conflict, treated, and then returned to active duty will not suffer any loss beyond the small amount of disability pay they may receive for that impairment. We have not included any cost for quality-of-life impairment. We have included the cost to families of caring for the wounded in the case of those with truly severe injuries or mental impairment. In short, we have been excessively conservative. Had we included the incremental unpaid medical costs to the families, and quality-of-life reductions, this number could be substantially higher.

However, there are still other significant costs of the war, some of which are hard to quantify but are nonetheless real. These include the broader costs to our economy and our nation, as well as the costs to our troops and their families.

Non-Quantified Social Costs

IN CHAPTER 2, we discussed the budgetary costs of filling the vacancies at home caused by the vast deployment of the National Guard and Reserve forces. More difficult to quantify is the price incurred by not keeping the Guard and Reservists at home. Many of these men and women normally work as critical "first responders" in their local communities: in the fire department, the police department, and as emergency medical personnel. The ramifications of pulling them out of the communities they serve were illustrated dramatically during the Hurricane Katrina debacle, when 3,000 Louisiana National Guard members and 4,000 Mississippi Guard members were stationed in Iraq as the hurricane hit.

The overstretched Reservists and National Guard are dealing with a further cost of the war: the fact that there is not enough equipment to supply Guard troops who remain at home. This had deadly consequences in the summer of 2007, when Greensburg, Kansas, was hit by sudden tornadoes, killing ten and injuring hundreds. The National Guard was operating with only 40–50 percent of its vehicles and heavy machinery: much of the equipment needed for rescue operations had been shipped to Iraq. As State Senator Donald Betts, Jr., of Wichita, put it: "We should have had National Guard troops there right after the tornado hit, securing the place, pulling up debris, to make sure that if there was still life, people could have been saved. The response time was too slow, and it's becoming a trend. We saw this after Katrina, and it's like history repeating itself."

The GAO had warned about exactly this problem in January 2007, when it issued a report on National Guard equipment shortfalls, noting: "The high use of the National Guard for federal overseas missions has reduced equipment available for its state-led domestic missions, at the same time it faces an expanded array of threats at home."[32] According to the GAO and the Guard, the Pentagon has stripped local Guard units of about 24,000 pieces of equipment in order to fully equip troops in Iraq. The GAO estimates that as much as 44 percent of such equipment now needs servicing or replacement.[33]

The full economic costs of the National Guard and Reserve deployment are thus far greater than any difference between what these individuals were paid and what they would have otherwise produced. When they are deployed overseas, we lose, of course, the enormously valuable services they provide in an emergency; but simply knowing that they are available should an emergency occur also is of enormous value. Economists refer to this as the "insurance" value of having them *ready* to respond. In our estimates, we do not measure either the economic costs of the loss of "insurance," or the economic and budgetary costs arising from any reduction in first-responder capabilities.

Fighting the war in Iraq with so many Reservists and Guard troops imposes costs on our nation and our local communities. But there is an additional cost to the soldiers themselves. Reserve and National Guard soldiers who have been called back to duty lose civilian wages during their deployment. Defense Department surveys in 2004 showed that 40 percent of Reservists and National Guard made less money while mobilized than they earned in their civilian jobs. Surveys of all Guard and Reserve personnel found that among mobilized troops whose pay was cut, the average annual reduction was $3,000, although some took pay cuts in the tens of thousands.

A RAND study in 2006 looked at the difference in the after-tax total compensation of Reservists and National Guard soldiers called to duty; it concluded that there was no significant difference between what they received before being called to duty and after. But the study had a number of technical flaws, including a failure to consider the extra costs that families had to pay as they were split apart.[34] More important, it did not include what these soldiers would have had to be paid to compensate them for undertaking the risks that they faced.[35] Most did not volunteer for even their first tour of duty, much less second tours and extended deployments. A full adjustment of the economic costs would include appropriate compensation for the risks taken.

But even a numerical tally of lost wages would not tell the full story. Reservists and National Guardsmen and women are encountering serious obstacles in their civilian career paths because of extended deployments. Although there are laws designed to protect the jobs of these deployed troops, many still come home unemployed if their companies skirt the law or cut jobs for other reasons.[36] The financial strain on self-employed Reservists—some of whom have gone into bankruptcy—has been particularly acute.

Guard members and Reservists have also faced problems ranging from payroll issues to denial of their veterans' disability benefits. Even in the early days of the war, a GAO study found that 95 percent of Army Guard soldiers from six case study units "had at least one pay problem associated with their mobilization."[37] Guard members and Reservists also are denied disability benefits more often than those in the regular forces—despite the fact that as a group they apply for fewer benefits. To date, 37 percent of the regular forces but only 21 percent of Reservists/Guard have applied to the VA for disability benefits. However, 16 percent of Reservists/Guard have been turned down, compared with only 6 percent of regular forces.[38]

There is an important reason to emphasize these costs: in future wars (or even in this war, if it continues), we should not rely as extensively as we have on our National Guard and Reserves—they are there for emergencies, and after five years, the conflict cannot be considered an emergency. But if we continue to rely on Reserve troops and Guard units, we should create a financial facility to help them, and to mitigate some of these costs.[39]

Earlier, we noted that there was an *opportunity cost* to having our National Guard over in Iraq: they were not at home to help in emergencies like Katrina. These were real costs. Having the National Guard is like having an insurance policy; but we have lost that insurance.

So, too, the reason that we pay, year after year, several hundred billions of dollars for our military is that it is there when we need it. It, too, is a kind of insurance, against an external threat. The fact that our military resources are devoted to Iraq and Afghanistan means that these resources are not available for addressing other threats—whether in Iran, North Korea, or elsewhere.

While we were focusing on weapons of mass destruction that did not exist in Iraq, North Korea acquired such weapons. Many analysts believe that our distraction in Iraq not only provided North Korea with an opportunity, which it seized, but that we provided North Korea with strong incentives: once it acquired these weapons, it would be more difficult for America to launch an attack.

Similarly, our willingness to strike preemptively against Iraq has delivered a clear message to Iran: the best way to deter U.S. military intervention is to develop a nuclear deterrent. Indeed, many analysts have concluded that the primary beneficiary of U.S. action in Iraq has been Iran, which is in a stronger geopolitical position than it has been for a long time.[40]

Tallying the Costs

THIS CHAPTER HAS focused particularly on the social and economic costs to our soldiers and their families that are not reflected in the budgetary totals. Some of these costs are easily quantifiable; others less so. Calculating only what we can, these costs add some $300–$400 billion to the total cost of the Iraq war.[41] (We add here only the economic costs that *exceed* the budgetary payments the government has already made for loss of life or compensation for injury.)

This brings our total costs—not including interest—to $2.0

trillion in the best case scenario, and $3.1 trillion in the realistic-moderate one.

Table 4.1 *The Running Total: Adding the Social Economic Costs—Iraq and Afghanistan*

Social Economic Costs	**Best Case**	**Realistic-Moderate**
	Social Economic Costs	
Value of Statistical Life—Deaths *(Net of death payments)*	$56	$64
Value of Statistical Injury—All other injuries	$180	$273
Societal, Family, and Other Medical Expenses	$55	$78
(less applicable disability benefits)	-$12	-$16
Other Social Costs	$16	$16
Subtotal Social Costs	**$295**	**$415**
	Plus Budgetary Costs of Iraq and Afghanistan Wars	
Total Operations to Date *(spent to date)*	$646	$646
Future Operations *(future operations only)*	$521	$913
Future Veterans' Costs *(Veterans Medical + Veterans Disability + Veterans Social Security)*	$422	$717
Other Military Costs/Adjustments *(Hidden defense + future defense reset + demobilization, less no-fly zone savings)*	$132	$404
Subtotal Budgetary Costs	**$1,721**	**$2,680**
TOTAL BUDGETARY + SOCIAL COSTS *(without interest)*	**$2,016**	**$3,095**

There is one further important cost: that to the overall economy. This war has not been good for the American economy or for the world economy, and we are likely to feel the ramifications for years to come. In the next chapter, we explain why this is so and attempt to quantify some of the adverse effects.

CHAPTER 5

The Macroeconomic Effects of the Conflicts

SINCE THE IRAQ war began, oil prices have gone from about $25 a barrel at the outset to more than $90, and as this book goes to press, they are rising still higher.[1] Americans have felt it at the gas pump and so has everyone else. Cooking fuel prices are higher in Indonesia and bus fares are more expensive in Ethiopia. But it does not stop there. Because of the knock-on secondary effects, higher oil prices affect almost every aspect of an economy. In oil-importing countries like the United States, higher oil prices lead to larger trade deficits and inflationary pressures. Central banks often respond to these pressures by raising interest rates. Since governments then have to spend more on importing oil and on interest payments on outstanding debt, it becomes harder to balance their budgets. Higher interest rates also lead to lower investment and consumer spending, declines in share prices, and a slowing of the economy. In America, the war has hurt the economy in other ways.

This chapter attempts to identify these macroeconomic costs and, where possible, quantify them.

First, however, we need to dispel the common myth that wars are good for the economy. This idea gained prominence in World War II. America (and much of the rest of the world) had been in a depression for years. There was a problem of *insufficient demand*. The economy's potential supply—what it could produce, if everyone were fully employed—exceeded what people were willing to buy, and so the economy stagnated and unemployment was high. World War II created a demand for tanks and armaments; the economy ran at full steam; everyone who wanted a job could get one—and the war even demanded that those who could work two shifts do so.

Today, no serious economist holds the view that war is good for the economy. The economist John Maynard Keynes taught us how, through lower interest rates and increased government spending, countries can ensure that the peacetime economy operates near or at full employment. But money spent on armaments is money poured down the drain: had it been spent on investment—whether on plants and equipment, infrastructure, research, health, or education—the economy's productivity would have been increased and future output would have been greater.

The question is not whether the economy has been weakened by the war.[2] The question is only *by how much*. Where you can put a figure on them, the costs are immense. In our realistic-moderate scenario outlined in this chapter, they total more than a trillion dollars.

Oil

MANY PEOPLE AROUND the world, not just in the Middle East, believe the U.S. government went to war because it wanted to get its hands on Iraqi oil.[3] We aren't going to discuss their arguments here. It is enough to say that if America went to war in the hope of securing cheap oil, we failed miserably. We did however succeed in making the oil companies richer. Exxon-Mobil and other oil companies have been among the few real beneficiaries of the war, as their profits and share prices have soared.[4] Meanwhile, the economy as a whole has paid a high price.

To estimate how high a price, we need to answer three questions: How much of the increase in the price of oil can be attributed to the war? What have been the direct costs to the U.S. economy from these price increases? And what have been the secondary effects—the effects on the overall macroeconomy?

Oil prices started to soar just as the war began, and the longer it has dragged on, the higher prices have gone. This certainly suggests the war has *something* to do with the rising prices. On this, almost all oil experts agree. But what fraction of the total price increase is due to the war? To answer this, we need to ask: What would the price have been had there been no war?[5]

Futures markets—which summarize what buyers and sellers of oil contracts think prices will be in a year or more—provide some insight. Before the war, they thought prices would remain in the range that they had been, $20 to $30, for the next several years.[6] Futures markets work on the basis of "business as usual," that is, they assume nothing out of the ordinary is going to happen. The war in Iraq was the most notable out of the ordinary event at the time prices began to rise, and it is hard to identify any other disruption that could be given similar credit for the changes in demand or supply, especially in 2003 and 2004. (The 2005 arrival of Hurricanes Katrina and Rita, however, did cause a large temporary drop in U.S. oil production, which in turn lifted prices.) Now, "business as usual" means that the turmoil that the Iraq war let loose will continue, and futures markets are betting that prices will remain high for the next several years.[7]

We conclude, accordingly, that a significant proportion of the increase in the price of oil resulted from the war. Exactly how much the war increased prices cannot be gauged with precision, so we are putting forward two estimates: a conservative one that assumes only $5 per barrel of the price increase is due to the war; and a more realistic one that assumes the figure is $10. (We have discussed these estimates with oil industry experts; and although they disagree on the relative importance of different factors in the soaring prices, they have all agreed that, if anything, we have underestimated the role of the Iraq war.) Our conservative estimate assumes the duration of these higher oil prices to be seven years; the realistic-moderate estimate eight years.

With these estimates in place, we can calculate the direct cost to the U.S. economy. The United States imports around 5 billion barrels a year,[8] which means that a $5 per barrel increase translates into an extra expenditure of $25 billion (a $10 increase would be $50 billion) *per year.*[9] Over the seven years projected in our conservative estimate, that is $175 billion.[10] For our $10 realistic-moderate estimate, which assumes the effect will last for eight years, the cost is $400 billion.

As oil prices reach $100 a barrel, and as futures markets continue to predict that high prices will persist years into the future, we feel that $5 to $10 a barrel for just seven or eight years is really too conservative. If even half of the difference between the current price ($95–$100 a barrel) and the price before the war ($25 a barrel) is attributed to the war, then the oil costs of the war today are $35 a barrel—not $10. More generally, attributing just half of the price increase in the post-Iraq world to Iraq over the period for which we have futures markets (2015) brings the *direct* costs of the oil price increase alone to somewhat in excess of $1.6 trillion.

Higher oil prices mean people have less money to spend on everything else. Since oil prices started their ascent, American families have had to spend about 5 percent more of their income on gasoline and heating than before.[11] Even governments—especially those on the state and local level, which must limit spending to revenues—have had to cut back other spending to pay the higher prices of oil imports. Paying Saudi Arabia, Russia, and Venezuela more for oil means that America is spending less on American goods. And, of course, this lower spending will cause the economy to produce less.

Put another way, if we took the estimated $25 billion we have been sending to Saudi Arabia and other oil exporters every year and instead spent it on American goods, output in the United States would be higher. The increased spending on goods made in America would, in turn, have increased wages and profits, the bulk of which would have been spent again in America, further strengthening the domestic economy.

While there is general agreement that spending $25 or $50 billion more on oil every year leads to a reduction in American gross domestic product and incomes, there is some disagreement on the size of the reduction. Economists call the extent to which a change in oil imports translates into a change in total output the *oil import multiplier.* A multiplier higher than 1 means that a $25 billion fall in demand for American goods generates a decrease in national output larger than that amount. Standard estimates of the multiplier are around 1.5.[12] For our conservative estimate, we assume GDP has gone down $25 billion × 1.5, or $37.5 billion, for seven years—a total of $263 billion.[13]

High oil prices dampened our trading partners' economies just as it dampened ours. As a result, our partners bought less from the United States. Econometric models that attempt to measure these global effects have come up with multipliers that are larger (sometimes by two or three times) than the 1.5 number we used in our conservative scenario. Theoretical analyses focused on long-run global effects also generate much larger multipliers. In order to stay on the cautious side, we use a multiplier of 2 to generate our realistic-moderate estimate.[14] We take our GDP reduction of $50 billion per year over eight years, apply the multiplier, and arrive at a total estimated reduction in GDP of $800 billion. We divide that $800 billion impact into three components: the $400 billion direct impact; a $200 billion conventional multiplier effect, through domestic "aggregate demand"; and a $200 billion *global multiplier effect*, which we refer to as the *global general equilibrium effect*. (Still more realistically, if we attribute $35 a barrel to the war, then the total oil impact of the war itself is in excess of $3 trillion.)

Of course, increased demand can lead to more production only if the economy has the capacity to produce more. Unfortunately, during most of the period of the war, our economy has been operating well below its potential. Throughout the period there has been sufficient excess capacity so that if consumers, for instance, had increased their demands for American goods—rather than spending money on foreign oil—output could have expanded to meet this increased demand.[15]

Government Spending

WRITING A WHOPPING yearly check to oil-producing countries has undoubtedly affected the economy, but so too has government spending on the war. Government money spent in Iraq does not stimulate the economy in the way that the same amounts spent at home would. We can ask, what would the country's output have been if even part of the money that was spent on building military bases in Iraq was spent on building schools in the United States? Such *expenditure switching* would have led to higher output in both the short run and the long.

Earlier, we described how reduced spending by consumers on U.S.-produced goods as a result of higher oil prices reduced the economy's output. By the same token, increased government spending, of say $1 billion, increases national output by an amount greater than $1 billion, by a factor which is called the *expenditure multiplier.*[16] But different kinds of expenditures have different multipliers. The multiplier—the bang for the buck, the increase in GDP for each dollar of government spending—is much lower for expenditures on Iraq than for other forms of government expenditure. Consider, for instance, $1,000 spent to hire Nepalese workers to perform services in Iraq. The spending does not directly increase the income of Americans, so we say there is no "first-round" effect on domestic GDP. There is, moreover, little further impact, except to the extent that the Nepalese buy goods made in the United

States. By contrast, $1,000 spent on university research in the United States registers a full $1,000 first-round impact and then further high impacts, as those in the university spend their money on goods and services, many of them made in America.

While the multipliers used to measure the effect of spending on GDP differ according to the type of spending, those associated with Iraq spending must be among the lowest. In our realistic-moderate scenario, we assume a small difference of 0.4 between a normal domestic government spending multiplier and an Iraq spending multiplier. Switching just $800 billion (over the fifteen years we project we will be engaged in Iraq)[17] to domestic investment would result in increased GDP of $320 billion. This is the number we use in our realistic-moderate estimate.[18]

Expenditure switching is one methodology used in *incidence analysis*, in which public sector economists attempt to ascertain the consequence of one policy or another. All of the methodologies are based on the simple premise that spending on Iraq displaces (or as economists put it, "crowds out"), in one way or another, some other kinds of spending. Each methodology tries to trace through the full consequences of this displacement. All of the results yield significant macroeconomic impacts. The expenditure-switching methodology assumes that Iraq war expenditures crowded out government investments. Other methodologies focus on the consequences of war expenditures displacing private investment or consumption.

When the government opts to let the deficit grow instead of reducing government investment, private investment is "crowded out." In chapter 2, we assumed that government did not reduce other expenditures, at least to a significant degree; the Iraq war simply led to larger deficits. As we explained there, there were convincing reasons to believe that to be the case. The reason we began with the expenditure-switching methodology was that the macroeconomics effects were easiest to see. But the macroeconomic effects of deficits are at least as great. As the United States runs a deficit year after year, the value of the national debt—what the U.S. government owes—increases. By the end of fiscal year 2008, the wars in Afghanistan and Iraq will have led to an increase in U.S. indebtedness in excess of $900 billion. In our realistic-moderate scenario, over the time horizon of this study (through 2017), the increased debt from just the increased military spending (ignoring veterans' benefits and health care), including the cumulative interest on the debt-financed war borrowing, exceeds $2 trillion.[19]

The economic analysis of the effects of these increased deficits is broken down into two parts. First, did Americans increase their savings in response to the increased deficits? Some theories (popular among supply-side economists) argue that deficits do not matter, because households just increase savings, with private savings increasing by a dollar for each dollar of increased deficits.[20] Even in normal times, the weight of evidence is against these theories—savings only increase to a limited extent.[21] In this economic episode, though, savings did not increase to offset the increased deficits at all, but actually fell—to levels not seen since the Great Depression.

That part of increased deficits which is not financed by increased savings either leads to less investment or to more borrowing from abroad. The budget deficits have played a role in the soaring U.S. borrowing from abroad—in 2006, America borrowed $850 billion. The richest country in the world could not live within its means—partly because it was fighting one of history's most expensive wars. The seriousness of this situation has attracted attention from David Walker, Comptroller General of the United States. He has warned that there are "striking similarities" between America's current situation and the factors that brought down Rome, including "an over-confident and over-extended military in foreign lands and fiscal irresponsibility by the central government."[22] Even so, standard estimates suggest that half or less of the shortfall is financed abroad. The rest comes out of domestic investment. As the private sector competes for funds with the government, private investment gets crowded out;[23] and again, this private domestic investment has a far greater multiplier than the Iraqi war expenditures. As a result, output is lower. This subtracts from the (rather limited) expansionary effects of the Iraq war itself, so much so that the net effect may be not only negative but greater than the adverse effects estimated in our expenditure-switching methodology.[24]

As important as these effects *during the war* are the effects in the *aftermath* of the war. The money spent on Iraq could have been spent on schools, roads, or research. These investments yield high returns. It could also have been spent more productively within the Department of Veterans Affairs, in its teaching and research programs, or in expanding medical facilities such as mental health clinics and TBI treatment facilities. Expenditures on the Iraq war have no benefits of this kind.

As a result of *not* making these investments, future output will be smaller. Earlier, we considered the *short-run* effects of growing the deficit as we have done. One of the reasons that there is such concern about growing deficits is that they crowd out private investment. With lower investment, the economy's potential output in the long run is diminished. If the previously estimated increased indebtedness of $2 trillion crowds out just 60 percent of this amount in private investment,[25] then the loss in investment is $1.2 trillion. And if this investment were to yield a return of 7 percent, and if we discount at the "social discount rate" of 1.5 percent, then the value of the forgone output is over $5 trillion; at a 4 percent discount rate, it is over $3 trillion; at a 7 percent discount rate, $1.2 trillion.[26]

Even if the increased borrowing is totally financed from abroad—so that there is no crowding out of domestic investment—America's wealth will be lower, by some $2 trillion. If America has to pay just 4.5 percent interest on this indebtedness, and manages to finance the increased interest payments (from then on) by increased taxes, taxes would have to be raised permanently by some $90 billion a year to finance the interest payments. Taxes will have to be raised, other expenditures will have to be crowded out, or the deficit will have to be increased still more—all unpleasant alternatives, each with adverse consequences. If, for instance, public investment expenditures are crowded out, it will mean that future output will be lower—by hundreds of billions, or even trillions, of dollars.[27]

Similar results are obtained in the "expenditure-switching" methodology. In that case, it is public investment, not private investment, which is crowded out. Assume, for instance, that of the $1.6 trillion of direct military costs of the war that we estimate in our realistic-moderate scenario, one half—$800 billion—was put into investments yielding conservatively a 7 percent real return.[28] That would mean that America's output would be greater by $56 billion a year—forever; every American family would, on average, have an income that was $500 greater, forever.[29] At a 7 percent discount rate, this amounts to $800 billion; at a 1.5 percent discount rate, to almost $4 trillion.

Not surprisingly, the different methodologies all yield large results for the total macroeconomic effect, or short run plus long run.[30] Simply to be conservative, we use the number $1.1 trillion, which is the same number used by the Joint Economic Committee.[31] There is no free lunch—and there are no free wars. In one way or another, today *and* in the future, we will pay for the war. In this particular war, the administration and Congress have chosen to push the bills onto future administrations, perhaps onto future generations. We believe that the numbers that we have used in our realistic-moderate scenario are almost surely a gross underestimate of the actual costs our economy will be paying.[32]

Other Macroeconomic Costs

OVER THE PERIOD from March 2003 to October 2007, stock prices have been doing well, and at first blush this seems inconsistent with the worries we have expressed in this chapter. But when you consider that, over the same period of time, wage increases have been moderate and corporate profits have surged, it is clear that we have *not* seen the kind of increase in stock prices we would expect given those facts. The U.S. economist Robert Wescott estimated in the years immediately following the beginning of the Iraq war that the value of the stock market was some $4 trillion less than would have been predicted on the basis of past performance.[33] Uncertainties caused by the war, the resulting turmoil in the Middle East, and soaring oil prices dampened prices from what they "normally" would have been. This decrease in corporate wealth implies that consumption was lower than it otherwise would have been, again weakening the economy.

The Federal Reserve sought, of course, to offset the adverse effects of the war, including those discussed earlier in this chapter. It kept interest rates lower than they otherwise might have been and looked the other way as lending standards were lowered—thereby encouraging households to borrow more—and spend more. Even as interest rates were reaching record lows, Alan Greenspan, then chairman of the Federal Reserve, in effect invited households to pile on the risk as he encouraged them to take on variable rate mortgages.[34] The low initial interest rates allowed households to borrow more against their houses, enabling America to consume well beyond its means.

Household savings rates soon went negative for the first time since the Great Depression.[35] But it was only a matter of time before interest rates rose. When they did so, hundreds of thousands of Americans who had taken on variable interest mortgages saw their mortgage payments rise—beyond their ability to pay—and they lost their homes.[36] This was all predictable—and predicted: after all, interest rates could not stay at these historically unprecedented low rates forever.[37] As this book goes to press, the full ramifications of the "subprime" mortgage crisis are still unfolding. Growth is slowing, and the economy is again performing markedly below its potential.

The Iraq war and especially the high oil prices have contributed to a weaker American economy; but these weaknesses have not been as apparent as they otherwise might because of low interest rates and lax lending standards.[38] If not for these policies, we would have seen more fully the adverse macroeconomic effects of the high oil prices, high deficits, and expenditure switching toward Iraq.[39] Output would have been lower and the depressing effects more obvious. We as a country have been living off of borrowed money and borrowed time. In earlier chapters, we showed how, by deficit financing, we have not paid the full *financial* costs of the war during the past five years. In this chapter, we have shown that neither did we pay the full *macroeconomic costs* of the Iraq war. *We will be paying those costs in the coming years.* Just as the country paid a heavy price for President Lyndon B. Johnson's guns-and-butter policies during the Vietnam War long after the war was over—in the form of inflation in the 1970s—so it is paying a heavy price for America's guns-and-butter policies today, and will be doing so for years to come.[40]

In our estimates, we have not included the long-run costs of the war's impact on the stock market or the "legacy of household debt" resulting from U.S. policies in this decade.[41] There is, however, little doubt that had the economy been stronger as a result of lower oil prices and patterns of expenditures that stimulated the economy more, the Fed would not have lowered interest rates as much and gone to such extremes to encourage debt-financed consumption. And with a smaller mountain of debt, the American economy would have been in a better position to face the challenges of the future.

IN TABLE 5.1 (at p. 130), we summarize the quantifiable macroeconomic costs. In the "best case" estimate, simply to be extremely conservative, we have excluded the macroeconomic consequences of expenditure switching, or the increased deficits, the global feedbacks, the supply-side effects (not just from reduced investment, but also from a labor force diminished by those killed and disabled, and those caring for the disabled), and the long-term growth impacts. These are, however, real costs to the economy. We have included these costs in our realistic-moderate estimates. But even here, we have excluded large costs that are hard to quantify: how greater global uncertainty dampened investment, in turn further reducing demand and output; the supply-side effects of resources (including labor) being diverted to fight the war; the knock-on effects on stock market prices; and the resulting lower aggregate demand.

The Iraq war has exacerbated international tensions. The war, whatever its initial aims, has not increased stability and security in the Middle East. It has not reduced the threat of terrorism. On the contrary, the threat seems to have increased, as evidenced by the number of recent terrorism incidents.[42] Disruptions at airports have become worse, not better. The bombings and attempted bombings in Bali, Spain, and the United Kingdom in recent years show again that the impact reaches around the world. Insecurity is, of course, bad for the economy—businesses dislike risk and work hard to keep it under control. Risk is bad for investment and growth.

All recent presidents have emphasized the virtues of international trade and its stimulating effect on the economy. But new barriers brought about by the increasing global tensions resulting from the Iraq war impede the flow of goods and services and people across borders. Some of the new trade impediments arise from the war on terror, but the Iraq war has worsened matters.

These impediments are not just an "inconvenience." Globalization has brought enormous benefits to the world. It has meant the closer integration of the countries of the world as goods, services, and labor move more freely across borders, largely as a result of lower transportation costs and communication costs, but also because of the reduction of man-made barriers.[43] We now have a new set of impediments to cross-border movements, offsetting many of the earlier gains, and the costs to America, and to our economy, may be particularly significant. America has reaped the lion's share of the gains from globalization, well out of proportion to the size of its economy. And just as America has gained so much from globalization, it stands to lose much.

The war has contributed to changing perspectives, which we describe at greater length in the next chapter. Much of the world has always had mixed views about the United States, from admiration for its successes and its democracy, to envy and resentment for the perceived abuses of its powers. Today, the mix of attitudes has changed, with a far greater weight toward resentment and anger for the United States' unilateralism. Guantánamo Bay and Abu Ghraib have altered admiration for its democracy and its strong advocacy of human rights: the focus is now on its hypocrisy and its double standards.

These changes in perspective have their economic consequences. Large numbers of wealthy people in the Middle East—where the oil money *and* inequality put individual wealth in the billions—have shifted banking from America to elsewhere. Singapore saw the opportunity, and grasped it. Others, like Dubai, are trying to follow suit. American firms, especially those that have become icons, like McDonald's and Coca-Cola, may also suffer, not so much from explicit boycotts as from a broader sense of dislike of all things American. Some American firms have been especially hurt badly, but they have also had a hard-to-quantify effect on the macroeconomy.

Lastly, we have not included in our estimates, especially in our conservative estimate, the full effects of the soaring national deficit and some of what now appear so clearly misconceived monetary policy responses to the weak economy—weaknesses for which the war was at least partly responsible.

Table 5.1 *The Running Total: Adding the Macroeconomic Costs—Iraq and Afghanistan*

Cost in billions	Best Case	Realistic-Moderate
Macroeconomic Costs		
Oil Price Impact	$263	$800
Budgetary Impact	$0	$1,100
Subtotal Macroeconomic Costs	**$263**	**$1,900**
Plus Budgetary and Social Economic Costs		
Total Operations to Date *(spent to date)*	$646	$646
Future Operations *(future operations only)*	$521	$913
Future Veterans' Costs *(Veterans Medical + Veterans Disability + Veterans Social Security)*	$422	$717
Other Military Costs/Adjustments *(Hidden defense + future defense reset + demobilization, less no-fly zone savings)*	$132	$404
Total Budgetary Costs	**$1,721**	**$2,680**
Social Costs Total	**$295**	**$415**
Total Budgetary and Social Costs	**$2,016**	**$3,095**
Total Budgetary, Social, and Macroeconomic Costs *(without interest)*	**$2,279**	**$4,995**

The Full Tally

BY ADDING THESE macroeconomic costs to the costs calculated in previous chapters, we can get a full tally of the costs of the war. The numbers are staggering. In the realistic-moderate scenario—the numbers that we believe (conservatively) best capture the costs of the Iraq venture, even without counting interest—the total for Iraq alone is more than $4 trillion; including Afghanistan, it increases to $5 trillion. Even in the best case scenario, where we have excluded most of the macroeconomic costs and have assumed a rosy scenario for the wind-down of the war, the cost of the Iraq war reaches $1.8 trillion, and the cost of the two conflicts together reaches close to $2.3 trillion without including interest.

But these are only the costs to the American economy. Our war on Iraq has imposed costs on others—numbers that themselves are in the trillions. We turn to these in the next chapter.

CHAPTER 6

Global Consequences

THE GLOBAL CONSEQUENCES of the invasion of Iraq are far-reaching. Iraq has borne the brunt of the damage, but the breakdown in most areas of central government there means it is difficult to secure reliable numbers with which to perform the type of cost analysis we have done for the United States.

Prior to the invasion, Iraq was a dictatorship and a miserable place to live for many of its people. Nonetheless, it had survived ten years of sanctions; it was a dysfunctional yet viable country. Five years after the United States occupied Iraq with the stated goal of bringing democracy to its people, the war has essentially ruined the country's economy, society, and sovereignty.

In global terms, the jump in oil prices since the start of the war dwarfs all the other economic costs. The higher oil prices assumed in our moderate scenario represent a direct cost to the world economy of approximately $1.1 trillion, taking into account the macroeconomic repercussions. In human terms, it is the loss of life and the destruction of Iraqi society that is the most egregious.

Meanwhile, costs continue to mount for the Iraqi people and their economy, as well as for the rest of the world.

For most Iraqis, daily life has become unbearable—to the point that those who can afford to leave their country have done so. By September 2007, a stunning 4.6 million people—one of every seven Iraqis—had been uprooted from their homes. This is the largest migration of people in the Middle East since the creation of Israel in1948.[1]

Half of these Iraqis—many of them women and children—have fled the country completely. Millions of people are finding temporary haven in Syria, Jordan, and other neighboring countries. Iraqis are also the leading nationality seeking asylum in Europe. According to the UN High Commissioner on Refugees, "thousands of the Iraqis [fleeing the country] are the victims of torture, sexual and gender-based violence, car bombings or other violent attacks and are in urgent need of medical care. The majority of Iraqi children are not attending school."[2]

However, the neighboring countries are themselves feeling the strain of accepting so many refugees. Syria, for example, will no longer accept Iraqis without visas. This has forced some Iraqis to return home, but in September 2007, there were still 2,000 Iraqis arriving at the Syrian border every day.[3] By late November 2007, despite the fact that the Iraqi government was offering to pay $700–$800 to refugees if they returned home, plus free bus and plane rides, the UNHCR pointed out that "large scale repatriation would only be possible when proper return conditions are in place—including material and legal support and physical safety. Presently there is no sign of any large-scale return to Iraq as the security situation in many parts of the country remains volatile and unpredictable."[4]

Inside Iraq, the situation is also dire. Over 2.2 million more

Iraqis have been displaced from their homes, often as the result of sectarian violence in their neighborhoods. As Syria tightened visa restrictions and few Iraqis can get visas for European countries, more people have been forced to move to safer areas within Iraq.

It is difficult to estimate the financial cost—let alone the human toll—of this humanitarian catastrophe. The countries that have accepted refugees have needed to provide food, water, sanitation, health care, shelter, transportation, legal assistance, protection, and education for millions of people. In the case of Jordan, for instance, the estimated cost is in excess of $1 billion.[5] In 2007, the UNHCR budget for caring for Iraqi refugees was $123 million, but this is a small fraction of the total budgetary cost. It does not even begin to take into account the impact on the economies of the countries that have been directly affected, such as Jordan, Syria, Egypt, and Lebanon.[6]

As we noted in chapter 1, America has shouldered only a small share of the burden of those refugees, relative to our population. This is not the only instance where other countries have borne a heavy burden. The United States knew that Iraq could pay for its own reconstruction only if its existing debts were forgiven. But most of these debts were held by other countries. America forgave the $2.2 billion ($4.1 including interest) owed to it by Iraq, but then pressured other creditors to forgive a combined $29.7 billion in a deal struck on November 21, 2004.[7]

The Cost of Iraqi Deaths and Injuries

AN OBVIOUS AND sobering cost to the country includes the deaths of Iraqi soldiers fighting on *our* side. We have always viewed those soldiers as substitutes for Americans; indeed, our emphasis has been on training them so that they could fight *instead* of Americans. Had they not done so, more Americans would have been needed to do battle and more Americans would have died. As we go to press, 7,697 Iraqi soldiers fighting alongside U.S. troops have been killed.[8]

Oddly, the U.S. government does not keep track of the number of Iraqi soldiers injured. As we saw in chapter 3, the number of troops injured in combat is more than eight times the number killed (counting all injuries, the ratio is 1:15). Conservatively estimating the number of Iraqis injured at just twice the number killed implies some 15,394 injuries thus far. Extrapolating for two more years of war, under a conservative scenario with the same death rate, raises that number to 23,946. Of course, as Iraqi troops take on a greater role, as assumed under the best case scenario, they may face an even higher death rate.

In writing this book, we have been reluctant to put a dollar value on the lives of the Iraqis killed in the war. It is unconscionable to make calculations based on the idea that an Iraqi life is worth less than an American one. If we value an Iraqi life as equal to an American life, then the total cost of Iraqi military deaths is $172.4 billion. Valuing an injury at 20 percent of the value of a life raises that number by an additional $69 billion. Salaries are lower in Iraq than in the United States, as is the average income, but the principle is the same: the Iraqi economy is poorer as a result of the loss of its young men.[9]

The military deaths and injuries in Iraq pale when compared to the number of civilian casualties. These include both innocent civilians killed by Coalition troops, who are counted as "collateral damage," and those killed in the civil war ignited by the invasion.

There are also "disappearances": by March 2006, some thirty to forty Iraqis were being kidnapped daily.[10] Many of those kidnappings ended with the victim's death.[11]

By December 2007, the official tallies of civilian casualties of the war had grown to 39,959.[12] But this number, large as it was, was a vast undercount. The Brookings Institution's *Iraq Index* puts the total at just shy of 100,000. The violence has risen to such a level that the Brookings researchers commented: "Starting in 2006, we have found it is no longer practical to differentiate between acts of war and crime."[13] During much of 2006, officially recorded deaths numbered more than 100 a day.[14] Beginning in 2007, a new category of killings was introduced into the tables: "extrajudicial killings" ("death penalty punishments," without the sanction of courts or government)—amounting to some 5,150 in the first seven months of 2007.

To this grim tally we must add the people who have become seriously ill or have died because Iraq's economy was destroyed and no adequate relief program was put in place. In difficult economic times, some people will become undernourished, and therefore less able to ward off disease. The absence of clean water and electricity, and the massive exodus of doctors (so that today Iraq has fewer than half the doctors it had at the beginning of the war) too have exerted their toll.[15]

One of the symptoms of the deteriorating living conditions in Iraq has been the outbreak of cholera—a disease which can occur when water supplies, sanitation, food safety, and hygiene practices are inadequate. People become infected after eating food or drinking water contaminated by the feces of infected persons. Overcrowded communities with poor sanitation and unsafe drinking water supplies are breeding grounds for *Vibrio cholerae,* the bacterium that causes cholera. Severe cholera cases present with profuse diarrhea and vomiting, which can lead to rapid dehydration and death if untreated. Cholera is widespread in parts of Africa, but it is rare elsewhere in the world. During 2006, there were fewer than 2,500 reported cases in the entire Asian continent (including India and China). In 2006, there were no cholera deaths in South America, North America, Europe, or Australia.[16]

Before the war, cholera was extremely rare in Iraq.[17] Now it is a serious health crisis. A cholera outbreak was first detected in Kirkuk, northern Iraq, on August 14, 2007. It has spread to nine out of eighteen provinces across Iraq. Over 3,315 cases have been confirmed—more than in all of Asia in 2006—and 30,000 people have fallen ill with acute watery diarrhea (cholera symptoms). At least fourteen have died of the disease,[18] which is continuing to spread across Iraq, especially in Kirkuk and Sulaymaniah provinces. An increasing number of cases have also been reported in the cities of Baghdad, Basra, Mosul, and Tikrit, and in the provinces of Diyala, Dahuk, and Wasit.

The World Health Organization has deployed epidemiologists to Iraq; it is sending 5 million water treatment tablets and has taken other measures to reduce the transmission of the disease. It is likely that the outbreak will eventually be controlled, but the WHO notes that in Iraq, "the overall quality of water and sanitation is very poor, a factor known to facilitate greatly cholera contamination."[19] The direct costs of controlling the disease are difficult to estimate. However, it will be an unwelcome additional cost to an organization whose annual budget of $3.3 billion (close to what we spend in Iraq during one week) is already stretched in dealing with global HIV/AIDS, tuberculosis, malaria, SARS, malnutrition, and many other conditions.

To fully understand the number of deaths that are attributable to the Iraq war, we need to look at what has happened to the total death rate in the country *after the U.S. invasion*. There are well-established methodologies for ascertaining changes in death rates, and a study conducted by researchers at Johns Hopkins University followed these methodologies; it looked at a scientifically chosen sample of villages, comparing death rates in those villages before the war and after.[20] This sampling approach is the same methodology used in political opinion polls. A sample of 1,000 can predict voting outcomes with a high degree of reliability, often with a margin of error of 3 percent or less, for a country like the United States. The Johns Hopkins study used a large sample (over 1,849 Iraqi households with 12,801 members) and went to great lengths to make sure that the reported deaths had actually occurred. As of July 2006, the study put the increase in fatalities at 654,965.[21] Since then, the pace of killing has increased. Assuming that the death rate remains at the level reported by the Hopkins study through March 2010, the total number of Iraqi deaths would exceed one million. As we noted earlier, we have no data for those seriously injured; but if we conservatively project that the numbers injured are double those killed, then that tally would exceed two million.[22]

Putting a value on Iraqi civilian casualties creates the same dilemmas as doing so for the military deaths and injuries. Using our methodology for American deaths generates a total cost of somewhat more than $8.6 trillion, which exceeds all the numbers we have previously calculated. The Iraqi economy is poorer, but again the principle is the same, except this: a society that has lost so many of its people is more than proportionately weakened.

As we have done elsewhere in this book, it may prove useful to consider the counterfactual: what would have happened if we had not invaded Iraq? Some studies, including those broadly supportive of the war, have suggested that 10,000 Iraqis a year likely would have died in the alternative "containment" scenario, under which UN sanctions would have continued as before the invasion. There seems to be no strong basis for that estimate; but even if it were true, it simply means a reduction of 70,000 from the projected one million deaths (with a corresponding decrease in the number of injured).

The most difficult aspect of the counterfactual concerns what would have happened at the end of Hussein's regime—since it would have eventually come to an end. Would another equally oppressive Baathist regime have replaced it? Would there have been a more democratic—but less violent—transition? Or would the country have broken apart in civil war? If one accepts the latter view, the American invasion simply precipitated the eventual splitting apart of the country. While there are by definition no certainties on "what might have been," it is clear that at a minimum the occupation exacerbated many of the long-standing tensions. By destroying the economic and political infrastructure, the American occupation meant that there was less reason for the country to hold together. Contemplating starting over from scratch, many Iraqis in those regions with oil thought they could do better on their own.[23]

The Cost to Iraq's Economy

THE WAR IN Iraq has dealt a heavy blow to the country's economy, which was facing serious difficulties even before the invasion. Iraq had spent eight years in a fruitless war with Iran. It had suffered a humiliating defeat in the Gulf War of 1991. The embargo on Iraqi oil, imposed by the United Nations and the United States after the first Gulf War ended in 1991, also had taken its toll. In 2001, Iraq's GDP was 24 percent lower than it had been ten years earlier (in purchasing power terms).[24] Like so many other Middle Eastern countries, Iraq's economy was dominated by oil—accounting for almost two thirds of the country 's GDP.[25] The country had a thriving middle class, and most Iraqis had high hopes for the future once their nation was freed from the burden of an embargo.

We noted earlier that Iraq's GDP, in real terms, is no higher than it was in 2003, in spite of a near quadrupling of oil prices; that at least one in four Iraqis are unemployed; and that Baghdad gets only nine hours of electricity per day—less than it had before the war.[26] Life in Baghdad's 130-degree Fahrenheit summers—outside the Green Zone in which the occupation authorities live—is oppressive. Oil exports have dropped and have yet to recover to their prewar level.[27]

The economic disaster is, of course, an integral part of the Iraqi debacle. It has been both cause and consequence: it has contributed to the insurgency, and the insurgency has had a devastating effect on the economy. In some places, destruction is outpacing construction. Some 59 percent of Iraqis view their economic conditions today as "poor," and only 11 percent as "good" or "excellent."[28] The failure to provide jobs and income has, rightly, lost the U.S.-backed government what little support it had. Worse, we have created an explosive combination of high levels of unemployed males between the ages of eighteen and thirty-five and ready access to arms.

The failure to provide adequate security, in turn, has made the reconstruction of the Iraqi economy nearly impossible. But the failure of the Iraqi economy is also the result of a fundamentally flawed economic strategy. Much attention has been given to the major military and political mistakes made by the Bush administration, especially in the critical days of the early occupation. Too little attention has been given to its flawed policies for the rejuvenation of the Iraqi economy.

Even before it had stabilized the country, even before there had been progress in reconstruction, the United States attempted to bring free market capitalism to Iraq. In September 2003, Paul Bremer enacted laws abolishing many tariffs on imports and capping corporate and income tax at 15 percent.[29] There has also been repeated talk of privatizing state-owned industry, despite the fact that the 1907 Hague Convention "Regulations Concerning the Laws and Customs of War on Land" bar occupiers from selling off a country's assets.[30] This privatization plan was part of the mantra of the Bush administration from the beginning.

In his powerful book *Imperial Life in the Emerald City*, *The Washington Post*'s Rajiv Chandrasekaran recounts an incident in which Thomas Foley, a Republican donor appointed in August 2003 to head private sector development in Iraq, boasted that he would privatize all of Iraq's state-owned enterprises within thirty days. Told that this was against international law, Foley replied: "I don't care about any of that stuff. . . . I don't give a shit about international law. I made a commitment to the President that I'd privatize Iraq's businesses."[31]

The benefits of privatization and free markets in transition economies are debatable, of course. But Foley and others like him failed to realize that, until Iraq was stabilized, anyone buying its assets would pay bottom dollar and then try to strip them, rather than sticking around to actually do business and invest in a dangerous country. And just when Iraqi firms needed the most help, the effect of U.S. policies was to expose them to free competition, with zero or very low tariffs. This was something that American industry would never have tolerated. The policies had the predicted effects. There has been little foreign direct investment outside of oil, and many businesses could not compete with the flood of imports and so shut down, resulting in even higher levels of unemployment.

The U.S. Treasury contributed to the debacle by insisting on tight monetary policies. A flood of dollars coming into the country from America—much of it unaccounted for—created shortages in certain parts of the economy. Prices rose. The Treasury responded in an almost mechanical way, encouraging Iraqis to raise interest rates and tighten credit. But the problem in Iraq was not a surfeit of credit. In fact, officials at USAID (the U.S. international aid agency) had been working hard trying to figure out how to stimulate small businesses, a major source of potential job creation. They concluded that a major impediment was lack of access to credit, and so they carefully designed a partial guarantee scheme that would enhance the flow of credit to small and medium-sized enterprises and hopefully help create more employment. But just as one part of the U.S. government was trying to expand Iraq's anemic economy by increasing the supply of credit, another part of the U.S. government, worried about "overheating," was working to decrease the supply of credit—even as the unemployment rate hovered between 25 percent and 40 percent.

America's policy of relying on contractors also unwittingly contributed to the failure of Iraqi recovery. U.S. procurement law requires the use of U.S. contractors, except in certain circumstances. In Iraq, much of the U.S. money spent on reconstruction went to high-priced American contractors rather than low-cost local Iraqi labor. California congressman Henry Waxman pointed out that non-Iraqi contractors charged $25 million to repaint twenty police stations—a job that the governor of Basra claims could have been done by local firms for $5 million.[32] This was not only wasteful but also led to resentment among Iraqis.

It was, however, not just a matter of resentment. It was in our interest to supply jobs for the large number of unemployed young Iraqi men (particularly given that, as we had disbanded the Iraqi army, many were left with arms—disgruntled armed young men who might easily be persuaded to join the insurgency). With more than one out of two Iraqi men out of work at some point after the invasion, Iraqis were begging for work. But American contractors focused on minimizing their labor costs,[33] and imported workers from Nepal and other low-wage countries who were cheaper than Iraqis. This is another example where the contractors' interests ran directly counter to America's national interest, which was to quickly create jobs and restore Iraq's economic strength.

Things might have been worse if the administration had been more successful in its liberalization and privatization agenda. But like so many other aspects of the Iraq agenda, it failed in the implementation of its policies just as it failed in their design. The laws of occupation blocked the most important component of the administration's privatization agenda—the oil sector.

No one, neither foreigners nor Iraqis, thinks of Iraq as a safe place to invest.[34] As long the insecurity is maintained, the prospects for Iraq's future economy are bleak.[35] We have not undertaken the ambitious task of calculating the loss to the Iraqi economy. And again, part of the calculation hinges on the counterfactual—what would have happened but for the war. Suffice it to say, no matter what assumptions one makes, it is hard to imagine a bleaker situation than the current one.

The Cost to the Rest of the World

IRAQ AND THE United States have been the biggest losers in this war; but many other countries have incurred heavy costs. First are the direct costs to U.S. allies that joined in the invasion as part of the "coalition of the willing." Second is the cost to the global economy—and to specific countries—of the increase in oil prices, including the resulting macroeconomic effects.

There is another set of costs, about which we will say little but which may ultimately be the most important. The Iraq war has contributed to a "clash of civilizations,"[36] a perception that there is a new crusade against Islam. Many in the Middle East see an American strategy of sowing dissension between Sunnis and Shiites as part of a grander strategy in this "new crusade." Regardless of the factual basis for such beliefs, the Iraq war has intensified feelings of animosity which are likely to be a source of conflict for years in the future.

The rhetoric about a global coalition notwithstanding, the war in Iraq has been largely an American venture, with some political cover provided by the United Kingdom. According to the White House, there were an impressive-sounding forty-nine countries in the "Coalition"; yet America provided 84 percent of the troops itself and paid the costs of many of the foreign troops.[37] Opposition to the war was so strong among the populations of many of these "allies" that it has played a role in unseating the governments of Italy, Spain, Poland, and Australia. By 2007, the United States was providing 94 percent of the troops; at least eighteen countries had withdrawn their troops; and our most important ally, the United Kingdom, had already begun major cutbacks. Increasingly, the "coalition of the willing" was becoming a "coalition of one."

The total of military deaths for the allies in Iraq as this book went to press stood at 306,[38] with a further 675 injured. Although these numbers will certainly rise before the war is over, the increase will probably be small, particularly since the United Kingdom, which provides the largest contingent, is rapidly reducing its presence in Iraq. If we apply the same yardsticks to valuing lives lost as for U.S. personnel, then the economic cost of these fatalities alone comes to $2.2 billion.[39] Including injuries would increase the total by at least 40 percent.

A full exposition of the budgetary expenditures of our allies is difficult. However, if we postulate that costs are roughly proportional to troop commitments, then given that they have been supplying between 6 percent to 16 percent of the troops, their direct operational costs so far may be of the order of magnitude of $30 to $90 billion. If we assume America has been waging the war in a "top-dollar" manner, with less attention to costs and more reliance on contractors, and take half of that number, we get a range of $15 billion to $45 billion—numbers that are more consistent with the budgetary figures provided by the United Kingdom government (see below). Future costs—including veterans' health care and disability—will increase that number further. Even where the United States has underwritten the short-term military costs, there will be a long trail of disability and health care costs that other countries will have to bear themselves.[40]

The Cost to Afghanistan

AFGHANISTAN HAS PAID a high price for our decision to invade Iraq. As Pennsylvania congressman Joseph Sestak, a veteran of the conflict in Afghanistan, has pointed out: "The war [in Iraq] was undertaken at exactly the wrong time. By not allowing us to first finish the work needed to fully secure peace in Afghanistan, the al Qaeda leadership that struck the United States on September 11 is still free. I know from first hand experience; I was first sent into Afghanistan two months after we began fighting there, and returned to the country a year and a half later. At the beginning of the war I saw what needed to be done to win the peace. I then later saw how much was still left to do in Afghanistan, as we turned our attention and valued resources toward Iraq, where the terrorist threat was not."[41]

Afghanistan, where the United States was successful at routing the Taliban in 2001 (despite managing to lose Osama bin Laden at Tora Bora), is facing increasing lawlessness outside of Kabul. One result of U.S. neglect since 2001 is that Afghanistan, which had reduced its production of heroin under the Taliban, since the war has become the largest supplier to the global heroin market.[42] Heroin production has been climbing every year since 2001. This money is widely reported to be finding its way into the Taliban's coffers, fueling resistance to the NATO-led forces. Meanwhile, suicide bombings (which used to be rare in the country) and other violence have become commonplace. Despite the presence of 50,000 foreign troops in the country, including NATO-led and U.S. contingents, the situation seems to be slipping out of control.[43] Afghanistan's defense minister has said that he would need 200,000 troops (nearly three times the 70,000 troops that are planned) to ensure long-term stability in the country.[44]

We have not counted the cost of suffering of the Afghan people, who after years of war with the Soviet Union, followed by a harsh life under the Taliban, had hoped that American involvement would bring peace and stability at last. Instead, 2007 has been the most violent year since the U.S.-led invasion of Afghanistan in 2001, with insurgency-related violence claiming nearly 6,200 lives.[45]

Costs to Great Britain

FROM THE BEGINNING, the United Kingdom has played a pivotal role—strategic, military, and political—in the Iraq conflict. In the run-up to the war in 2003, the U.K. prime minister's support was indispensable to George Bush. At a time when the United States faced loud opposition from France, Germany, Russia, China, and the United Nations, Tony Blair visited Washington and spoke in favor of military action against Iraq to a joint session of the Congress. His support was critical in enabling the Bush administration to convince Congress to authorize the war.

Blair helped Bush in two ways. First, in the eyes of the average American voter, Blair personified "sensible" world opinion. Britain had a long history of military experience in Iraq, dating back to World War I.[46] French opposition was presented by the media not as a reasonable difference of opinion but as symptomatic of France's untrustworthiness as an ally. Blair's stance allowed the White House to maintain its argument that there was a "coalition of the willing" ready to help the United States invade Iraq. This was politically essential since the United Nations opposed the action.

Second, Blair was critical in creating bipartisan support for the war in Washington. Democrats remembered his close relationship with Bill Clinton. Many saw him as a kindred spirit. This was one of the reasons why Democrats (including Hillary Clinton, John Kerry, John Edwards, and the rest) fell in line behind Bush's rush to war with so little protest. Indeed, it is arguable that if Blair had urged the United States to postpone action for six months to allow more UN inspections (or if he had chosen to play the role of honest broker who forged a consensus between the Americans and the Europeans), Blair and the United Kingdom might have thwarted the administration's invasion plans in March 2003. Perhaps history would have been different.

Instead, Britain facilitated every aspect of the war. Militarily, the United Kingdom contributed 46,000 troops, which was 10 percent of the total force. The British Ministry of Defence noted that, while overall planning for the operation was led by the United States, "the UK was fully involved, including through personnel embedded in US Central Command in Tampa and elsewhere."[47] Unsurprisingly, then, the British experience in Iraq has paralleled that of the United States—rising casualties, increasing operating costs, poor transparency over where the money is going, overstretched military resources, and scandals regarding the squalid conditions and inadequate medical care for some of its severely wounded veterans.

Before the war, Chancellor of the Exchequer Gordon Brown set aside £1 billion for war spending. As of late 2007, the United Kingdom had spent an estimated £7 billion (U.S. $14 billion) in direct operating expenditures in Iraq and Afghanistan (76 percent of it in Iraq). This includes money allocated from a supplemental "Special

Reserve," plus additional spending from the Ministry of Defence.[48] As in the United States, the Special Reserve comes on top of the regular defense budget, which has also increased, and which covers ordinary costs such as military salaries. The British system is particularly opaque: funds from the Special Reserve are "drawn down" by the Ministry of Defence when required, by arrangement with the Treasury, without specific approval by Parliament.

As a result, British citizens have little clarity about how much is actually being spent. As the Iraq Analysis Group notes, "With no standard reporting procedure in place, it is extremely difficult to trace where sums are going. While the Special Reserve has been fairly well publicized, information such as how much of the Reserve is being spent in Iraq as opposed to the wider 'war on terror' has not been put into the public domain. It should not be the case that this information has to be discovered through Freedom of Information requests." Moreover, Britain (like the United States) will face heavy costs to restock its military once the conflict—or Britain's part in it—is over.

British Casualties and Veterans

AS OF THE end of 2007, the United Kingdom had some 5,000 troops in Iraq and some 7,000 in Afghanistan. It was planning to halve the number in Iraq and to increase deployments in Afghanistan.[49] British casualties in Iraq included 174 deaths, 206 serious injuries, and 2,372 other injuries requiring hospitalization. In Afghanistan, casualties included 82 deaths, 89 serious injuries, and 957 other injuries requiring hospitalization.[50] These figures include a significant number who were medically evacuated as a result of disease, wounding, and non-combat injuries. It does not include those suffering long-term psychological problems such as PTSD.

Wounded veterans in the United Kingdom are provided with more generous compensation than is typical for the United States, including lump-sum payments of up to £285,000 for serious multiple injuries. Additional financial support includes a guaranteed income payment based on soldiers' salary, index-linked and tax-free for life.[51] In addition, the U.K. "standard of proof" for making claims is based on the "balance of probabilities," which is the accepted approach in other U.K. claims law, such as the Criminal Injuries Compensation Scheme, and in the civil courts. Veterans can claim the lump-sum payments within five years, and longer for certain late-onset illnesses such as cancer, mental illness, and PTSD. The result is that the United Kingdom will face a significant cost in providing disability benefits for its disabled servicemen and women as a consequence of the Iraq and Afghan conflicts.

Medical care in the United Kingdom is provided free by the National Health Service, and wounded British soldiers are cared for in specialist units within the NHS. However, in 2007, shortly after *The Washington Post* revealed horrific conditions at Walter Reed Army Medical Center, the British Sunday newspaper *The Observer* discovered wounded British troops who were enduring vile conditions at Birmingham's Selly Oak Hospital. The newspaper published letters to the Ministy of Defence from the families of British soldiers describing deplorable conditions, including how the youngest soldier wounded in Iraq, Jamie Cooper, eighteen, was forced to spend a night lying in his own feces after staff allowed his colostomy bag to overflow. His parents wrote that their son had been "sent to Iraq straight from training with no real military knowledge and [is] not receiving the care and attention that is needed for his recovery."[52] Letters from parents described "grubby" surroundings, unbearable noise levels, and inadequate visiting facilities. Parents reported that they were being left no choice but to give up their jobs in order to care for their sons. In the United Kingdom, "Selly Oak" now conjures up the same images of disgrace and shame that "Walter Reed" has taken on in America.

The British public reacted with outrage to the Selly Oak revelations. The Royal British Legion, which has 600,000 members (British veterans), put forward a motion questioning medical treatment for the first time in its eighty-six-year history. The British media has provided wide coverage of the lack of adequate medical care for troops, especially for those with mental health problems, the difficulties in making the transition from the army to civilian medical care, and the cover-ups in the total number of injured.[53] Official figures show that since 2003, 2,123 troops have been treated for mental health problems resulting from deployment in Iraq, but army charities claim many more cases have fallen through the net.[54] The government is also using private health care providers to treat returning servicemen where the waiting times for NHS treatment are too long. It is not clear how widespread this practice is, but there is evidence that it may add billions of pounds in costs to the medical bill for British veterans.[55]

Even senior officers currently serving in the British forces are speaking out in protest at how the war has been conducted. General Sir Richard Dannatt, Chief of the Army General Staff, described in a 2007 report how underfunding, undermanning, and overstretching had left British troops feeling "devalued, angry, and suffering from Iraq fatigue."[56] He concluded that "the tank of goodwill now runs on vapour; many experienced staff are talking of leaving." General Dannatt also emphasized (as we did for the United States) that the Iraq war has meant the United Kingdom is less prepared to face other external security threats.

Backbenchers in Parliament have repeatedly criticized the government's handling of the conflict, with regard to underfunding of troops, lack of housing for military families, and the growing strain on the armed forces in general. Lord Astor of Hever's recent comments in the House of Lords provide a flavor of the British sentiment:

> I am sure that all noble Lords will have seen elements of General Dannatt's staff briefing team report. The bleak reality, based on interviews with thousands of soldiers, is an Army at the end of its tether. There is a profound level of dissatisfaction with the conditions under which the soldiers have to live and serve—that leave is often cancelled or constrained because of operational overstretch and that housing is often inadequate. We are sending soldiers out to Afghanistan to fight pretty much 24 hours a day. . . .
>
> Many noble Lords . . . including the noble and gallant Lords, Lord Guthrie [former Chief of the Defense Staff, head of all UK armed forces], Lord Boyce [former First Sea Lord, head of the Royal Navy] and Lord Bramall [also former Chief of the Defense Staff], have argued that these conditions are largely the result of a decade of underfunding by this Government. It has not been lost on the armed services that the Government are willing and ready to risk more on bailing out the financially inept bank, Northern Rock, than is spent on the entire defence budget.[57]

The strain on the military is appearing in the officer corps. The number of officers leaving the army and the RAF early are at a ten-year peak, with recent surveys showing that this is mostly due to the frequency of deployments and the "inability to plan ahead" in their lives.[58] In November 2007, Lieutenant Colonel Stuart Tootal, the commander of 3 Para,[59] reflected the mood of the rank and file when he resigned in protest at the troops' poor pay, the lack of equipment for recruits to train with, the state of army housing, and the lack of dedicated facilities for injured soldiers. Colonel Tootal led his men in some of the war's most intense fighting in southern Afghanistan's Helmand Province, for which he was awarded the Distinguished Service Order. During his six-month tour between April and October 2007, Colonel Tootal said he had to contend with lack of food, water, and ammunition, as well as insufficient helicopter support.[60]

Prime Minister Gordon Brown has announced that Britain will reduce its troop level to 2,500 by the spring of 2008, although it appears likely that this number will remain in Iraq for the foreseeable future.[61]

Social and Economic Costs in the United Kingdom

IN ADDITION TO the costs of military operations, replacing military equipment, caring for veterans, and reinvesting in the armed forces, Britain also faces economic and social costs. Keith Hartley, at the Centre for Defence Economics, University of York, has written extensively on this topic. Hartley points out that "there are costs to the UK civilian economy through such impacts as higher oil prices, possible recession effects and the need for higher defence spending which has to be financed through either higher taxation or reduced public spending in other areas."[62]

in terms of families who leave jobs to care for wounded soldiers, long waiting times for care, poor medical conditions that require the families to take up residence at hospitals, and diminished quality of life for those thousands left with disabilities.

By the same token, there are macroeconomic costs to the United Kingdom as there have been to the United States, though the long-term costs may be less, for two reasons. First, the United Kingdom did not have the same policy of fiscal profligacy. And second, until 2005, the United Kingdom was a net oil exporter. Going forward, as its production declines, it will have to import more, and the adverse effects of the higher oil prices will be felt more strongly. As in the United States, the weaknesses in the economy that might otherwise have shown up as a result of the higher oil prices did not evidence themselves because the United Kingdom, like the United States, had a housing bubble, which fueled high levels of consumption. The mortgage problems that first became apparent in the United States have had even greater repercussions in the United Kingdom, with the first major run on a bank in more than a century, requiring a bailout which could be as much as 50 billion pounds. Because net imports into the United Kingdom remain so uncertain, we have not included any explicit estimate of the macroeconomic costs; but using plausible numbers, the macroeconomic costs could easily double or triple the overall economic costs. For instance, some standard estimates put projected imports of oil in 2010 at 500,000 barrels per day; if half the forecasted difference between the price of oil then and the prewar price is attributed to the Iraqi war, then the increased oil bill—the income transferred from those in the United Kingdom to oil exporters—is $6.4 billion; with a multiplier of just 1.5, this translates into a macroeconomic cost, for 2010, of $9.6 billion. For to oil exporters—is \$6.4 billion; with a multiplier of just 1.5, this translates into a macroeconomic cost, for 2010, of \$9.6 billion. For the period of the study for which we have futures prices, 2003 through 2015, the figures easily accumulate to mind-boggling totals of \$100 billion or more. Had the war been fought somewhat earlier, when the United Kingdom was an oil exporter, it would have been among the beneficiaries, along with Venezuela and Iran. As it is, it joins the United States as one of the big losers from the war.

Total Cost Estimates for the United Kingdom

WE HAVE ESTIMATED the costs to the United Kingdom to date, assuming that British forces in Iraq are reduced to 2,500 in 2008 and remain at that level through 2010. We expect that British forces in Afghanistan will increase slightly, from 7,000 to 8,000 in 2008, and remain stable for the subsequent three years. Future spending estimates are based on these assumptions. We also estimate a cost of \$1 billion for military reset costs, based on comments by Lord Astor of Hever in *Hansard*, November 2007. We anticipate that the increased defense spending in the Ministry of Defence budget that has characterized the war period will continue through 2008, and then taper within three years. However, this may well underestimate the costs of demobilizing and transporting back to the United Kingdom the enormous amount of equipment that is currently based in Iraq. The House of Commons Defence Committee has recently found that despite the cut in troop levels, Iraq war costs will increase by 2 percent in fiscal year 2008 and personnel costs will decrease by only 5 percent. Meanwhile, the cost of military operations in

Afghanistan is scheduled to rise by 39 percent. The estimates in our model may be significantly too low if these patterns continue.[63]

We assume that those who have been "very seriously injured or wounded" in Iraq and Afghanistan will qualify for the maximum lump-sum payments, as well as lifetime benefits and pensions; and that servicemen and women who are recorded as "seriously injured or wounded" will receive lesser lump sums (we assumed 25 percent), as well as lifetime benefits. We estimated that half of the remaining number of soldiers who were hospitalized with wounds, injuries, or disease will not receive any lump-sum benefits, but will qualify for the lowest level of lifetime veterans' disability benefits.

We have assumed a value of statistical life (VSL) of $7.2 million (as in the United States) for soldiers who were killed or "very seriously" injured or wounded (less the lump-sum payment); and 20 percent of that amount for those who were "seriously" injured or wounded.[64] We have not attributed a cost to those who were otherwise hospitalized.

Based on this set of assumptions, the budgetary cost to the United Kingdom of the wars in Iraq and Afghanistan through 2010 will total more than £18 billion (U.S. $30.6 billion). If we include the social costs the total impact on the United Kingdom will exceed £20 billion.

Other Global Costs

THE MOST DIRECT global cost imposed on the rest of the world results from the increase in the price of oil, a price paid by all oil importers. Of course, the costs to some have been a benefit to others—namely, the oil exporters. The losers include traditional U.S.

Table 6.1. *U.K. Iraq War Costs (2007) Through 2010 in pounds sterling (thousands)*

Military Spending	
Spent to Date	8,738
Future Spending	7,015
Veterans' Disability and Medical Payments	2,265
Total Budgetary Costs	**18,017**
Social Costs of Death and Disabilities ***(Net of Budgetary Costs)***	**2,076**
TOTAL COSTS	**20,094**

allies in Europe and Asia. Those who have gained are, by and large, dictators in the oil-producing countries—including some who have been quite open about using their increased wealth to advance an agenda that is anti-American and in some cases anti-Western. This redistribution of global economic power is not something to be enthusiastic about. Indeed, it is hard to think of anything else that the United States could have done that would have been, on a global scale, so much against its own interests.

In chapter 5, we described how higher oil prices have hurt America. Higher oil prices have also hurt the economies of Europe, which import some 3.7 billion barrels a year.[65] If $5 per barrel of the increase in the price of oil is attributable to the Iraq war, the increased oil cost they will pay will total $129 billion in the best case (conservative) scenario of a seven-year war-related price surge, while the total paid by Europe, Japan, and other OECD-importing countries together will amount to $235 billion.[66] In our more realistic estimate, based on an increase of $10 per barrel over eight years, the total comes out to $295 billion for Europe and $539 for

Europe, Japan, and other OECD-importing countries—more than half a trillion dollars.[67]

Europe has been hampered from offsetting the dampening effects of high oil prices by its Growth and Stability Pact, which limits the size of deficit spending, and even more so by a European Central Bank focusing exclusively on inflation.[68] Higher oil prices have led to higher inflationary pressures, and thus to higher interest rates that, in turn, slow growth. That is why the appropriate *oil price multiplier* is higher in Europe than in the United States. Still, if we use a conservative multiplier of 1.5, we get a total cost to Europe of $194 billion in the best case scenario. More reasonably, we should use a multiplier of 2 (see the discussion in chapter 5), obtaining our realistic-moderate estimate of $590 billion for Europe.

Japan's ability to respond to the depressing effect of higher oil prices is hampered by a different set of constraints. High deficits and a huge debt-to-GDP ratio (in excess of 164 percent)[69] constrain fiscal stimulation. With interest rates near zero, further monetary stimulation is a virtual impossibility. If we use a multiplier of 1.5, the cost to Japan in the best case scenario is $101 billion; using the more realistic scenario (with a multiplier of 2), it is $307 billion.

Putting it all together, in the best case scenario, the total cost to oil-importing advanced industrial countries other than the United States (Europe, Japan, South Korea, and others) in the best case scenario is $354 billion, but in the more realistic-moderate scenario, the cost of the increase in the price of oil to our allies in Europe, Japan, and elsewhere in the advanced industrial countries will amount to some $1.1 trillion.

The problem is that the increases in income generated to the oil-producing countries do not fully offset these depressing effects. Just as America's oil companies have done well by the war, so too have the oil sheiks of Saudi Arabia, Hugo Chavez in Venezuela, and Mahmoud Ahmadinejad in Iran. Arms sales to those who control oil assets—and those who would seek to control them—have increased, another reason that the defense industry and arms firms have never had it so good. But, even with their profligate spending, these countries' "marginal propensity to consume"—the fraction of the income that is spent on goods and services—is lower, and hence global GDP is lower. Oil-producing countries know that the high oil prices almost surely will not last, so prudence requires that they set aside a large fraction of the bonanza—one of the reasons that the world has been awash with liquidity.

Another major group of "losers" from the war and the surge in oil prices which followed are poor oil-importing countries all over the world. A study by the International Energy Agency, for instance, showed that the post–Iraq war increase in oil prices for a sample of thirteen African importing countries had the effect of lowering their incomes by 3 percent—more than offsetting all of the increase in foreign aid that they had received in recent years, and setting the stage for another crisis in these countries.[70] Given the high cost of transportation in many of these countries, the higher fuel prices are translating into higher food prices.

In short, there have been global losers and winners in the Iraq war. Our long-standing friends in Europe and Japan are among the global losers. But net, the world is a loser—and by a considerable amount.

Global Peace and Security

THE DREAM OF the U.S. invaders was to create a stable, prosperous, and democratic Middle East. But America's intervention in Iraq is laying the foundations for precisely the opposite result—and the consequences of America's Iraqi venture for global peace and security extend beyond the Middle East. It has helped feed extremism throughout the Islamic world and beyond. This growth of extremism has made the task of leaders in moderate Islamic republics all the more difficult. They have been forceful in encouraging Bush to withdraw, knowing that if the war continues, they will face an increasingly hard time containing more fundamentalist forces.[71]

America's standing in the world has never been lower. Anyone who has traveled abroad knows this. It is also confirmed by every poll and opinion survey. Of course, there have always been mixed feelings: envy mixed with admiration, respect for American democracy and its advocacy of human rights mixed with resentment toward its brashness and overconfidence. But the positives have outweighed the negatives in most countries. This was true not just of traditional allies, such as Great Britain (where 83 percent of the population had a favorable rating of the United States in 1999–2000) and Germany (78 percent), but even in Islamic countries, such as Indonesia (75 percent), Turkey (52 percent), and Morocco (77 percent). Franklin D. Roosevelt, John F. Kennedy, and Bill Clinton were global heroes, even more in some places abroad than they were at home. The war has dramatically changed this picture: compared to 2002, favorable ratings of America are now lower in twenty-six of thirty-three countries surveyed by the Pew Research Center.[72] The situation has worsened in most Muslim countries in the Middle East and Asia—and even among historically steadfast U.S. allies.

By 2007, favorable ratings had fallen to 9 percent in Turkey and 29 percent in Indonesia.[73] That same year, confidence in President Vladimir Putin's leadership exceeded that of President Bush in Canada, Britain, Germany, and France. In chapter 1, we noted that citizens of many countries saw America in Iraq as a greater threat to global peace than Iran. More remarkably, another recent Pew Survey showed that in every country surveyed, the U.S. presence in Iraq was viewed as a greater threat to world peace than North Korea. In short, all over the world, the United States was viewed as a greater danger than the countries President Bush included in his "axis of evil."[74] In Indonesia, a moderate Islamic republic, 80 percent of the public reported being either "very" or "somewhat" worried about America as a military threat to their country. Indeed, a vast majority of those in Islamic countries—and a majority among many of our allies—believe that the Iraq war has made the world a more dangerous place. In Islamic countries, majorities (in some cases, large majorities) see America's motives as dominating the world and gaining control of Middle East oil.[75] Most disturbing is that America is no longer seen as a bastion of civil rights and democracy. The Iraq war "for democracy" has almost given democracy a bad name. Some 65 percent of those in Germany, 66 percent of those in Spain, and 67 percent of those in Brazil expressed a dislike for American ideas about democracy; but these numbers were still more favorable than the reactions in Islamic countries such as Palestine, where the number stood at 71 percent, Pakistan at 72 percent, and Turkey at 81 percent. Even among our former allies in the United Kingdom and Germany, America was seen as doing a bad job in advancing human rights: 78 percent in Germany said so, while only 16 percent said America was doing a good job. Before the war, 61 percent in Germany thought it was doing a good job.

Why does this matter? In earlier chapters, we discussed (but did not quantify) how changing perceptions of America have hurt U.S. businesses and the U.S. economy. It is inevitable that those who see the Bush administration and its conduct of the war unfavorably also begin to see America and its conduct of business in the same light. It is no surprise that the countries that have been most critical of American ideas about democracy are also most critical of American ways of doing business: a majority of those in Germany and France have an unfavorable view, while some 83 percent of those in Turkey do.

But there is a far larger cost. Globalization has made countries more interdependent. Many of the world's most pressing problems—from climate change to the AIDS pandemic to poverty—are global in nature and cannot be solved by any one country acting alone. Wars and conflict in one part of the world can easily spill over to another. The Iraq war has shown that even the sole remaining superpower, a country that spends almost as much on defense as all other countries combined, cannot impose its will on a country with 10 percent of the population and 1 percent of its GDP—at least not without inflicting a cost on itself greater than it is willing to pay.

America has done a good job in selling the idea of democracy—so good that there is a global consensus that decisions about how to run the world need to be made in a way that pays at least some respect to democratic principles and the rule of law. But, in its march to war, the United States trampled on these very same principles.

While the world has become more interdependent and integrated, there are markedly different views about how to approach the myriad global problems facing us. One thing agreed on by all is that real leadership is required. Today, there is a serious lack of confidence in American leadership. And whether it will be easy or difficult to restore that confidence will, in part, depend on who is chosen to be the next American president, and how forthright he or she is in rejecting not just the Bush administration's conduct of the war but the process by which the United States entered the war.

The costs and consequences of the failure to restore American leadership—both to America and to the world—are likely to be enormous. Democracy does provide an important check on wars—only the American electorate has been able to put a check on the military adventurism of the Bush administration. Americans may overestimate their importance in providing leadership, and certainly, in areas like global warming, key agreements have been made without us. Still, America looms so large in the global economy that it is hard to imagine progress on any of the key issues facing the world without its playing a pivotal role.

This book has emphasized the costs of the war in Iraq: the *economic costs* as well as the *opportunity costs*—the diversion of funds that could have been used in so many other and better ways. In the long run, though, the squandering of America's leadership role in the international community, and the diversion of attention from critical global issues—including issues like global warming and nuclear proliferation in North Korea that simply won't go away on their own, and that cannot simply wait to be addressed—may represent the largest and most long-standing legacy of this unfortunate war.[76]

CHAPTER 7

Exiting Iraq

THROUGHOUT THE CONFLICT, President Bush has said that Iraq is just about to turn the corner; stability is about to be restored . . . if only we stay a little bit longer. At any moment, one can identify some indicators that are looking better but others that are looking worse. Violence in one place may be going down, but it may be going up in others. Five years into the war, statements that the country is just about to turn the corner—even when they come from the professional military—ring hollow, especially when seen within the broader landscape. Of course, in the uncertain world of Iraq, nothing is certain; it is *possible* that staying longer could make a difference. But the likelihood of this—five years into the war—looks small.

Unfortunately, five years after the invasion, with hundreds of billions having been spent and thousands of casualties, things are not much better. In 2007, Iraq ranked 178th out of 180 countries worldwide in terms of corruption. Only Somalia and Myanmar (formerly Burma) were worse.[1] Iraq's top anticorruption official fled the country after thirty-one of his agency's employees were killed in a three-year period.[2] The U.S. troop "surge" appears to have improved the security situation in Baghdad, but the violence has migrated to other regions. On December 2, 2007, suspected al Qaeda militants attacked the Shiite village of Dwelah, killing thirteen Iraqis (including three children), torching homes, and forcing hundreds of families to flee.[3] Al Qaeda has moved into northern Iraqi regions such as Diyala with its usual brutality. On December 3, 2007, three young women in Diyala Province were murdered for refusing to marry members of al Qaeda.[4] Meanwhile, radical Sunni and Shiite extremists are still killing dozens of civilians every month in areas beyond where U.S. forces are located. And tensions are high in the north, with Turkish forces attacking Kurdish separatists. For the United States, 2007 proved the deadliest year of the war.[5]

On the political front, Iraq now has a religious government—whereas it had secular governments for eighty years prior to the U.S. invasion. This vastly complicates the challenges of bringing political stability to different parts of society. So far, Iraq's own government has not been able to unite the country. Furthermore, the Iraqi government plans to cut the number of items in the food ration from ten to five in January 2008 due to "insufficient funds and spiraling inflation," which could cause even more social unrest.[6]

For the United States, the skyrocketing costs of the war are driving the tempo of decisions and limiting the scope of action. America *might* have been able to bring a greater semblance of peace and security to Iraq had we been willing to commit sufficient military resources in 2003.[7] But from the start, we have fought the war without inconveniencing ourselves too much. We paid a small group of Americans to bear the burden.

Today, America is engaged in a debate about our exit strategy. Few argue, at least openly, for a permanent Iraq occupation, even if U.S. troops were to retreat to a set of safe military bases scattered around the country.[8] Few argue that we should expand our commitment and draft young Americans to go to war over Iraq. The question, then, centers on how and when to withdraw. Staying longer may not make things better; it could make them worse. The majority of Iraqis, in fact, believe that the security situation will get better once the U.S. military withdraws.[9] While the British have enjoyed a better reputation, as they prepared to withdraw from Iraq, the majority of the Iraqis from Basra, the part of the country the British occupied, view their occupation unfavorably: 85 percent believe that it had an overall negative effect, 56 percent that it contributed to the overall level of militia violence, and two thirds think security will improve after the British turn over control of the province to Iraqi forces (in mid-December 2007). Only 2 percent believe that the British have had a positive effect on the province.[10]

Opponents of a rapid exit policy point to the chaos and violence that might follow. According to them, the country would likely split into three regions. The largest part, the Shiite south, might fall within Iran's orbit of influence. Saudi Arabia and other Sunni governments might then come to the assistance of the Sunni center, providing the wherewithal for continued conflict. The Kurdish-controlled north might break away, and Turkey, long adamant that there should not be a separate Kurdish state, might intervene to prevent it.[11]

These outcomes have frightened most U.S. politicians from declaring support for an immediate withdrawal. But the analysis should not begin with this scenario. The relevant questions are simple ones: Would things be better, or worse, if we were to leave in six months, a year, or two years? Would the situation improve enough to justify the costs—both the human toll and the economic one—of staying? A number of experts have already suggested that chaos is virtually inevitable whether we withdraw today or withdraw in two years' time.

While there is a heated political debate about when and how we should exit, the Bush administration seems to be preparing for a long-term presence. The United States has established hundreds of military bases in Iraq since 2003. Many of these have been handed over to the Iraqis, but several are massive compounds that appear to be designed for long-term U.S. occupation. The largest include Al-Asad, the main supply base for troops in Al Anbar Province, about 120 miles west of Baghdad (housing about 17,000 troops and contractors); Al-Balad (also known as Camp Anaconda), which is the U.S. military's main air transportation and supply hub (housing about 22,500 troops and several thousand contractors); Camp Taji (which has the largest shopping center in Iraq); and Al-Talil, in the south, a key stopping point for supply convoys from Kuwait. The United States has also been constructing a huge new embassy complex in Baghdad, which is more than six times the size of the UN complex in New York.

These key U.S. bases are vast. Al-Balad/Anaconda is 4.5 miles wide and 3 miles long—requiring two bus routes. Al-Asad and Al-Talil are even bigger: nearly 20 square miles each. Even in the vicinity of Baghdad, the base complex Victory/Liberty is so big that it accommodates a 140-mile triathlon course. At the center of these bases are large and sophisticated military airfields, with double runways of 10,000–12,000 feet that can accommodate many aircraft, including fighters, drones, helicopters, and large transport planes.

The bases are largely self-sufficient in terms of utilities, including power, phone systems, heating/cooling, and hospital facilities protected by highly fortified perimeters. Whereas clean water, electricity, or quality medical care are in short supply in the rest of the country, the bases are islands of fully functioning amenities. They include sports facilities, department stores, fast-food restaurants (including a 24-hour Burger King, a Pizza Hut, and Baskin Robbins ice cream outlets), a Hertz Rent-a-Car, movie theaters, air conditioning, satellite Internet access, cable television, and international phone service. The bases have reinforced concrete buildings, hardened protective bunkers, extensive concrete barracks for troops, large internal road systems, and elaborate electronic systems that are rarely, if ever, installed in temporary basing facilities. It is difficult to break out from DOD accounts precisely how much has been spent on constructing these bases, but it runs easily into the billions of dollars. Much of the construction has been built by U.S. contractors. The House Appropriations Committee noted in a March 13, 2006, report that the budgetary requests for the bases were "of a magnitude normally associated with permanent bases."[12] Congress voted overwhelmingly against the use of funds for constructing permanent bases in the 2007 supplemental defense bill; however, construction has continued because the Bush administration has parried whether the current bases are considered "permanent."

Although Americans have differing views of our intentions, Iraqis see our actions as suggesting a long-run presence—if only for forays from protected fortifications. But whatever our intentions, we may not have the final say, unless we are willing to spend even more economic, and political, capital.

The calculations in this book form an essential part of an analysis of an exit strategy. The *stated* cost of our staying in Iraq for another month at current levels is now in excess of $12 billion. Based on our analysis, the total costs are probably twice that—some $25 billion per month. Staying another two years would thus cost some $600 billion. The human toll is even greater—far larger than the dollar sums paid in compensation to bereaved families. There are also the opportunity costs: more money and energy spent in Iraq means we have less to spend elsewhere.

Finally, there are the political costs—the continuing decline in American standing around the world and the increasing disillusionment of American citizens with foreign entanglements. Iraq has proved such a humiliating failure that, when we finally do leave, many Americans may be tempted to withdraw from engagement in the world anywhere else. This may yet prove to be the ultimate tragic cost of Iraq, because (as we argued in the previous chapter) American leadership is important for addressing a host of global problems confronting the modern world.[13]

The prospects of a fundamental change of direction in the next year or two are at best questionable. The Iraq Study Group report put it forcefully: "Despite a massive effort, stability in Iraq remains elusive and the situation is deteriorating. . . . The ability of the United States to shape outcome *is diminishing* [italics added]."[14] Although the number of insurgents through much of 2004–06 was estimated at 20,000, by March 2007, the number of Sunni insurgents alone (including "part-time supporters") was put at 70,000.[15] While the surge did manage to reduce the civilian death toll *compared to the period before the surge,* it still remains high, especially outside of Baghdad. In Baghdad by August 2007, deaths were down to 550 (a three-month toll of 2,050, still almost twice that of the first three months of 2006); the overall rate for the country remains high (800 in October, for a three-month total of 3,300, compared to 2,250 for the first three months of 2006).[16] Even with the surge, the number of insurgent attacks was higher by the end of 2007 than it was two years earlier—rising from 62 per day in early 2005 to 91 in late 2007.[17]

As this book goes to press, there is some optimism that, at last, the surge may eventually have an effect in reducing the number of violent attacks and deaths.[18] It is, of course, impossible to know whether this is more than a temporary lull. But even if an increased presence of U.S. troops were to succeed in reducing the scale of violence, what does it mean? It does not mean that *without* the American presence, violence would be contained. It does not mean that an American departure would be accompanied by any less violence next year than would have been the case this year. It may simply mean there is a degree of rationality in the insurgents' strategy. Knowing that there is a good chance that America will leave after Bush departs, it makes sense for the insurgents to lie low, to husband their resources, to wait until after his departure. If U.S. troops are required to maintain the peace, is America willing to commit, for years to come, 100,000 or more troops to Iraq? Is it willing to add that number and more (to provide the logistical and other support) to the size of the standing forces, so that America is able to meet the other challenges it faces around the world?

In short, five years into the war, we have not created a safe and stable Iraq. Despite our failures in the region, a number of delusions continue to surround the prospect of America's departure from Iraq.

Departure Delusions

THE FIRST DELUSION posits that we cannot leave before our "mission is accomplished" because it would lead to a loss of American credibility. Our enemies would know that we don't have staying power and, in the future, they would be less afraid of our might. Our role in the world would be compromised, and we would wield less influence. The world without the United States acting as a credible policeman would be an increasingly dangerous place. Our supporters in Iraq would be annihilated, and, given all the brutal militia and terrorists now actively killing and kidnapping in Iraq, our withdrawal would make the flight from Saigon look easy by comparison.

The "credibility" argument is a sign of sloppy reasoning. Yes, there will be some loss of credibility if we depart now; but if our analysis is correct, the alternative—staying another year or two or three—will not reduce significantly the chaos and violence that will follow our departure. Then, our "loss of credibility" will be even greater. If we leave now, we will have shown that America could not prevail even with five years of fighting; in two more years, we will have shown that America could not prevail even after seven years.

There is a related risk. If we delay departure, we may not be able to choose the timing. We have pushed for democracy in Iraq. But, apart from the Kurdish north, there is overwhelming opposition to the presence of American forces. Overall, 78 percent of Iraqis oppose our presence. This opposition is as high as 97 percent for the population in Sunni areas and 83 percent in the Shia areas.[19] The democratically elected government could, at any time, ask us to leave. It is almost inconceivable that we would remain in the country under these circumstances. The departure could hardly be more ignominious, as we left with our tail hanging between our legs.[20]

The second delusion is even more dangerously flawed: that if we leave before our mission is accomplished, those who sacrificed their lives will have died in vain. The fallacy in this reasoning is one of the central tenets of economics. There is a set of simple aphorisms that describe this point, including: "Let bygones be bygones." To economists, these expenditures are known as *sunk costs*. In fact, there is an old joke among economists about a driver asking for directions to some destination. The reply? "I wouldn't start from here." None of us would have chosen to begin from here—but here we are. So the question is, what do we do, given where we are now? It makes no sense to send even more young Americans to die in vain.

A third delusion is that we "owe" it to Iraqis to help rebuild their country, given the damage we have inflicted, and that we should not leave until we have finished the task. As the expression goes, "You broke it, you fix it." We obviously cannot bring back to life those who have been killed; but in this view, it would be immoral if we were to leave before we at least repaired the damage inflicted on the Iraqi economy. Yet having accomplished so little in the past five years—we were not even able to spend the Iraqi reconstruction funds effectively or to improve living conditions for average people, despite spending three times the amount per Iraqi that the United States spent per European in the Marshall Plan—there is little reason to believe that much progress is in store in the next year or two.

Even if, by staying longer, we do succeed in reducing temporarily the level of violence, there is little assurance that violence might not flare up after we depart. Vaunted "benchmarks"—like the creation of an effective coalition government—may provide an illusory guide to what will happen *after* we depart: there may be a broad consensus among Iraqis about the desirability of getting the United States out of the country, but not on the aftermath.

Conversely, a high level of violence does not *necessarily* mean that that level will be all the greater upon our departure. Indeed, as we have already noted, most Iraqis believe that we have contributed to the violence and that the level will fall after our departure. Our presence in Iraq may be impeding reconciliation efforts that are almost surely a precondition for successful reconstruction. If that is the case, a speedy departure would save *both* American and Iraqi lives. We should accept some responsibility for what we have done; but there are many ways to help Iraq, including support for multinational reconstruction efforts (probably not managed by Halliburton or other U.S. contractors with a demonstrated record of failure).

Misguided Exit Strategies

STAYING IN IRAQ in order to maintain our credibility, or so that those who have already died will not have died in vain, or so that we can finally repair the damage from our invasion, are three of the more obviously fallacious reasons offered for remaining. More thoughtful—but also flawed—are two widely discussed strategies for framing our exit. The first holds that the U.S. government needs to define some reasonable objectives and then leave as soon as we can credibly claim to have accomplished those objectives. But are there any objectives for which there is a reasonable possibility of accomplishment within, say, a two-year horizon? The art of setting goals lies in making sure they are attainable. Otherwise, only disappointment can result.

When we went into Iraq, the Bush administration offered a well-articulated objective: A free Iraq would inspire the creation of newly democratic states in the Middle East that would join the United States in the war against terrorism and perhaps even be willing to sign a peace agreement with Israel. The reality of the Middle East is now dominated by the increasing popularity of extremist factions such as Hezbollah, Hamas, and the Muslim Brotherhood (in Egypt). Where there has been a democratic election—in Palestine—the voters supported the terrorist-linked Hamas Party.

Today, even the more modest goal of a stable and democratic Iraq appears unattainable.[21] Few experts ever expected a strongly unified state; but some hoped that Sunnis, Shiites, and Kurds would see mutual benefits in creating a workable federal system with high degrees of autonomy. Yet even this hope has eluded the country, and there are few signs of progress. A broader consensus now supports plans to define more limited benchmarks for Iraq and to threaten to leave if the country fails to meet them. These goals are far short of a democratic flowering of the Middle East; they focus on intermediate steps in Iraq that are supposed to indicate progress toward achieving more fundamental goals—steps like the passage of an oil law dividing revenues, or the creation of an effective domestic police force.

A simple notion underlies this approach: If we set clear goals, Iraqis will have a strong incentive to act in a concerted way to satisfy them. If they do not succeed, we should wash our hands of the whole matter. In both the Democratic and Republican parties, there seems to be some faith that this will work. But this approach is also flawed: it treats the Iraqi government and people as if they were a single, rational individual. In fact, there are almost surely members of the current Iraqi government who want it to fail. If they believe that the United States will carry out its threat of withdrawal, the prospect provides them with increased incentives to engage in delaying tactics. To the extent that the U.S. policies coincide with the interests of one group or another, it is almost inevitable that others will believe that they could cut a better deal if America left. Thus, the benchmark approach is almost doomed to failure.

Moreover, our threat of withdrawal has not been credible.[22] If Bush himself were to order U.S. forces out of Iraq, it would be admitting defeat *on his own watch*. No president wants to do this; not Johnson during Vietnam, and certainly not George W. Bush. For those in Iraq who favor U.S. withdrawal, their best strategy is to persuade America's voters that the price of staying in Iraq is too high. Vietnam understood this and ultimately convinced the United States to leave.

The Political Economy of Leaving

THE DIFFICULTY THAT Bush has faced in leaving Iraq provides an example of a widely discussed phenomenon. This phenomenon, known as "the risk of escalating commitment," states that *those undertaking a war—or any other failed project—have a tendency to extend commitments when they should be cutting their losses*. The risk of escalating commitment has several root causes. Earlier, we noted that rational decision making includes "treating bygones as bygones." But there is extensive evidence that in large organizations, this often does not happen. The problem is particularly severe because *those making the decisions do not fully bear the consequences of their mistakes*. In the case of Iraq, although the probability of salvaging the war may be small, leaders may undertake a strategy with a low probability of success because the potential gain from saving *their* reputation is large (whereas if they fail, their reputation will not be much lowered). They do not bear the brunt of the costs—either the economic costs or the cost in lives.

In December 2006, President Bush was given a clear opportunity to change course: the bipartisan Iraq Study Group results, combined with strong voter reaction in the 2006 election, provided an opening for an early exit. Many Republicans hoped that a quick withdrawal would reduce the likelihood that Iraq would be a pivotal issue in the 2008 election. With voter sentiment more than two to one against the war, Republican leaders had every reason to want the issue off the table. Instead, the president remained adamant about staying in—even as one after another member of his own party urged a major change in course.

Bush's stance will place his successor in a difficult position. If the new president orders a rapid departure, he (or she) will be blamed for the chaos that might follow. Bush and his team will say (and believe) that had his successor shown the resoluteness that he had shown, things would have turned out differently. If no rapid departure is ordered, the Iraq war will quickly become the new president's war. At that point, the risk of escalating commitment will again set in. If thousands more Americans are killed and wounded, the new president will have to explain his (or her) mismanagement of the war. The war will sap the energy of the next administration and divert attention away from the myriad other critical problems that our country faces.

The prescription, then, is clear: Unless there is a marked change in the likelihood of peace and security as a result of the continued presence of U.S. troops between the time these words are written and the new president comes into power, there should be a rapid withdrawal. Americans will need to be told the ugly truth: there is no easy way out of the tragedy that has unfolded in Iraq.

Why America's Continued Presence May Make Matters Worse

BY NOW, A massive amount has been written on the sources of America's failure, based on the disastrous consequences of a few key decisions. Paul Bremer's decision to dissolve the Iraqi armed forces, combined with the failure to secure munitions supplies and to restart the economy, created large numbers of disaffected, unemployed, and armed Iraqi soldiers—an explosive recipe for creating an insurgency.[23] The de-Baathification program—firing those affiliated with Saddam Hussein's party, even if they had joined the party only out of necessity—not only increased disaffection but also deprived the country of people capable of managing vital parts of the economy. The deployment of troops to protect the oil ministry and production facilities, while failing to safeguard Iraq's magnificent antiquities and stores of munitions, reinforced cynicism that the invasion was simply a ploy for taking over lucrative resources. Rumsfeld's refusal to allow competitive bidding for billions of dollars of reconstruction money—instead, relying on the usual cabal of Washington Beltway defense contractors—led to delays that resulted in a plummeting standard of living and squandering of our only real opportunity to win the hearts and minds of the Iraqi people.

There was, however, a more fundamental problem with America's military strategy—a lesson we should have learned from Vietnam. We had a number of contradictory stances: we wanted to "shock and awe" Saddam Hussein's followers into subservience, but at the same time, we knew that we had to win their backing. We wanted to promote democracy, but we knew that America was not popular in the Middle East. Similarly, the Bush administration never fully grasped that a majority of the citizens—the Shiites—might not only favor a radical Islamic government (of the kind that we were opposing in Iran and Afghanistan), but even see itself as an ally of Iran. As we have noted, our intervention has led, for the first time in the history of modern Iraq, to a religiously inclined government, making the task of national reconciliation and forming a unified, if federal, government, all the more difficult. Stiglitz raised these dilemmas with one of the senior Bush officials responsible for Iraqi reconstruction shortly before his departure for Iraq in 2003. The official acknowledged that there might have to be a re-education of the Iraqis; he assumed that we could do that—and that we had the time to do it. America's decades of steadfast and often one-sided support of Israel had earned the enmity of almost all Arabs, whether Sunnis or Shiites—it was one thing that united them. And since Bush had taken office, relations deteriorated further, spurred on by actions such as Bush's unremitting backing of Israeli prime minister Ariel Sharon, who was anathema in the Arab world.

We miscalculated the consequences of our actions and their costs—and we designed our policies in ways that were self-defeating. Even with the best of strategies, we might have been defeated; but with the strategy that we adopted, failure was almost inevitable. We expected that our presence in Iraq would galvanize Iraqis to support our efforts; but our presence changed the environment in ways that instead incentivized many Iraqis to oppose us.

First, the administration assumed a *partial equilibrium model*, which did not take into account that the supply of those fighting us was *endogenous,* that is, it could be affected by what we did.[24] With a fixed supply, killing one enemy would reduce the number of enemy soldiers by one. With a supply that responds to actions, killing one enemy could actually increase the number of enemy soldiers. There is a general consensus now that U.S. actions led to an increase in the supply of insurgents. In particular, al Qaeda had no significant presence in Iraq before our entry—the secularist Hussein would not have tolerated such a strong fundamentalist group. Today, it appears to be one of the main sources of the insurgency. Indeed, our very presence in Iraq provides fuel for the insurgency. America is seen not as the liberator, but as the occupier. In any country, it is noble to fight for one's freedom against the occupier.

What is clear is that any occupation government—or at least any government that we approve of—almost surely will be viewed as a puppet and may well not survive our departure. Like it or not, we have become toxic. The United States has no credibility, and neither does any government that we help install. Nor does the current government have enough credibility in Iraq to bring all the disparate groups together. Iraq risks joining the list of failed states—countries whose governments are unable to provide the basics required for society to function, including maintaining law and order. With each senseless killing, the cycle of recrimination and revenge continues, and with it the likelihood that more violence and chaos will erupt upon our departure.

The fact that our presence, which should have united Iraqis against us, has failed to bring the various factions together illustrates the depth of the fissures in Iraqi society. But even if those within the country could unite temporarily in their common cause against the United States, it does not mean that they will act in a concerted way after we leave. Some analysts suggest that, once we leave and the Iraqis can turn their attention toward living with each other, they will find common ground. That may be the case—though there is little evidence to support such a sanguine view—but it is also possible that the fissures that have increased during the five years of our occupation run so deep that reconciliation will not be easy; the risk is that the longer we stay, the deeper the fissures, and the harder the task of national reconciliation.

Second, much of our thinking about Iraq was inflected with the old-style deterrence thinking that dominated military strategy during the Cold War. A strong America deterred the USSR from using its weapons. An aggressive America in Iraq would, in this theory, deter opposition. But again we applied the model incorrectly, and again it became increasingly clear that the model itself was inappropriate.

Deterrence theory is based on the assumption that all participants behave rationally. In a *rational* model, an individual makes the decision to join the insurgency or not by looking at the consequences—what are his or her "life prospects" in each of the alternatives. That in turn is affected by perceptions of the likely winner and what a "victory" might look like. In Iraq, there is no reason to join the side of the occupying forces and the government that the United States installed. The United States has not been able to create jobs, get the economy working, or maintain law and order. We noted such serious mistakes as dissolving the army and excluding former Baathists from key positions. Those left jobless by these moves had no incentive to support the current government but every reason to support the alternative: the insurgency. The larger the number of individuals in the insurgency, the higher the probability of its success, and therefore the more individuals that will continue to join it.

In any war, there is "collateral damage"—the loss of life and property of innocent bystanders. In this war, where winning the support of the Iraqi people was critical, the magnitude of the collateral damage—and the degree of sensitivity of the United States to it—required careful attention. America might view an individual who is unlucky enough to be in the wrong place at the wrong time and so dies as "unfortunate"; but the Iraqis may see such "accidents"—when they occur frequently—as evidence of a pattern of deliberate disregard for Iraqi life and property. It is easy for the opposition to exploit such perceptions. They can also make it easier to recruit insurgents, or at least enhance one's willingness to help insurgents.[25] The U.S. military keeps detailed count of its own dead and injured[26] and goes to enormous lengths to rescue American soldiers if they are in danger. This stands in marked contrast to how Iraqis are sometimes treated. The readiness of the Bush administration to discount the only studies using statistical techniques to estimate "excess" deaths of Iraqis—studies that show deaths in excess of half a million[27]—reinforces perceptions that there is a double standard.

These arguments are reinforced by the failure of judicial procedures. If good individuals are treated badly (e.g., tortured), then there is little incentive to be good. One risks being tortured whether one supports the insurgency or not. What may matter is the differential accuracy of the two "judicial" systems. If *they* punish only those who are complicit with the occupation, and *we* punish many who are not complicit with the insurgency, individuals have an incentive to join the insurgency. What matters is the relationship between our punishment and their punishment, and, most important, the accuracy with which punishments are levied.[28]

There may exist a tipping point, such that when that threshold (measured in terms of the fraction of the population in the insurgency) is crossed, the equilibrium to which the society converges is *not* the one in which groups co-exist peacefully within a single country.[29] That is, as more people join the insurgency, the likelihood of success for the American vision of a united Iraq diminishes.

No one wants to be on the losing side of any conflict. What is true for Iraq is also true for America, and the Iraqi insurgents know this: The fact that the United States has not been able to "pacify" the country after five years may not have discouraged Bush and Cheney. No doubt, they believe their own rhetoric of optimism. But to most Americans—increasingly, even to many American troops—the prospects of an American "victory" are dim. To many, our ambition at this point should be more modest: to leave with dignity. The remaining questions are tactical: how fast we can get our troops home and the implications of various levels of withdrawal; they are no longer strategic questions about how to succeed and win.

These conclusions about our ability to deter the insurgents are strengthened once one takes into account certain other "non-rational" behavioral responses. For the Iraqi side, the fact that individuals are willing to commit suicide means that the usual kinds of deterrence strategies not only may be less effective, but may even be counterproductive.[30]

Every society is likely to react strongly against outsiders who are insensitive to cultural mores. Most of our young soldiers, Marines, sailors, and airmen have performed with great sensitivity, showing empathy to the Iraqi and Afghan people and their terrible plight. Letters we have received show how much our troops want to improve the situation and how hard they are working to alleviate the suffering of local communities. The stories that circulate in the Iraqi media and by word of mouth are the exceptions: cases of U.S. soldiers detaining, interrogating, humiliating, and even torturing innocent Iraqis. But these stories have shaped Iraqi public opinion. Naturally, Iraqis are outraged and our enemies, such as al Qaeda, are clever at exploiting this outrage.

The asymmetry here is that the wrongful conviction of an innocent creates a martyr, which is not offset by the rightful conviction of the guilty (or even the rightful release of the innocent). That is why we should be attentive to procedures associated with arresting and holding those accused of wrongdoing. U.S. policy has conspicuously failed to do this. We are currently holding 26,000 alleged "insurgents" in U.S. custody, with another 37,000 in Iraqi custody.[31] But it is not clear how we define insurgents. Many of those imprisoned may have been indifferent to the United States before we arrested them; internment may make them into active insurgents when they are released.

In addition, we have greatly harmed our own interests by asking Iraqis to share our antipathy to "insurgents." For example, during the battle of Fallujah, Iraqi doctors said that the United States opened fire on emergency workers, stretchers, vehicles, and hospitals—supposedly because they were treating wounded who included a number of insurgents. Dr. Salam Ismael, a surgeon working in Fallujah shortly after the first U.S. sieges on the city, describes the intense frustration in a recent British documentary film. "How did we know who was an insurgent and who was not?" he asks. "Do you think we could stop a person with his leg blown off to ask if he was a member of an insurgency faction? And even if he was—I swore the Hippocratic oath to treat anyone, regardless if he is American or Iraqi, insurgent or not."[32]

There is a growing sentiment that things have gotten to the point where we cannot turn them around, at least not without commitments of resources and personnel well beyond the levels that America is willing to make. The tipping point has been reached. Staying another two years will simply add another 1,000 or more American bodies to the 4,000 who have already died in vain, and another 10,000 or more casualties to the 60,000 who have already been injured. When framed the correct way—not *whether* we should leave, but *when* we should leave—exit becomes simpler. It is a bleak situation. Leaving sooner rather than later is the only way to stop it from getting worse.

As this book goes to press, there is in America a wave of relief: the "surge" seems to have succeeded in reducing violence, especially in Baghdad, and with the reduced violence and the increasing economic problems facing the nation, the war in Iraq has ceased to be the number one issue for many voters. But, as we noted, it is not that the violence has ceased: every week there are reports of attacks that kill twenty-five or more people, attacks that almost anywhere else would be headline news. It is only that in Iraq, we have become so inured to massive violence that when it becomes slightly less pounding, it seems acceptable. Nor does reduced violence today tell us much about what will happen after our departure, whether that departure occurs in six months or six years. The military would like to claim credit for the reductions in violence—the surge of troops. To the extent that this is the primary cause, it is troubling: does it mean we will have to maintain these troop levels to sustain the relative quiet? There are also numerous other factors (e.g., the willingness of Iran to provide support), many of which are outside our control. In short, we are unconvinced that the observed reduction in violence has fundamentally changed the analysis of this chapter. The critical question remains: Will matters be substantially better *upon our departure* two, or six, years from now, enough better to justify the deaths and casualties in the interim?

CHAPTER 8

Learning from Our Mistakes: Reforms for the Future

THE FAILURES IN Iraq, like the earlier failures in Vietnam, will have a chastening effect. Almost surely, America will be more loath to get involved in another venture of this kind; it will, or should, proceed more cautiously in getting involved in another war that could turn into a quagmire. But with all the precautions and caveats, the United States will, someday, go to war again, and so we need to start thinking *now* about how to avoid the problems that have contributed to the failures of this war. We can, and must, put in place reforms that will help us the next time around. We can already identify some of the reforms that, if implemented, can help us avoid future mistakes. Some of these would improve the information and decision-making process—including budgeting. Others relate to the care of soldiers when they come home. The lack of planning and attention to our veterans is a grave error, but thankfully, one of the easiest to correct.

One of the fundamental lessons of this war is the failure of institutions such as the U.S. Congress and the United Nations to provide adequate checks and balances. The founding fathers were keenly aware of the abuse of executive powers, and they designed a system of government based on principles of checks and balances. There is a cost to these checks and balances—they often slow down the pace of making needed change; but the benefits—reducing the likelihood of abuses, or even costly mistakes—are well worth it.

At the time the U.S. Constitution was written, there was little need for limits on the president's ability in the conduct of foreign policy. The United States was a new country and relatively powerless. France and England were the major powers of the time. Our founding fathers gave Congress control of the purse strings and that, in theory, was enough to check the power of the president and to prevent abuse. In the run-up to the Iraq war, we discovered that the existing checks were ineffective. The president's party had a majority in Congress, and he controlled the sources of information. There is evidence that those in the administration manipulated this information to exaggerate the threat from Saddam Hussein. The president claimed that the nation's security was at grave risk, and so Congress took him at his word and voted for the war.[1]

Our checks and balances failed at home, and there was no one abroad that was willing or able to stop us from the early and mad decision to invade Iraq.[2] There are today no international institutions that can provide an adequate check against a major country determined to go to war, even if it is plainly contrary to international law. The United Nations was created after World War II to prevent armed aggression, but it failed here. According to the UN Charter, states are only entitled to take up arms in self-defense or if the Security Council authorizes force. But we ignored the United

Nations and the great majority on the Security Council. The Iraq war was not claimed to be self-defense and it was not authorized by the Security Council. Nor was justification claimed on the grounds of "humanitarian intervention," the use of force to prevent massive violations of fundamental human rights. The U.S. invasion amounted to an act of aggression and violated international law.

The U.S. stance of ignoring the United Nations was shortsighted. There may well come a time when other countries decide to wage war and we will need the United Nations to help us stop them. For this reason, it is important that international law be respected, so that it can act as a check on any one country's ambitions. It is in the United States' interests to have international law respected as much as it is anyone else's.

There are other reasons why it is desirable to have international checks on the power of the U.S. president. In recent years, economists have drawn attention to a phenomenon they call the *agency problem*: the interests of those delegated to make a decision on the part of others (the agent) often do not coincide well with those in whose interests they are supposed to be working, or with those who will have to bear the costs of the decisions. In the case of the Iraq war, it is young people sent to fight who bear the biggest burden. As we saw in the last chapter, this discrepancy between national interests and those of the president extends to virtually every major strategic decision, including whether or when to leave. If U.S. forces withdraw and Iraq implodes, then President Bush will be blamed. But if we stay, there is always the chance that history will judge him more kindly: events could somehow turn out more favorably or the blame could be shared with a future administration. The scope for abuse is increased when information is imperfect—part of the reason that governments often like secrecy, and part of the reason that every modern democracy has tried to circumscribe secrecy, through the passage of Freedom of Information Acts.[3]

The first set of reforms that we propose involves making sure that citizens and their representatives have better information as we go to war—including information about the estimated human and financial costs of the venture. In the case of the Iraq war, we believe that faulty information, not just about the supposed threat from Saddam Hussein's regime but also about the realistic cost of an invasion, was a key factor in ensuring congressional support for the invasion.

The second set of reforms focuses on treating our soldiers and veterans fairly. In January 2005, Under Secretary of Defense for Personnel and Readiness Dr. David Chu caused outrage in the veterans' community when he told the *Wall Street Journal* that the amounts being spent on veterans' pensions, health insurance, and benefits for widows "have gotten to the point where they are hurtful. They are taking away from the nation's ability to defend itself."[4] Yet his statement is an accurate reflection of how this administration has approached war funding. It has not flinched at asking for ever higher amounts of cash to pay troops while they are in combat, and it has not balked at the astronomical demands of private contractors such as Halliburton and Blackwater Security. We have behaved as if there were a direct conflict of interest between funding the war and taking care of the veterans after they come home. This has resulted, as we described in chapter 3, in funding shortfalls at the Veterans Health Administration, a backlog of 400,000 pending disability claims at the Veterans Benefits Administration, and hundreds of thousands of returning veterans having to cope with unnecessary bureaucratic roadblocks and red tape.

. . .

WE PROPOSE A number of reforms designed to ensure that we have better information in the event the United States considers marching into war, or as we continue with any prolonged conflict.

Reform 1: *Wars should not be funded through "emergency" supplementals*

Wars are sometimes not expected. It is understandable that at least some of the initial spending may be unanticipated; but there is no reason why a war should be financed by "emergency" appropriations for two years—let alone five. As we have pointed out, emergency funds are not subject to regular budget caps and—more important—they do not require the same level of budget justification as regular appropriations and are not subjected to the same level of scrutiny. With emergency supplementals, the analysts in Congress and the Congressional Budget Office do not have sufficient information or time to evaluate the request. As a result, the normal checks and balances designed to ensure financial accountability are circumvented. We would urge Congress to enact legislation limiting the use of emergency funding to the first year of a conflict.[5]

Reform 2: *War funding should be linked to strategy reviews*

If the administration resorts to emergency appropriations more than twice, or more than one year after initiation of a conflict, Congress should presume that the war is going worse than was expected. The administration should be required to explain why the conflict is going badly, identify what changes in strategy will be implemented, and estimate their budgetary implications.

Reform 3: *The administration should create a comprehensive set of military accounts, which include the expenditures of the Department of Defense,* *the State Department, the Department of Veterans Affairs, and the Department of Labor, as well as Social Security and health care benefits that arise from military service*

This set of budget accounts should be transparent, and presented on both a cash and an accrual basis—costs not just for the next ten years, but for the next forty. The costs of war continue long after combat has ceased, but they are hidden by the government's "cash" accounting system and can remain so for a long time. There are a variety of budgetary tricks (besides cash accounting) by which an administration can obfuscate the real costs—which may be particularly tempting to an administration if, say, the war is unpopular.

In every war, the administration should be required to provide a set of budget accounts that not only include current expenditures in detail but take into account the cost of replacing equipment and supplies used in the war effort and the need to provide long-term medical care and disability benefits to soldiers. The budget accounts should also provide for the long-term costs of any structural changes in the DOD budget, such as increased combat pay and benefits. Any likely impact on other departments, such as the departments of State, Energy, and Health and Human Services, as well as large agencies such as the Social Security Administration, should also be reported.

Reform 4: *The Department of Defense should be required to present clean, auditable financial statements to Congress, for which the Secretary of Defense and the Chief Financial Officer are held personally accountable*

Unbelievable as it seems, basic information about outlays—what has actually been spent on them—is not available. President Bush has not presented, on a regular basis, an accounting of how much the war in Iraq has cost us. It is only through hard work that we—and others—have been able to piece together the accounts. The DOD classifies more than $25 billion in its annual Operations and Maintenance budget as "other services and miscellaneous contracts"—a catch-all category which the Congressional Research Service criticizes as being "too vague to be useful." The accounting systems at the Pentagon are so poor at tracking expenditures that the department has flunked its financial audit every year for the past decade. Every responsible party looking at the costs of the war—including the CBO, the CRS, the Government Accountability Office, the Iraq Study Group, and the department's own auditors and Inspector General—have found numerous discrepancies in the DOD figures.

The department is required under the Chief Financial Officers Act and the Financial Management Integrity Act to prepare financial statements that meet certain minimal standards of transparency and accountability.[6] Since the enactment of these reforms, almost all the cabinet-level departments (with the exception of the Department of Homeland Security, which was created by merging twenty-two agencies and has not yet consolidated all of those accounts) have been able to produce "clean" financial statements that are approved by outside auditors. This has required a great deal of hard work at all these departments. Despite efforts by some of the career staff in the Pentagon, the leadership at DOD has not made the kind of intense, sustained effort (nor requested funds to do so) that would lead to a "clean" opinion—that the accounts provide an accurate description of the department's spending.

It is ironic that Congress is willing to tolerate such lax standards and limited accountability. Just four years ago it enacted (almost unanimously) the Sarbanes-Oxley Act, which requires CEOs to take personal responsibility for their companies' financial statements and imposes criminal penalties for violations. The act also demands a high standard of transparency in financial statements and offers protection to whistle-blowers. Sarbanes-Oxley was passed in 2002 in response to the corporate accounting scandals of the late nineties at Enron, WorldCom, and Tyco, whose senior officers are now behind bars. If the Defense Department were held to similar standards of accountability, Defense Secretary Donald Rumsfeld and his former deputy Paul Wolfowitz might be held personally liable for some of the profiteering and financial lapses at the Pentagon during their stewardship.

Holding the Secretary of Defense and the Chief Financial Officer more personally accountable would likely spur the needed change.[7] We urge Congress to begin by insisting on enforcement of the existing rules: require all major departments to file financial statements that cover their assets, liabilities, inventories, systems, and contracts.[8] If this does not produce results, Congress should enact a mini–Sarbanes-Oxley for government that holds cabinet officers accountable for financial matters in their departments.[9]

Reform 5: *The administration and the CBO should provide regular estimates of the micro- and macroeconomic costs of a military engagement*

The large disparity between the budgetary and the total economic costs of war means that there is need for a comprehensive accounting of the cost to the economy. The attempt to keep the budgetary costs of this war down has increased costs elsewhere. There are thousands of economists in the federal government—serving at the Office of Management and Budget, the CBO, GAO, the Joint Economic Committee in the House of Representatives, and throughout government. Despite this capacity, the federal government has made only limited efforts to understand the full economic costs of war—and only after outside prodding. This should be made a matter of routine. The CBO should be given responsibility for preparing an economic report that addresses the main categories of these costs, along the lines provided in this book, and in a way that is sufficiently transparent that outsiders can validate its conclusions. Future costs that should be identified include future health care and disability payments over the lifetime of the injured, replacement of destroyed and depreciated equipment, and "resetting" the military to its prewar capacity.

Reform 6: *The administration should be required to notify Congress of any procedural changes that might affect the normal bureaucratic checks and balances on the flow of information. The Freedom of Information Act (which enshrines the basic principles of citizens' right to know what their government is doing) should be strengthened, with a more narrow carving out of exceptions, and with congressional oversight on these exceptions*

Information about the war effort has been concealed, disguised, or delayed during the Iraq conflict. This includes basic data—such as the number of soldiers injured, the amount of time they wait to see a doctor in the VA system, and the number of suicides and desertions among soldiers deployed to the conflict. Veterans' organizations have been forced to use the Freedom of Information Act to find these things out. We urge that Congress require that such data be made accessible.[10]

There were a number of other aspects of this war that were unusual, that have diminished the extent to which Americans feel the full pain of war. Two of these require careful review.

Reform 7: *Overall, Congress should review the heavy reliance on contractors in wartime. In particular, the use of contractors for "security services"* *should be limited, both in number and in duration, with a detailed justification provided for why the military itself cannot provide these services. Careful attention should be paid to hidden costs borne by the public, of the kind uncovered in this book, such as the payment for disability and death through government-provided insurance*

The war in Iraq is proving to be a wake-up call regarding the role of contractors. In Iraq and Afghanistan, we are using contractors to perform many of the tasks formerly done by military or civilian government employees. They are used not only in support roles but in key strategic positions, such as prison interrogators, bomb defusers, top-secret intelligence gatherers for the CIA, and armed bodyguards for U.S. officials. They have landed lucrative contracts to rebuild infrastructure and to feed American troops. Much of this work has been poorly managed and inadequately monitored, and yet private contractors have become indispensable to the war operation.

There are serious fundamental flaws with this reliance on the private sector. First, contractors are motivated by different incentives than civil servants. Whether they are giant corporations like Bechtel and General Electric or individual security guards who can earn $16,000 a month in Iraq, contractors are driven by making money. It is unrealistic to assume that they will be motivated by the same concern for the public interest as civil servants or soldiers. The current system relies on civil servants to manage contractors and hold them accountable. But—as has become painfully evident in Iraq—few civil servants, even in the military, have the training or skills to do this effectively; and we have simply not hired enough civil servants to provide adequate oversight.

Second, the taxpayer does not appear to be getting value for money. One of the main reasons for outsourcing is that the private sector is widely assumed to be more efficient. But in Iraq, much of the reconstruction funds went to high-priced American contractors rather than low-cost local labor. The GAO and other government watchdogs have repeatedly documented cases of over-billing, overpayment, and outright profiteering during the Iraq war. This has increased the operational costs. And a large percentage of military contracts in this war have been awarded without full competition. Giant contractors have become adept at gaming the system. Once firms win big contracts—often using low-ball initial cost estimates—the government becomes so dependent on their services that it's almost impossible to get rid of them.

Third, the risks of losing control may well outweigh budgetary considerations—as, say, in the interrogation of military prisoners. But the pendulum has swung so far in favor of contracting out that the Pentagon typically even hires contractors to perform audits of other government contractors. In Iraq, this issue is compounded by the contractors' murky legal status. Under the Geneva Conventions, they are non-combatants; but many of those working in Iraq carry arms and work as paramilitary security forces, or they are involved in training military security forces. Yet they are not always subject to the same discipline and accountability as U.S. troops.

The extensive and growing dependence on contractors is likely to accelerate even further. At the Department of Defense, 50 percent of civilian military workers will soon be eligible to retire. Many of those retirees, still in their mid-fifties, will end up in the "revolving door," working for contractors after their obligatory one-year abstinence from government-related work.

Above all, our dependence on contractors has limited the extent to which America has felt the human toll of the war. The all-volunteer Army, National Guard, and Reservists perform heroically, but the percentage of the U.S. population bearing the cost of a conflict is the lowest ever.[11] Rather than making more Americans share the burden, we hired, contracted, and required those who were in the armed forces, National Guard, and Reserves to work for longer. This is not only unfair; in the long run, it may even be costly, as it renders volunteering less attractive. Congress should undertake an extensive review of the entire philosophy and implications behind this privatization of the military.

Reform 8: *The military should not be permitted to call upon the National Guard or the Reserves for more than one year, unless it can demonstrate that it is not feasible to increase the requisite size of the armed forces*

We are supposed to call upon the Reserves and the National Guard in times of emergency. Five years into a war, we cannot credibly claim that in Iraq it is still an emergency. We have already seen the consequences of a first-responder National Guard that is overseas instead of able to take action quickly at home. Limiting the deployment of these troops to one year will compel the military to present alternative approaches. National Guard and Reserves would only serve more than one twelve-month tour if the military can convincingly prove that it cannot meet the force requirements any other way.

In the event National Guard or Reserve troops do serve more than one tour, the military would be required to pay double wages on a second tour of duty and triple on a third. Double pay should be given to any individual required involuntarily to extend his or her time in service beyond the originally contracted amount.

This will provide incentives for the military not to use the National Guard or Reserves for repeated tours of duty; not to force those who have signed up for four years duty to do a fifth or sixth;

and will also compensate those called up and who have had the time of their service extended for the huge burden imposed on them.

Finally, the military should provide a compelling case that there are indeed significant cost savings and improvements in military effectiveness from imposing such a large burden on so few individuals, rather than sharing the burden more broadly.

It may, of course, be the case that military recruiters are not able to raise the additional troops required in an all-voluntary army, or at least may not be able to do so without raising compensation and lowering standards. But that should itself be sending an important message to our policymakers. Americans are patriotic. They volunteered in droves for World War II because they thought it was a just war. If America's young men and women are saying that they are unwilling to fight in a conflict in which political leaders in Washington have got the nation engaged, our political leaders should listen to their message.

Reform 9: *There should be a presumption that the costs of any conflict lasting more than one year should be borne by current taxpayers, through the levying of a war surtax*

War has become too easy for America.[12] The average American was not asked to risk his own life, or the life of his children, in Iraq. Nor has he been asked to pay higher taxes. The war has been financed by debt. The combination of a volunteer army and a war financed by debt made it initially possible for most Americans to support the war, without ever asking: would they be willing to sacrifice their lives or the lives of their children to fight this war? Would they be willing to pay $25,000 of their own family's money (and their children's money) to fight this war?[13] The incentives of average Americans to act as the check and balance against the abuse of presidential power was short-circuited. We believe that, at a minimum, the financial costs of running the war should be borne by its current citizens, not simply transferred to the next generation.[14] This means that current revenues must cover current spending; a war tax should be levied to fund such expenditures. The tax would fund both current operations and additional contributions to the Veterans Benefit Trust Fund that we propose later in this chapter.[15]

As the United States has emerged as the sole superpower, with an imbalance of military power even greater than the imbalance in economic power (spending 47 percent of the total for the entire world on armaments), there is no last line of checks against its abuse of military power—other than the active involvement of its citizens. The fact that the death and destruction occurs from bombs dropped from 50,000 feet, on people who are neither seen nor heard, most of whom can be written off as "collateral damage," should not make the act of killing any easier.

THE NINE REFORMS just described are designed to make it more likely that we make intelligent decisions about going to war—good information is required to make good decisions, and it is important that Americans know, and confront, the costs of war. The United States will almost surely go to war again. Americans may disagree about whether or when to do so. On one issue, however, almost all concur: we should treat those who fight for their country well—better than they have been treated by the Bush administration. The next nine reforms are designed to ensure that this happens.

Reform 10: *Shift the burden of proof for eligibility (presumption) for health care benefits and disability from soldiers to government*

If a veteran claims a war-related disability, then the veteran should be *presumed* to be entitled to that claim. It should be up to the Department of Veterans Affairs to provide evidence that the veteran is not eligible. We should think about veterans' disability claims the same way we do taxes: the IRS automatically accepts nearly all tax filings from everyone, and then audits a subset to detect and deter fraud. For veterans, we should require that all returning servicemen and women have a complete medical examination on their discharge from the military, especially for traumatic brain injury and post-traumatic stress disorder. Any disabilities apparent at that time should automatically qualify the veteran for benefits. The department can then accept claims immediately. Several studies by the Inspectors General of the VA and DOD have found almost no fraud among veterans' claims. Nevertheless, the VA can then audit a sample of claims later on, adjusting payments where necessary.[16]

The current system sets up an unfair battle between the government and the veteran—with the presumption (and the resources) on the side of the government. In the current conflict and in the Gulf War of 1991 the VA eventually approved 88–90 percent of all claims (at least in part), paying them retroactively. It makes more sense to approve the claim up front rather than force disabled veterans to wait between six months and two years before approving a claim.

Reform 11: *Veterans' health care should be viewed as an entitlement, not a matter of discretion*

Veterans Health Administration expenditures should not be part of the discretionary budget (in the same way that Social Security and Medicare benefits are not part of the discretionary budget), subject to annual appropriations. If the Veterans Health Administration cannot provide the health care veterans are entitled to in its medical facilities, then veterans should have access to the Medicare program, paid for by the VA's (non-discretionary) budget. The fact that these costs may be higher (especially when it comes to rehabilitation, a VA specialty) should provide the administration with an incentive to expand VA health facilities.

Reform 12: *A Veterans Benefit Trust Fund should be set up and "locked," so that veterans' health and disability entitlements are fully funded as obligations occur*

There are always pressures to cut unfunded entitlements. So, when new military recruits are hired, the money required to fund future health care and disability benefits should be set aside ("lockboxed") in a new Veterans Benefit Trust Fund. We require private employers to do this; we should require the armed forces to do it as well. This would mean, of course, that when we go to war, we have to set aside far larger amounts for future health care and disability costs, as these will inevitably rise significantly during and after any conflict.

Reform 13: *National Guard and Reservists who fight overseas must be eligible for the Benefits Delivery at Discharge program and other all military benefits programs*

There is mounting evidence that National Guard and Reserve veterans are being rejected for disability benefits more frequently than active duty forces, even though fewer file claims (cf. chapter 4). This may be due to the fact that they have not been eligible for the Benefits Delivery at Discharge program, and the DOD should move immediately to make them eligible. In addition, National

Guard and Reserve troops who have served overseas should be eligible for the same benefits as the military, such as low-cost loans for homes and education.

Reform 14: *A new office of advocacy should be established to represent the interests of veterans*

The military chain of command rightfully requires that troops take orders from their superiors. Especially in times of conflict, there cannot be the usual bargaining that marks the ordinary employer-employee relationship. But this means that the interests of the ordinary individual serviceman or woman may be given short shrift. Someone should be speaking out for their interests, both while they are serving and afterward.

This office would provide a lifeline to young men and women who are currently at the mercy of wrongheaded policies and decisions by the huge, impersonal military establishment. Just one example is that the military has been demanding that combat-wounded veterans repay a portion of their enlistment bonuses if they fail to serve out their full tours of duty as a result of their injuries. This legal but morally offensive policy was discovered by the Dole-Shalala Commission and would be reversed by legislation that has just been passed by the Senate. But there are hundreds of obscure regulations that can have adverse consequences. Ordinary rank-and-file members of the military need someone who can speak up on their behalf.

Reform 15: *Simplify the disability benefits claims process, especially for veterans with PTSD*

The actual process of claiming disability benefits is outdated, paper-intensive, and needlessly complicated. Every commission, panel, and organization that has looked into this subject has reached the same conclusion. In 2007, the National Institute of Medicine published an exhaustive 300-plus-page critique of the current system, which urged a radical overhaul and modernization of disability benefits.[17] The Dole-Shalala Commission also recommended a major restructuring of the disability claims process. Veterans' organizations have some disagreements about the precise characteristics of the new system, but most agree that the current one has become unworkable. This situation will worsen in the next few years as the number of complicated claims increases, and as a large number of the most experienced claims adjudicators retire from the VA.

We urge extensive revisions of the claim form itself, of the rating scale, and of the formula for calculating disabilities, as well as modernization of the medical terminology and conditions rated. The current 26-page form, with its detailed requirements for documentation for each disabling condition, should be shortened to a one-page document modeled on the IRS "short form" for taxes. We also urge the VA to consider a radical simplification of categories, based on five levels: not disabled; mild disability; moderate disability; severe disability; and very severe disability. This would replace the current ten-step percentage increment scale, which is highly subjective and applied inconsistently in different regional offices. We recommend that current veterans be grandfathered into the new system at the nearest equivalent ranking on the five-step scale, rounded to the higher equivalent. The new system not only would reduce errors, inconsistencies, and complexity, but also would make it easier to train new claims adjudicators. The problems with the current formulas and medical conditions are well documented in the National Institute of Medicine report and we urge adoption of its recommendations.

In addition, there is an urgent need to fast-track the process for filing for disability for those suffering from post-traumatic stress disorder. This should be a top priority. The current system, which is geared to physical ailments that are immediately apparent, is especially cruel to those suffering from PTSD because the illness seldom manifests itself immediately. Filling in forms and securing detailed documentation is not easy even for people in full mental health. The veterans with PTSD are at higher risk of homelessness,[18] substance abuse, underemployment, domestic violence, suicide, and other social problems. Since PTSD is fast becoming endemic among returning troops, it is essential that this system be reformed by automatically approving (a presumption of service connection) all disability compensation claims where the veteran was deployed to the war zone and was diagnosed with PTSD.

Reform 16: *Restore medical benefits to Priority Group 8 veterans*

In 2003, former VA secretary Anthony Principi suspended all veterans who were in the lowest-priority category, "Priority Group 8," from eligibility for VA medical care. His intent was to free up scarce resources for the higher-priority veterans, those who are disabled or have a very low income. However, this decision meant that at least 400,000 veterans since 2003 have been denied access to care.[19] These veterans are not rich; a veteran earning $30,000 a year can be disqualified from access to VA care because of his income.[20] While we understand that Principi was attempting to preserve access for the most needy, the fundamental problem is that we are not fully funding the VA so it can provide care to all veterans who wish to participate. We urge that Congress restore the funding and capacity necessary to the VA health care system so that Priority Group 8 veterans can be accepted.

Reform 17: *Harmonize the transition from military to veteran status, so that it becomes a truly "seamless" transition*

Perhaps no issue has been as roundly criticized as the apparent inability of the DOD and VA to work together to provide a seamless transition for soldiers from military to veteran status. This is a particular disgrace since it is not a rare occurrence. It has caused untold suffering, as was revealed in the Walter Reed Army Medical Center outpatient fiasco. The Dole-Shalala Commission, the Gates Commission, the Commission on the Future for America's Veterans, and other groups of the DOD and VA remain unable to fix this problem. But most of the reforms needed are straightforward common sense, and many of them were outlined in a set of recommendations by the Department of Veterans Affairs' "Seamless Transition" Task Force in 2004.[21] They include better coordination in the medical and payroll systems between the DOD and VA; better access to DOD facilities for VA employees; and synchronization of the DOD disability ratings with the VA system, as well as more trust and information sharing at all levels between the two departments.

Reform 18: *Increase education benefits for veterans*

During World War II, America made a contract with its troops that enabled an entire generation of veterans to gain access to a good education after the conflict. The G.I. Bill covered the full cost of a college education, including tuition, books, and a living stipend. Current education benefits (provided under the Montgomery G.I. Bill of 1984) are less generous. Today's active duty forces can receive up to 75 percent of tuition costs at a public college or university, with no provision for books or living expenses. Moreover, in order to qualify, a service member must pay an upfront premium of $1,200 within the first year of military service; otherwise, he or she is not eligible to receive education benefits at all. There are eleven individual states which provide free tuition to home state veterans at their state colleges and universities. But for veterans from the other thirty-nine states, the cost of a good education may well be out of reach.

Today's military is all volunteers: some have not even completed high school. In an effort to bolster recruiting, we have hired more soldiers from the lower socioeconomic quintiles, and fewer from the top. We have doubled the number who lack a high school diploma.[22] Having already spent $3 trillion to wage this war, one of the best investments we could make would be to substantially increase education benefits to the post–World War II G.I. Bill levels as an investment in our young men and women who have fought for America.

EVEN UNDER THE best of circumstances, the United States will be spending many billions more in Iraq in the coming decade. Already it is committed to providing Iraq with long-term security guarantees; to training, equipping, and arming the Iraqi Security Forces; and to fighting "Al-Qaeda, Saddamists and all other outlaw groups."[23] This virtually guarantees that U.S. troops will be required to maintain a presence in Iraq for the foreseeable future. Our hasty decision to invade Iraq in 2003 has long-term implications that will be paid for by generations of Americans to come.

The eighteen major reforms that we propose in this final chapter will help us avoid becoming embroiled in another Iraq or Vietnam in the future. Our system will not be fail-safe. Even the best and the brightest make errors of judgment, and America's political system does not always ensure that the best and brightest reach the pinnacles of decision making. But these reforms would make such mistakes less likely. At the very least, they would ensure that if we do become embroiled in another such conflict, we will do so with our eyes open and with an ability to deal with some of the long-term social and economic problems that follow.

Wars should not be undertaken without an appreciation of the likely human and economic costs and without plans to treat our troops and veterans in the way they deserve. War inevitably involves not just the killing and injuring of enemy combatants; it also harms innocent bystanders who are unlucky enough to be in the wrong place at the wrong time. In Iraq, this human suffering, euphemistically referred to as "collateral damage," now includes hundreds of thousands of civilian deaths, 2 million international refugees, and a further 2 million who have been displaced within the country.

GOING TO WAR is not to be undertaken lightly. It is an act that should be undertaken with greater sobriety, greater solemnity, greater care, and greater reserve than any other. Stripped of the relentless media and government fanfare, the nationalist flag-waving, the reckless bravado, war is about men and women brutally killing and maiming other men and women. The costs live on long after the last shot has been fired.

APPENDICES

President's Letter to the Speaker of the House of Representatives on the Emergency Appropriations Act

October 17, 2001

Dear Mr. Speaker:

In accordance with provisions of Public Law 107-38, the Emergency Supplemental Appropriations Act for Recovery from and Response to Terrorist Attacks on the United States, FY 2001, I ask the Congress to consider expeditiously the enclosed proposals, totaling $20 billion, to enable the Government to continue to provide assistance to the victims of the September 11th attacks and to deal with the consequences of the attacks.

Public Law 107-38—legislation crafted and enacted with strong bipartisan cooperation—provided a total of $40 billion in emergency funding to the Emergency Response Fund.

The $40 billion in emergency expenses enacted in Public Law 107-38 was provided to assist victims of the attacks and to deal with other consequences of the attacks, including the costs of: (1) providing Federal, State, and local preparedness for mitigating and responding to the attacks; (2) providing support to counter, investigate, or prosecute domestic or international terrorism; (3) providing increased transportation security; (4) repairing public facilities and transportation systems damaged by the attacks; and (5) supporting national security.

As required by Public Law 107-38, on September 18th, I designated the entire $40 billion as an emergency funding requirement. Today, I hereby request and designate these individual proposals as emergency funding requirements pursuant to section 251(b)(2)(A) of the Balanced Budget and Emergency Deficit Control Act of 1985, as amended. In addition, I hereby designate the funds in or credited to the Defense Cooperation Account during FY 2002 as emergency requirements pursuant to section 251(b)(2)(A) of such Act.

I am proud that we have continued to work together with such bipartisan spirit in the weeks following the despicable attacks on our Nation. Since final estimates of the total resources needed to address the consequences of this tragedy will not be known for months to come, I urge the Congress to enact—without delay—these specific requests that address immediate, near-term needs and that represent currently defined and certain requirements.

My Administration does not intend to seek additional supplemental funding for either domestic or defense needs for the remainder of this session of Congress. If further requirements become clear, we will work with the Con-

gress to address additional needs in the Second Session of the 107th Congress. In addition, we will assess the manner in which our FY 2003 Budget will address further needs as they relate to the September 11th terrorist attacks.

The details of these actions are set forth in the enclosed letter from the Director of the Office of Management and Budget. I concur with his comments and observations.

Sincerely,
GEORGE W. BUSH

Evolving DOD Web Sites for Operation Iraqi Freedom

CHART 1

THIS IS THE official DOD casualty total, which can be easily found on the regular DOD Web site. It includes both hostile and non-hostile deaths but provides wounded statistics only for those wounded in combat (hostile wounds).

Operation Iraqi Freedom (OIF) U.S. Casualty Status*

Fatalities as of: December 26, 2007, 10 a.m. EST

OIF U.S.Military Casualties by Phase	Total Deaths	KIA	Non-Hostile	WIA RTD**	WIA Not RTD**
Combat Operations—19 Mar 03 thru 30 Apr 03	139	109	30	116	429
Post Combat Ops—1 May thru Present	3,749	3,057	692	15,742	12,424
OIF U.W. DoD Civilian Casualties	8	7	1		
Totals	**3,896**	**3,173**	**723**	**15,858**	**12,853**

**Operation Iraqi Freedom includes casualties that occurred on or after March 19, 2003, in the Arabian Sea, Bahrain, Gulf of Aden, Gulf of Oman, Iraq, Kuwait, Oman, Persian Gulf, Qatar, Red Sea, Saudi Arabia, and United Arab Emirates. Prior to March 19, 2003, casualties in these countries were considered OEF.*

***These columns indicate the number of service members who were Wounded in Action (WIA) and Returned to Duty (RTD) within 72 hours and WIA and Not Returned to Duty within 72 hours. To determine the total WIA figure, add the columns "WIA RTD" and "WIA Not RTD" together. These figures are updated on Tuesday unless there is a preceding holiday.*

CHART 2

THIS WAS DOD'S hard-to-find full tally before DOD changed the format. As of January 6, 2007, it listed the "Total Number of 'non-mortal casualties,'" including hostile and non-hostile deaths; combat woundings; and non-hostile wounds, injuries, and diseases that were serious enough to require medical transport. As of January 6, 2007, the number of non-mortal casualties was 47,657 for Iraq. The chart no longer exists in this format.

Global War on Terrorism—Operation Iraqi Freedom

By Casualty Category Within Serivce (March 19, 2003, Through January 6, 2007)

Casualty Type	Total	Army	Navy***	Marines	Air Force
Killed in Action	1,843	1,201	42	585	15
Died of Wounds*	562	411	1	150	
Died While Missing in Action	7	7			
Died While Captured	2	2			
Total Hostile Deaths	**2,414**	**1,621**	**43**	**735**	**15**
Accident	383	260	10	103	10
Illness	57	48	7	1	1
Homicide	12	8	1	1	2
Self-Inflicted	96	81	2	13	
Undetermined	6	5	1		
Pending**	30	17		13	
Total Non-Hostile Deaths	**584**	**419**	**21**	**131**	**13**
Total Deaths	**2,998**	**2,040**	**64**	**866**	**28**
Wounded—No Medical Air Transport Required	16,164	9,944	386	5,627	207
Wounded—Medical Air Transport Required****	6,670	4,751	130	1,738	51
Non-Hostile Injuries—Medical Air Transport Required****	6,640	5,299	214	857	270
Diseases—Medical Air Transport Required****	18,183	15,710	509	1,163	801
Total—Wounded	**22,834**	**14,695**	**516**	**7,365**	**258**
Total—Medical Air Transported	**31,493**	**25,760**	**853**	**3,758**	**1,122**
Total—Non-Mortal Casualties	**47,657**	**35,704**	**1,239**	**9,385**	**1,329**

*Includes died of wounds where wounding occurred in theater and death occurred elsewhere.
**Pending means final category to be determined at a later date.
***Navy totals include Coast Guard.
****Reported by Deployment Health Support Directorate (through December 4, 2006).

CHART 3

THIS IS DOD'S current list of casualties, in the new format. It lists hostile and non-hostile deaths, hostile woundings, and non-hostile medical air transports. To find the total non-mortal casualties (previously listed as "Total Number of Non-Mortal Casualties"), you must add the "Wounded—No Medical Air Transport Required" plus "Total Hostile and Non-Hostile Medical Transports." As of December 8, 2007, this number was 58,846 for Iraq (available at http://siadapp.dmdc.osd.mil/personnel/CASUALTY/OIF-Total.pdf). Similar charts were altered for Operation Enduring Freedom (Afghanistan).

Global War on Terrorism—Operation Iraqi Freedom

By Casualty Category Within Serivce (March 19, 2003, Through December 8, 2007)

Casualty Type	Total	Army	Navy***	Marines	Air Force
Killed in Action	2,451	1,720	58	647	26
Died of Wounds*	699	522	1	176	
Died While Missing in Action	7	7			
Died While Captured	2	2			
Total Hostile Deaths	**3,159**	**2,251**	**59**	**823**	**26**
Accident	461	328	11	110	12
Illness	71	58	7	3	3
Homicide	20	12	3	3	2
Self-Inflicted	132	113	4	15	
Undetermined	8	7	1		
Pending**	26	6	2	18	
Total Non-Hostile Deaths	**718**	**524**	**28**	**149**	**17**
Total Deaths	**3,877**	**2,775**	**87**	**972**	**43**
Total—Wounded (WIA)	**28,661**	**19, 364**	**599**	**8,357**	**341**
Wounded—No Medical Air Transport Required	19,970	12,906	435	6,370	259
Wounded—Medical Air Transport Required****	8,691	6,458	164	1,987	82
Total—Non-Hostile Related Medical Air Transports	**30,185**	**25,373**	**974**	**2,494**	**1,344**
Non-Hostile Injuries—Medical Air Transport Required****	7,963	6,316	278	1,037	332
Diseases/Other Medical—Medical Air Transport Required****	22,222	19,057	696	1,457	1,012
Total—Medical Air Transports (Hostile and Non-hostile)	**38,876**	**31,831**	**1,138**	**4,481**	**1,426**

*Includes died of wounds where wounding occurred in theater and death occurred elsewhere.
**Pending means final category to be determined at a later date.
***Navy totals include Coast Guard.
****Reported by Force Health Protection and Readiness.

On Methodologies

THERE ARE A large number of technical issues that we have had to address in analyzing the costs of the Iraq war. In this technical appendix, we examine several critical issues and explain some of the underlying reasons for our approach and our conclusions. It should be added that many of these issues are very complex—whole tomes have been written on them—and in this short appendix, we cannot do full justice to them.

Oil has been at the center of the war from the onset. Many believe we went to war to get an assured supply of inexpensive oil for the United States and its oil companies. We begin by explaining both why that belief is so widespread and why the quest for an assured supply of oil could, or at least should, never have been the basis of a *rational* strategy. But whatever our motives, the consequences have been the opposite: oil prices have soared. In the third section, we explain why we believe that the war should be given "credit" for much of the rise—and why our assumption, attributing but $5 or $10 per barrel of the rise for seven or eight years—is excessively conservative.

In the 1970s, soaring oil prices played a central role in the macroeconomic disasters of that decade. This time, so far, the effects have been more muted; we explain why this is so but also why the effects are still significant, far greater than just the effect of the hundreds of billions of dollars that have been transferred to the oil-exporting countries.

In the text, we argue that one of the effects of the soaring oil prices was to dampen the economy; had prices been lower, output would have been higher. But was there scope for expanding production? In the fourth section, we explain why there was scope, and why, more generally, had we spent the money in ways that would have stimulated the economy more (than the dollars squandered on Iraq), the economy could (and would) have been stronger.

Many of the macroeconomic effects of the war are hard to quantify—for instance, markets dislike uncertainty and the turmoil in the Middle East has clearly contributed to uncertainty. And while most of our analysis has focused on the effects of the war on aggregate demand (the amount Americans have to spend on goods at home is reduced because we are spending more on oil), there are also *supply-side effects.* As labor gets diverted to the war effort, as the numbers of casualties mount, and as the war has diverted resources away from needed investments in both the public and the private sector, the economy's productive potential is diminished. We discuss, and provide some quantification of, these effects.

One of the main points stressed in this book is that there are bills that will be coming due for decades—including payments for disability and medical benefits. But how do we value these future costs? While all agree that a dollar in the future is worth less than a dollar today, the extent to which future costs are "discounted" is important (though changing the discount rate within a plausible range will not change the overall assessment, that this conflict will impose enormous economic costs, almost surely greater than every other war the

United States has fought except World War II). In the final section, we explain the appropriate methodology for discounting.

Was the War About Oil?

LARRY LINDSEY, HEAD of Bush's National Economic Council, claimed that "The successful prosecution of the war would be good for the economy" (cf. chapter 1). A key reason for this claim was the belief that it would keep oil prices low. As the *Wall Street Journal* editorial that same day argued, "the best way to keep oil prices in check is a short, successful war on Iraq."[1]

This commonly accepted view was articulated clearly by Alan Greenspan, former chairman of the Federal Reserve. "If Saddam Hussein had been head of Iraq and there was no oil under those sands," Greenspan said, "our response to him would not have been as strong as it was in the first Gulf War. And the second Gulf War is an extension of the first. My view is that Saddam, looking over his 30-year history, very clearly was giving evidence of moving towards controlling the Straits of Hormuz, where there are 17, 18, 19 million barrels a day" passing through.[2] Greenspan noted in his memoirs that the fact that the war was "largely about oil" was "politically inconvenient."[3]

There are other reasons that have caused many around the world to conclude that oil was the underlying *motive* for the war. When America went into Iraq, it went to great efforts to protect the oil assets, even as it failed to protect Iraq's priceless antiquities, or (even more surprising from a military perspective) munitions supply. Moreover, while the weapons of mass destruction were put forward as the war's rationale, there was at the time another country that was truly threatening to develop weapons of mass destruction:

North Korea. But North Korea did not have oil and North Korea was not invaded. While America was focusing its attention on Iraq, North Korea became a nuclear power. Some interpreted the energy Bush put into getting debt relief for Iraq as motivated by oil: Iraq's debt overhang cast a legal pallor over Iraq's oil sales; creditors might go to courts to seize Iraqi oil in payment for what was owed. Only by ridding Iraq of this debt would it be possible for Iraq to sell its oil easily on global markets. The fact that Bush had long-standing ties to the oil industry and was knowledgeable about world oil markets, and that Iraq had one of the world's largest reserves, made it plausible that oil was one of the factors on the president's mind as he invaded Iraq.

From another perspective, however, the notion that the U.S. oil companies would be able to get Iraq's oil for themselves was never very realistic. Some may have looked forward to a quick privatization of Iraqi oil, to be purchased on the cheap. But under the laws of occupation, that was not permitted (cf. chapter 6). Especially if there was more than a grain of truth in American promises about creating a democracy, there was little reason to believe that Iraqi politicians would simply execute America's wishes. Oil is a global commodity, and they would have been under great pressure to get top dollar for their oil; American companies would have had to compete on an even footing with those from every other country. There is a limit to the number of regime changes that America could have engineered to get a government willing to execute its wish.

Moreover, there were other nations, such as Russia, claiming to have legal contracts that entitled them to develop some of Iraq's oil resources. America could not simply assume that because it occupied Iraq, it could easily make these other claimants disappear. Indeed, when the Iraqi government, guided by U.S. legal advisers, cancelled a Russian contract, Russia retaliated by threatening to cancel its agreement to forgive $13 billion in Iraqi debt.[4]

In short, to the extent that oil did motivate the invasion, it was not based on a realistic analysis of the prospects of America gaining access for itself to an assured supply of oil. The belief that the United States invaded Iraq to get hold of its oil has, in fact, impeded reaching agreement on an oil law, viewed by many as critical for a future political settlement in the country. A response to the government's draft oil law by 419 leading Iraqi academics, engineers, and oil industry experts stated, "it is clear that the government is trying to implement one of the demands of the American occupation," and went on to argue that the law "lays the foundation for a fresh plundering of Iraq's strategic wealth and its squandering by foreigners, backed by those coveting power in the regions, and by gangs of thieves and pillagers."[5]

The Impact of the War on the Price of Oil

WHILE WE HAVE argued that the Iraq war's disruption to the supply of oil is the single most important factor contributing to the soaring price, some analysts blame high global demand for oil, in particular from China. In this appendix, we explain why we believe the war is pivotal.

Before the Iraq war, China had had two decades of robust growth, and most analysts expected this to continue—with an accompanying increase in the demand for oil. And although global growth in 2003 and 2004 was stronger than many market analysts had anticipated, it was not markedly so. This can explain only *some* of the oil price rise. Moreover, well-functioning markets are not only supposed to anticipate changes in demand but to respond to changes in demand by increasing supply.[6] Errors in one year are quickly corrected the next. It was anticipated that demand would be increasing in the coming years but that there would be a corresponding increase in supply, mostly from the Middle East—the low-cost supplier.

With oil this expensive, you would expect other oil-producing countries to start producing more. Many have (marginal) production costs far lower than current market prices.[7] The anticipation of these supply-side responses would, in turn, drive down futures. The fact that there has not been this expected supply-side response, and that current and future oil prices are still so high, needs explaining. We think the Iraq war is a key part of the explanation.[8]

Had there been no war, and had the price of oil increased as a result of an unexpected increase in demand, the international community could have allowed Iraq to expand production, and this too could have brought down the price. Even if this had not happened, it is likely that production elsewhere, especially in the Middle East, would have increased. But the instability there has increased the risk of investing in that region; and because costs of extraction are so much lower in the Middle East, there has not been a commensurate supply response elsewhere. If stability is restored, prices will fall, and these investments elsewhere would turn a loss.[9]

Analyses of the Macroeconomic Impact of Higher Oil Prices

HERE, WE EXPLAIN why spending, say, $25 billion more on oil imports reduces GDP by a great deal—almost surely far more than the $37.5 billion we assume in our conservative scenario. That is, we explain why we think the oil multiplier (the ratio of the impact on GDP to the increased spending on oil imports) is greater than 1.5.[10]

The International Monetary Fund, for instance, has constructed econometric models that yield results with full effects (achieved over several years) that are almost four times as large as our estimate.[11] Other studies suggest even larger multipliers.[12]

There are two possible explanations for the large discrepancies between the standard analyses, which often yield multipliers around 1.5, and these results. The first has to do with the analysis of global general equilibrium results. What gives rise to the multiplier is that money spent in the United States is spent again; as people buy goods and services, GDP is raised still more; and the higher GDP leads to still more expenditures, which in turn lead to still further increases in GDP. What limits the multiplier are leakages—money not spent "domestically" but taken out of the system, saved or spent abroad, or by government. In either case, the feedback of income into further expenditures stops. But if we take a *global* perspective, then the money spent abroad is part of the global economic system. Money spent, for example, on imports from Europe raises incomes in Europe, and some of that income is spent on imports from America. Thus, America still benefits. This would make the multiplier considerably larger.

Higher oil prices have depressed income in our major trading partners, Europe and Japan, and that has meant they have bought less from us than they otherwise would have, which in turn has increased the impact of higher oil prices on the U.S. economy.[13] In Europe, inflationary pressures from higher energy prices most likely contributed to interest rates being higher *than they other-*

wise would have been, especially given the European Central Bank's single-minded focus on inflation. This has further weakened their economies—with knock-on effects on America's.[14] The European Union's Stability and Growth Pact limits the ability of European governments to run deficits, which has meant they have not been able to respond adequately with fiscal policy; on the contrary, increased government spending on energy has meant there was less to spend on domestically produced goods and services, again contributing to the weakening of aggregate demand. In short, the direct effects of higher oil prices weakening Europe's economy were made worse by these fiscal and monetary policy responses—enhancing the adverse effects on the U.S. economy.[15]

Second, standard analyses also focus only on short-run impacts—how higher oil prices today affect output today. But in this book, we are not concerned with these short-run impacts but with the total impact, year after year. When viewed from this long-run perspective, again, leakages are smaller. Money not spent this year (that is, savings) is spent in later years, stimulating income in those later years.[16] The total impact of the oil price is accordingly much greater than the *current* impact (measured by the conventional multiplier).[17]

All these factors help explain why the "correct" multiplier, taking into account the full global effects, realized over many periods, may be a lot more than that generated by the models focusing only on the American economy in isolation (which generate multipliers of around 1.5), and why higher numbers such as those generated by the IMF model are reasonable.[18] They also explain why we are confident that the multiplier we used in our moderate scenario is, in fact, highly conservative.

Was There Scope for Increasing Production?

WE HAVE ARGUED that had the United States not spent so much on oil and on the war in Iraq, our GDP would have been higher. The increased spending on American goods would have increased production. But that would have only been possible if production *could* have been increased. We explain here why we believe that throughout the Iraq war period, there was scope for increasing production—in some years by a considerable amount.

America has been operating below its potential. Potential output is defined as that output above which the rate of inflation starts to *increase.* In the late 1990s, America had an unemployment rate of 3.8%, and there did not appear to be any significant increases in inflation. In the Iraq war period, the unemployment rate has averaged more than 5%,[19] suggesting that the economy could have expanded without inflationary pressures. It was lack of demand that was limiting output. There are two further pieces of evidence that support this view. First, the real unemployment rate—including disguised unemployment—has been high, markedly higher than, say, in 2000. Many Americans are working part time, involuntarily, because they cannot get full-time jobs. Many have dropped out of the labor market simply because they have found looking for work too discouraging—and are not included in the unemployment figures. And some have gone on disability because disability pays better than unemployment, and those who can get a doctor's excuse do so.[20]

Second, pressure in the labor market is so weak that workers' real wages (that is, taking into account inflation) have been falling relative to worker productivity—they are markedly below what they were at the beginning of the decade, or at the beginning of the war.[21]

If this analysis is correct, then there was ample scope for America to have expanded its output considerably—and certainly by the amount that it would have, had America not had to spend some $25 to $50 billion a year on imported oil, and had it switched some of the war spending to investments or other areas that would have stimulated the economy more.[22]

The Non-Quantifiable Macroeconomic Impacts of Higher Oil Prices

IN THE TEXT, we described the major quantifiable macroeconomic costs—arising from higher oil prices, switching government spending from productive investments to war expenditures, and increased deficits. We believe, however, that they represent an underestimation—perhaps a major underestimation—of the total costs to the economy. Here we examine this by looking at two categories of macroeconomic costs not considered in our earlier analysis.

First, the analysis of the cost of the higher oil price *assumes that the only cost of the higher price is the increased transfer of dollars abroad to the oil exporters*. It ignores adjustment costs and assumes that if the price increase is reversed, the damage is over. To put it another way, this simple model implies that if first the price goes up by $10 for one year, and then down by $20 for one year, and then is restored to its previous level, there is no cost. This is wrong. There is a cost to this volatility. The technology, for instance, that is best adapted to one set of prices will not be that appropriate for another. And these costs can be significant. This is consistent with macroeconomic studies which show large asymmetries between the impacts of increases and decreases in oil prices.[23] Thus, *this analysis of a seven- to eight-year period of high prices provides a significant underestimate of the true economic costs.* We have not, however, provided an estimate of this additional cost.[24]

Second, most of our analysis focused on how the war—and the resulting oil price increases—dampened the American economy through demand-side effects. Because we were spending more money importing oil, and spending money in Iraq rather than at home, aggregate demand was lower. Earlier in this appendix, we argued that during most of the war period the economy could have produced more, if only there had been more demand.

Virtually all economists are agreed on two propositions. The first is that there is no such thing as a free lunch: While the Bush administration may have tried to persuade the American people that it could fight a war without any *economic* sacrifices, economists know otherwise. The second is that because Bush tried to fight the war without increasing taxes, the Iraq war has displaced private investment and/or government expenditures, including investments in infrastructure, R&D, and education: they are less than they would otherwise have been.[25] The result is that the economy's future potential and actual output over the long term will be lower, and in chapter 5, we have calculated by how much.[26]

Some economists, however, think that the supply-side effects—effects of the war on the economy's production potential—are equally important even in the short run. If, for example, it were true that America's economy was producing at its full potential, then those men and women from the National Guard and the Reservists sent to Iraq are not available for work in civilian jobs.[27] These supply-side effects mount with the war: as the war continues, so do the casualties, producing increasing numbers who are partially or totally disabled and will never fully return to the labor force. Many of the returning veterans suffer from mental health conditions, which will interfere with their ability to be productive members of the labor force. We noted too in chapter 3 that many spouses and other family members have had to drop out of the labor force to care for returning disabled veterans, especially those needing medical care—in about one of five cases for a seriously injured veteran.[28] We estimate that for the year 2006, the civilian labor supply has been reduced by approximately 140,000. Standard macroeconomic analyses suggest, at least in the short run, that GDP may fall (in percentage terms) by more than the value of the reduced employment. As the economy shrinks because of the lack of availability of labor, profit opportunities are also lost; and new bottlenecks appear. That is why the *systemic* cost may be so much greater than the direct costs of forgone labor.[29]

It is important to remember that the total number of servicemen and women involved in the Iraq conflict includes not just the 140,000–170,000 pairs of boots on the ground at any one time, but the far larger number who are between deployments, or based in military bases prior to being shipped to the theater. It also includes those providing logistical support. For the National Guard, we can argue that all of those mobilized are in effect part of the war effort, whether they are in active deployment or simply waiting to find out whether they will be required overseas.

Civilian GDP (GDP exclusive of what is being spent in Iraq) will be reduced too by the American contractors in Iraq. These are workers not available for producing consumer goods that individuals enjoy today or the investment goods that lead to future economic strength.[30]

Assuming that the loss in output is just proportional to the loss in labor implies for 2006 alone a loss of $13 billion, a total loss in GDP that is much larger than just the opportunity costs of these workers—the "microeconomic" costs discussed in chapter 4. Going forward, the losses to the labor force from those killed and disabled in the war will continue to increase, as will those who will have to drop out of the labor force to take care of them. It is likely that the number of Reservists and National Guard that are called upon will be further reduced; but, with prospects of large numbers permanently stationed in Iraq, the size of the military is likely to increase by some 92,000. This means that these supply-side losses to GDP are likely to continue, and even increase. Moreover, we should not really be focusing on the effect of the war on GDP—which values the bombs dropped in Iraq the same way as a newly built school or the salary of a research scientist making a breakthrough cure for some debilitating disease. We should really be looking at GDP *net of resources spent on Iraq*.

The most thorough analysis of the costs of the war using a comprehensive macroeconomic model was that of Allen Sinai, using the Sinai-Boston model with approximately 950 equations, and incorporating financial variables and their links to the "real" economy.[31] He estimated that without the war (and ignoring the impact of the war on oil prices), real GDP growth would have been 0.2 percentage points higher, on average, over the period mid-2002 to mid-2005. The unemployment rate would have been 0.3 percentage points lower, on average, and almost 900,000 more non-farm payroll jobs per year would have been created. Assuming that impacts in future years are similar, the estimated macroeconomic effects are considerable—in excess of $200 billion.

Sinai calls attention to a further impact: there is a significant effect on government deficits. He calculates that the federal budget deficit would have been substantially lower. Tax receipts (personal and corporate, including capital gains, excise, and social insurance) would have been higher because of a better economy and a better stock market.

Determining the Discount Rate

IN THE TEXT, we argued that the appropriate discount rate should be 1.5%. That is the (real) rate at which government is able to borrow, which is why it is appropriate to use for purposes of evaluating impacts on the government budget. In chapters 4 and 5, however, we considered broader economic effects.

The debate about the appropriate discount rates has been contentious and confusing. There are two approaches. One focuses on how individuals trade off consumption (income) in different periods. The fact that individuals are willing to lend at 1.5% (real) interest means that this is their *intertemporal trade-off,* and so, in evaluating the impact on the well-being of individuals in society, this would seem to be the appropriate discount rate.

Other analysts argue that we should discount at the rate of the *opportunity cost*, the returns the funds might have generated had they been invested elsewhere. The calculations in the text take into account the opportunity cost of the funds; we analyze what GDP or national income might have been had the funds been spent, say, on investment, rather than on the war in Iraq. The question, though, is having analyzed the changes in output or consumption which might have been generated, how do we value an increase in consumption in the future *relative* to an increase in current consumption? The fact that individuals seem willing to trade off consumption today for that in the future using a 1.5% discount rate suggests this is the appropriate rate.

Three factors complicate this analysis. The first is that future consumption may not be enjoyed by the same individual but by future generations. How, in other words, should we evaluate *at the margin* consumption of the current generation versus that of future generations? A long philosophical tradition, dating back at least to the Cambridge economist Frank Ramsey in the 1920s, has argued that there is no justification for weighing future generations less than the current generation (except for a small factor, taking into account the risk of the extinction of the human race; and taking into account that because of productivity increases, future generations will be better off).[32] In short, having calculated the changes in consumption that could have been generated, using a plausible value of opportunity cost (say, 6% to 8%), one then discounts these numbers back to present dollars using a low discount rate (say, 1% or 1.5%).[33]

Uncertainty presents the second complication. Some analysts discount at higher rates because the future is uncertain. This is an inappropriate, and potentially even dangerous, approach when it comes to valuing future uncertain costs. Discounting at a high rate (even 7%) means that we can effectively ignore such risks in the distant future. But if anything, the uncertainty should make us pay more, not less, attention to these risks. Our future health care and disability liabilities are examples of costs which, if anything, ought to be weighed more heavily because of the risks they represent: the uncertainty should, if anything, lead us to discount them at a lower rate. (Technically, the appropriate procedure entails converting costs and benefits into certainty equivalents, which increases costs and reduces benefits by the amount individuals would have been willing to pay to eliminate the risk, and discounting the certainty equivalents at the appropriate discount rate, say, 1.5%.) If uncertainty is increasing over time, this procedure entails increasing costs and decreasing benefits (relative to their average or mean values) over time. That is why, in the conservative approach taken here, when we evaluate the benefits that might have been generated by increasing investment had we not gone to war, we have looked at the consequences of using a higher discount rate, though in evaluating future costs (veterans' health and disability), we have focused on the lower 1.5% rate.

The third complication is taxes on capital income. This introduces a discrepancy between individuals' intertemporal trade-offs (how they value consumption today and in the future) and the return to capital (the opportunity cost). In *evaluating* the effects of the Iraq war, say financed by deficit, as we have noted, the appropriate procedure is to estimate what output would have been, and then (ignoring uncertainty and intergenerational effects) to discount the differences at individuals' time preferences. Thus, if before-tax rates of return are 7%, and the marginal tax rate is approximately 40%, then the appropriate discount rate is approximately 4% (0.6 × 7%).[34]

List of Commonly Used Acronyms

CBO—Congressional Budget Office, provides the U.S. Congress with analyses, information, and estimates required for the congressional budget process

CPA—Coalition Provisional Authority, the U.S.–led body that governed Iraq from April 2003 to June 2004

CRS—Congressional Research Office, provides policy analysis to the U.S. Congress

DOD—U.S. Department of Defense

EIA—Energy Information Administration, an independent agency within the U.S. Department of Energy that develops surveys, collects energy data, and analyzes and models energy issues

FOIA—Freedom of Information Act, the federal law that establishes the public's right to obtain information from federal government agencies

GAO—Government Accountability Office, an independent, nonpartisan agency that works for Congress and investigates how the federal government spends taxpayer dollars

GWOT—Global War on Terror, a term used by the Department of Defense to describe its worldwide campaign against terrorism. The GWOT includes Operation Iraqi Freedom (OIF),

Operation Enduring Freedom in Afghanistan (OEF), and Operation Noble Eagle (ONE)

IAEA—International Atomic Energy Agency, an international organization within the United Nations system that works for the safe, secure, and peaceful uses of nuclear science and technology

IED—Improvised explosive device, a device placed or fabricated in an improvised manner and designed to destroy, incapacitate, harass, or distract; it is often devised from non-military components

ISAF—International Security Assistance Force, a UN-mandated international force, led by NATO, that is supposed to assist the Afghan government in extending and exercising its authority and influence across the country

MRAP—Mine-resistant ambush-protected vehicles, designed to protect the occupants against armor-piercing roadside bombs

OECD—Organization for Economic Cooperation and Development, comprised of the advanced industrialized countries, that provides and analyzes statistics and economic and social data

OEF—Operation Enduring Freedom, refers to ongoing operations in Afghanistan, as well as some anti-terror operations in other countries in the region

OIF—Operation Iraqi Freedom, refers to the invasion of Iraq, the defeat of Saddam Hussein's regime, and the subsequent military, peacekeeping, rebuilding, and counterinsurgency operations in Iraq

OMB—Office of Management and Budget, a White House office that assists the president in overseeing the preparation of the federal budget and supervises its administration in executive branch agencies

ONE—Operation Noble Eagle, provides enhanced security at military bases

Operation Herrick—Code name for British operation in Afghanistan, including the British contribution to the International Security Assistance Force (ISAF) and support of the U.S.–led Operation Enduring Freedom

Operation Telic—Code name for all British operations in Iraq since 2003

PTSD—Post-traumatic stress disorder, an anxiety disorder that can develop after a person's exposure to a terrifying event or ordeal in which grave physical harm occurred or was threatened

TBI—Traumatic brain injury, which is caused by a blow or jolt to the head or a penetrating head injury that disrupts the normal function of the brain

UNHCR—Office of the United Nations High Commissioner on Refugees, mandated to lead and coordinate international action to protect refugees, and to resolve refugee problems worldwide

USAID—United States Agency for International Development, an independent federal government agency that extends development assistance to other countries

VA—Department of Veterans Affairs; two of its major branches are the Veterans Health Administration (VHA) and the Veterans Benefit Administration (VBA)

VSL—Value of statistical life, a systematic procedure that economists have developed for valuing a life lost

WHO—World Health Organization, the directing and coordinating authority for health within the United Nations system

Notes

Preface

1. These numbers include more than 28,600 troops wounded in combat in the Iraq war (referred to as Operation Iraqi Freedom [or OIF]) plus over 1,800 troops wounded in combat in the Afghanistan conflict (referred to as Operation Enduring Freedom [or OEF]), plus more than 36,500 troops who were medically evacuated from the two combat theaters as a result of serious non-battle injuries or illness (such as vehicle crashes and exotic diseases). These figures do *not* include troops who suffered non-battle injuries, illness, or disease but were treated in theater and not evacuated. As we note later, the military has considerable discretion in classifying any injury as combat-related. For Iraq casualties, see Defense Manpower Data Center, Statistical Information Analysis Center, "Global War on Terrorism—Operation Iraqi Freedom; By Casualty Category Within Service, March 19, 2003 Through December 8, 2007," obtained by Veterans for Common Sense under the Freedom of Information Act, available at http://siadapp.dmdc.osd.mil/personnel/CASUALTY/OIF-Total.pdf. (This is reprinted as part of our Appendix.) For Afghanistan casualties, see Defense Manpower Data Center, Statistical Information Analysis Center, "Global War on Terrorism—Operation Enduring Freedom; By Casualty Category Within Service, October 7, 2001 Through December 8, 2007," available at http://siadapp.dmdc.osd.mil/personnel/CASUALTY/WOTSUM.pdf.
2. By the first half of fiscal year 2007, approximately 264,000 returning veterans had sought care from VA medical centers and clinics (the federal government's accounts are based on a fiscal year that begins on October 1). Of these, about 38% (100,282) have received at least a preliminary diagnosis of a mental health

condition, and 20% (52,000) a preliminary diagnosis of PTSD—Statement of the Honorable Patrick W. Dunne, Rear Admiral, U.S. Navy (Ret), Assistant Secretary for Policy and Planning, U.S. Department of Veterans Affairs Before the Committee on Veterans Affairs, U.S. Senate, October 17, 2007.

3. Prewar, 12.9 million had access to potable water; by early 2006 (the latest date for which data is available), only 9.7 million did so—Michael O'Hanlon and Jason Campbell, *Iraq Index: Tracking Variables of Reconstruction and Security in Post-Saddam Iraq,* Brookings Institution, October 1, 2007, www.brookings.edu/iraqindex, p. 48. In 2004, the Coalition Provisional Authority established a goal to improve peak generation capacity to 6,000 mw per day by the end of June 2004. However, by the end of 2006, peak generation capacity for the year averaged only 4,280 mw per day. In March 2006, the State Department also set a goal to achieve twelve hours of power per day both in Baghdad and nationwide—Government Accountability Office, "Rebuilding Iraq: Integrated Strategic Plan Needed to Help Restore Iraq's Oil and Electricity Sectors," GAO-07-677, May 2007 (http://www.gao.gov/new.items/d07677.pdf). By November 2007, Baghdad was still getting an average of only 9 hours of electricity, markedly lower than the 16–24 hours it got prewar—O'Hanlon and Campbell, *Iraq Index: Tracking Variables of Reconstruction and Security in Post-Saddam Iraq,* November 12, 2007, p. 36.
4. The Gulf War conflict is officially referred to as Operation Desert Storm and Operation Desert Shield (covering the period from August 2, 1990, to March 31, 1991). Additionally, one pilot is listed as missing in action, and as we will see in the case of the Iraq war, there were also many out-of-combat accidents—235 Americans died in these—Department of Veterans Affairs, "America's Wars," November 2007, at http://www1.va.gov/OPA/fact/docs/amwars.pdf.
5. The Gulf War cost $94 billion (in 2007 dollars). The United States paid only $7 billion of that amount; Saudi Arabia, Kuwait, and other countries reimbursed the United States for the remainder—Testimony by Amy Belasco, Specialist in U.S. Defense Policy and Budget, Congressional Research Service, Statement before the House Budget Committee Hearing on "The Growing Budgetary Costs of the Iraq War," October 24, 2007.
6. Veterans Benefits Administration, Annual Benefits Report, Fiscal Year 2005 (released September 2006), adjusted for inflation and cost-of-living increases (in 2007 dollars).
7. The United States has spent over $1 billion in research related to Gulf War illnesses, primarily in medical research grants funded through the departments of Defense, Health and Human Services, and Veterans Affairs—Authors' calculation based on FY 93–FY 07 budget of the U.S. government.

8. Department of Veterans Affairs, "Gulf War Veterans Information System," May 2007, released June 30, 2007 (http://www1.va.gov/rac-gwvi/docs/GWVIS_May2007.pdf).
9. Eric Schmitt, "Troops' Queries Leave Rumsfeld on the Defensive," *New York Times*, December 9, 2004, p. A1.
10. Official combat operations in Iraq lasted from March 19, 2003, to April 30, 2003. The United States spent $46 billion in Iraq during the full fiscal year 2003 on military operations, equivalent to around $55 billion in 2007 inflation-adjusted dollars—"Estimated Costs of U.S. Operations in Iraq and Afghanistan and of Other Activities Related to the War on Terrorism," Testimony of Robert A. Sunshine, Assistant Director for Budget Analysis, CBO, before the House Budget Committee, July 31, 2007.
11. Government Accountability Office, "VA Health Care: Preliminary Findings on the Department of Veterans Affairs Health Care Budget Formulation for Fiscal Years 2005 and 2006," GAO-06-430R, February 7, 2006.
12. In February 2007, the outpatient facility at Walter Reed Army Medical Center was found to be infested with mold and vermin, and suffering from shortages of staff and basic hygiene. See Dana Priest and Anne Hull, "Soldiers Face Neglect, Frustration at Army's Top Medical Facility," *The Washington Post*, February 18, 2007, p. A1.
13. The Iraq war is referred to as Operation Iraqi Freedom (OIF); the Afghanistan War is referred to as Operation Enduring Freedom (OEF). These two operations, together with Operation Noble Eagle (ONE), which provides embassy security and related activities, constitute what is officially called the Global War on Terrorism (GWOT), even though, at least at the onset, there was no connection between Iraq and the terrorist attacks of 9/11. U.S. troops in Afghanistan also include those involved in NATO-led operations.
14. The typical household refers to the median, the household in the "middle," such that half of the households in the country have a higher income, half a lower income—Table H-6. Regions-All Races by Median and Mean Income: 1975 to 2006, US Census Bureau, Current Population Survey, Annual Social and Economic Supplements, at http://www.census.gov/hhes/www/income/histinc/h06ar.html.
15. "2007 Annual Report of the Board of Trustees of the Federal Old-Age and Survivors Insurance and Federal Disability Insurance Trust Funds," May 1, 2007, available at http://www.ssa.gov/OACT/TR/TR07/tr07.pdf.
16. See www.costofwar.com.
17. See "Education for All: Meeting Our Collective Commitments," World Education Forum, Dakar, Senegal, April 26–28, 2000. Goal #2 of the Millennium Development Goals is universal primary education; recent studies estimate

that "putting every child in the world in a good-quality primary school would cost between $7–$17 billion per year." Nancy Birdsall, Ruth Levine, Amina Ibrahim, et al., "Toward Universal Primary Education: Investments, Incentives, and Institutions," Task Force on Education and Gender Equality, Millennium Project, 2005, pp. 8–9 (http://www.unmillenniumproject.org/documents/Education-complete.pdf).

18. U.S. Census Bureau, Current Population Survey. While median incomes have been declining, average household income has been increasing. Large disparities between median and average income are associated with large income disparities. If a few people at the top get richer and richer, the *average* income rises, but median income can remain unchanged or even decrease. Today, average (mean) household income is more than a third greater than median income.
19. For instance, one critic suggested that even in peacetime, there are casualties in the armed forces, e.g., automobile accidents. Not all of the seeming war casualties should accordingly be blamed on the war. Even though the U.S. government has to pay for all soldiers' deaths and injuries, regardless of how they occur, we agree that it is important to understand the incremental numbers. To do this we have now compared the number of accidental, non-hostile casualties in the Army for the five years prior to Iraq to the years following the invasion. We found that accidental, non-hostile deaths have increased by more than 50%. We explain this new analysis in chapter 3.
20. Steven Davis, Kevin Murphy, and Robert Topel, "War in Iraq versus Containment," American Enterprise Institute, Washington, DC, February 15, 2006, prepared for the CESifo Conference on "Guns and Butter: The Economic Causes and Consequences of Conflict," Munich, Germany, December 9–10, 2005 (http://www.aei.org/publications/pubID.23916/pub_detail.asp).
21. Hans Blix, the UN diplomat responsible for the UN inspections to ensure that Iraq did not have WMD, had forcefully concluded that it was highly unlikely such weapons existed. He plaintively asked, "Are reports from [the United Nations] totally unread south of the Hudson?"—"Blix Questions Coalition's Expectations for WMD Discovery," Global Security Newswire, June 18, 2003 (http://www.nti.org/d_newswire/issues/newswires/2003_6_19.html#1).

Chapter 1: Is It Really Three Trillion?

1. In FY 2008, the United States is slated to spend more on its military than the next forty-two highest-spending countries combined, accounting for 47% of

the world's total military spending—"National Security Spending," Center for Arms Control and Non-Proliferation, at http://www.armscontrolcenter.org/policy/securityspending/ (accessed October 16, 2007).

2. Anthony Cordesman and Abraham Wagner, *The Lessons of Modern War.* Vol. II: *The Iran-Iraq War* (Washington, DC: Center for Strategic and International Studies, May 1990).
3. Eric Hooglund, "The Other Face of War," *Middle East Report*, no. 171, *The Day After* (July–August 1991), pp. 3–7, 10–12.
4. See Pew Global Attitudes Project, "Global Opinion Trends 2002–2007: A Rising Tide Lifts Moods in the Developing World," July 2007 (http://pewglobal.org/reports/pdf/257.pdf), and "America's Image in the World: Findings from the Pew Global Attitudes Project," Remarks of Andrew Kohut to the U.S. House Committee on Foreign Affairs, Subcommittee on International Organizations, Human Rights, and Oversight, March 14, 2007.
5. "The Iraqi Public on U.S. Presence and the Future of Iraq," a WorldPublic Opinion.org Poll conducted by the Program on International Policy Attitudes, September 27, 2006, at http://www.worldpublicopinion.org/pipa/pdf/sep06/Iraq_Sep06_rpt.pdf.
6. Even though the price of oil has soared. See O'Hanlon and Campbell, *Iraq Index: Tracking Variables of Reconstruction and Security in Post-Saddam Iraq*.
7. For a discussion of these estimates and of the other indicators of what has happened to Iraq's economy and society, see chapter 6.
8. "The binding section of the population does not exist anymore. The middle class has left Iraq"—Sabrina Tavernise, "Iraq's Middle Escapes to Poverty and Pain Abroad," *International Herald Tribune*, August 11–12, p. 6. The article goes on to argue, in what is now accepted as common wisdom, "The poorer they grow and the longer they stay away, the more crippled Iraq becomes, making it difficult for anyone to put the country back together again." Such arguments provide part of the case for an early exit.
9. The Office of the UN High Commissioner on Refugees (UNHCR) puts the internally displaced at 2.2 million—UNHCR, "Statistics on Displaced Iraqis around the World," September 2007, at http://www.unhcr.org/cgi-bin/texis/vtx/home/opendoc.pdf?tbl=SUBSITES&id=470387fc2. Approximately one in seven Iraqis have been forcibly uprooted—UNHCR, "Iraq Situation Response," July 2007. http://www.unhcr.org/cgi-bin/texis/vtx/home/opendoc.pdf?tbl=SUBSITES&id=46a4a5522. See also Elizabeth Ferris, "Security, Displacement, and Iraq: A Deadly Combination," Brookings-Bern Project on Internal Displacement, August 27, 2007, at http://www.brookings.edu/~/media/Files/rc/papers/2007/0827humanrights_ferris/20070827.pdf.

10. "Asylum Seekers to Sweden During 1984–2006" and "Resident Permits to Relative (Family Ties) by Citizenship 1986–2006," Swedish Migration Board. See also "U.S. Humanitarian Assistance for Displaced Iraqis," Press Release, U.S. Department of State, October 5, 2007.
11. CRS estimates the military costs (in FY 2007 dollars) of previous wars as: Vietnam, $670 billion; Korean War, $295 billion; and Gulf War $94 billion (total costs, mostly paid by allies). These are military costs, not including veterans' medical care and disability compensation and other budgetary costs—Belasco, Statement before the House Budget Committee Hearing on "The Growing Budgetary Costs of the Iraq War." By contrast, in our "best case" scenario, we estimate the operating costs for this war will be around $855 billion.
12. In a separate study, the Congressional Research Service cites a figure of $4.7 trillion in 2002 dollars (equivalent to $5.4 trillion in 2007 dollars) for World War II, and $577 billion for World War I ($410 billion net of war loans to our allies, in 2002 dollars, or $476 billion in 2007 dollars)—Stephen Daggett and Nina Serafina, "Costs of Major U.S. Wars and Recent U.S. Overseas Military Operations," CRS Report to Congress, October 3, 2001. See also a study by Yale professor William Nordhaus, "The Economic Consequences of a War with Iraq," chapter 3 in his paper, *War with Iraq: Costs, Consequences and Alternatives* (New York: American Academy of Arts and Sciences, 2002), pp. 51–86. He cites numbers for World War I and World War II that are (in current dollars) considerably smaller. These imply, of course, that relative to these previous wars, Iraq is even more expensive.
13. Amy Belasco, "The Cost of Iraq, Afghanistan, and Other Global War on Terror Operations Since 9/11," CRS Report for Congress, July 16, 2007, order code RL33110. This report puts the cost in FY 2006 per troop at $390,000, that is, in 2007 dollars, around $400,000 per troop.
14. Letter from CBO director Peter Orzsag to Congressman John Spratt, February 1, 2007.
15. Congressional Budget Office, "Some Implications of Increasing U.S. Forces in Iraq," April 2007, http://www.cbo.gov/ftpdocs/80xx/doc8024/04-24-Iraq.pdf.
16. Bob Davis, "Bush Economic Aide Says Cost of Iraq War May Top $100 Billion," *Wall Street Journal,* September 16, 2002, p. 1.
17. In an interview with George Stephanopoulos on ABC *This Week,* January 19, 2003.
18. House Budget Committee transcript, *Hearing on FY 2004 Defense Budget Request,* February 27, 2003.

19. The Bush administration was, however, not alone in providing these vast underestimates. The Congressional Budget Office (the independent office of Congress that estimates the costs of various proposals and bills) estimated the costs of a two-and-a-half month conflict at approximately $50.99 billion (in 2007 dollars), and $1.74 to $4.64 billion per month of occupation. While Bush's "Mission Accomplished" speech might have suggested a short occupation, even a five-year occupation would have led to a figure of $104.4 to $278.4 billion, still markedly below the actual level of expenditures.
20. Transcript of interview with Andrew Natsios, USAID Administrator, on ABC's *Nightline*, with Ted Koppel, April 23, 2003.
21. Davis, "Bush Economic Aide Says Cost of Iraq War May Top $100 Billion."
22. The total will be the $645 billion spent to date (inflation-adjusted to 2007 dollars to account for inflation and what economists call the "time value" of money) plus the approximately $200 billion requested for FY 2008, which brings us to $845 billion in 2007 dollars. These amounts do not include the cost of disability compensation paid to veterans so far, nor does it include some intelligence funding—Belasco, "The Cost of Iraq, Afghanistan, and Other Global War on Terror Operations Since 9/11." This covers funding in 25 separate funding bills, including: P.L.107-117, 107-206, 1207-115, 108-7, 108-11, 108-106, 108-199, 108-287, 109-13, 108-447, 108-287, 109-148, 109-102, 109-108, 109-54, 109-114, 109-234, 109-289, 110-5, the FY 2007 Continuing Resolution (PL 110-28), and $2 billion in "unidentified transfers" into DOD.
23. Belasco, Statement before the House Budget Committee Hearing on "The Growing Cost of the Iraq War."
24. Unless Congress enacts specific restrictions, funds approved for the DOD are appropriated for particular *types of* expenses (e.g., military personnel) rather than designated for particular operations like the war in Iraq.
25. "Baseline funds" simply refers to the funds that would have been spent normally, in the absence of the war.
26. According to the CRS estimates, at least three quarters of the personnel and direct operational military expenditures are for operations in Iraq; by contrast, medical costs and disability compensation are closely related to the number of injuries, of which 89% have occurred in Iraq. Accordingly, in our analysis we have attributed 75% of military costs to Iraq, and 89% of veterans' disability costs, Social Security disability compensation, and medical costs to the Iraq war—Injury data from DOD sources (OIF/OEF U.S. Casualty Status, at http://www.defenselink.mil/news/casualty.pdf) and Hannah Fischer, "United

States Military Casualty Statistics: Operation Iraqi Freedom and Operating Enduring Freedom," CRS Report RS22452, August 17, 2007.

27. Belasco, Statement before the House Budget Committee Hearing on "The Growing Cost of the Iraq War."
28. More than 531,000 Reservists and National Guard personnel had been mobilized (notified of possible deployment) as of June 30, 2006, and more than 378,000 had been deployed by that date. Because most Guards and Reservists have reached the end of their eligibility period, they composed 34% of the force in 2005 but had declined to 23% by December 2006—"DOD and the Services Need to Take Additional Steps to Improve Mobilization Data for the Reserve Components," GAO-Report to Congressional Committees, GAO-06,1068, September 2006, and Belasco, "The Cost of Iraq, Afghanistan, and Enhanced Base Security Since 9/11."
29. In that sense, even most of the costs—including any future benefits, such as medical care—of the Reservists and National Guard that have been mobilized but not deployed either to Iraq or Afghanistan should be attributed to the Iraq war.
30. This figure does not even count the number of subcontractors, that is, those the contractors themselves may hire to perform their work—Renae Merle, "Census Counts 100,000 Contractors in Iraq," *The Washington Post,* December 5, 2006, p. D1. Probably a more accurate estimate is the "more than 160,000" provided by Brookings Institution scholar Peter W. Singer, in "Can't Win With 'Em, Can't Go to War Without 'Em: Private Military Contractors and Counterinsurgency," Brookings Institution, September 2007. In contrast, the number during the Gulf War was 9,200—Katherine Peters, "Civilians at War," *Government Executive,* July 1, 1996.
31. John M. Broder and David Rohde, "State Department Use of Contractors Leaps in 4 Years," *New York Times,* October 24, 2007, p. A1.
32. To put some perspective on this number, the State Department suggested that the family of one of the Iraqis killed be compensated with a $5,000 payment to "put this unfortunate matter behind us quickly"—compensation for a "wrongful death" that amounted to less than five days' pay of the Blackwater security guard—House Committee on Oversight and Government Reform, Memorandum re: Additional Information About Blackwater USA, October 1, 2007.
33. A few have suggested that the comparison is unfair. After all, the government winds up paying for disability and medical costs for injured veterans, the costs of which are significant. But the argument is disingenuous. As we point out in chapter 3, it turns out that the figures cited for the cost of contractors do not include the costs of insurance, which the government bears; and, even after

paying for the insurance, for those injured or killed in combat, the government still picks up the tab.

34. Contractors are not always bound by the Uniform Code of Military Justice (UCMJ), and by and large, they appear exempt from prosecution by Iraqis for crimes committed there—Stephen M. Blizzard, "Increasing Reliance on Contractors on the Battlefield; How Do We Keep from Crossing the Line?" *Air Force Journal of Logistics*, vol. XXVIII, no. 1 (Spring 2004). From 2006 onwards military contractors have been bound by the UCMJ, but State Department contractors (like Blackwater) are still not. See John Broder and James Risen, "Armed Guards in Iraq Occupy a Legal Limbo," *New York Times*, September 20, 2007, p. A1.
35. On September 17, 2007, after a particularly bloody encounter in which Blackwater contractors were accused of killing seventeen civilians, Iraq's government threatened to suspend Blackwater's license, and the U.S. Congress felt impelled to hold hearings. See, e.g., Sabrina Tavernise, "U.S. Contractor Banned by Iraq Over Shootings," *New York Times*, September 18, 2007, p. A1. The FBI has since found that fourteen of the seventeen shootings were unjustified—David Johnston and John M. Broder, "FBI Says Guards Killed 14 Iraqis Without Cause," *New York Times*, November 14, 2007, p. A1.
36. At least ninety investigations have been opened, alleging misconduct involving billions of dollars of contracts for everything from the supply of food to weapons. The criminal investigative arm of the DOD is investigating allegations of fraud, profiteering, and disappearance of weapons. These investigations have already led to five federal criminal indictments and ten persons convicted of felonies, nineteen companies and persons suspended from doing business with DOD, and four individuals and one company barred permanently from contracting with the U.S. government—Statement of Thomas F. Gimble, Principal Deputy Inspector General, Department of Defense, before the House Armed Services Committee, on "Accountability During Contingency Operations: Preventing and Fighting Corruption in Contracting and Establishing and Maintaining Appropriate Controls on Material," September 20, 2007.
37. Contrast the requested $19 billion with the statements of Andrew Natsios (p. 8), who on behalf of the Bush administration, only a few months earlier, had assured Ted Koppel and the American people that the reconstruction costs would not top $1.7 billion.
38. DOD Office of the Inspector General, "Human Capital," Report on the DOD Acquisition Workforce Count (D-2006-073), April 17, 2006.
39. House Committee on Oversight and Government Reform, Memorandum re: Supplemental Information on Iraq Reconstruction Contracts, February 15, 2007.

40. Office of the Special Inspector General for Iraq Reconstruction, "Oversight of Funds Provided to Iraqi Ministries Through the National Budget Process," Report No. 05-004, January 30, 2005.
41. Center for Public Integrity, "Outsourcing the Pentagon: Halliburton Co.," http://www.publicintegrity.org/pns/db.aspx?act=cinfo&coid=964409007. Halliburton is the largest private contractor operating in Iraq, through its Kellogg, Brown & Root subsidiary. It holds three large contracts: the Logistics Civil Augmentation Program (LOGCAP), through which it provides support services to the troops; the Restore Iraqi Oil (RIO) contract, to rebuild oil fields throughout Iraq; and the Restore Iraqi Oil 2 (RIO 2) contract to rebuild oil fields in southern Iraq—House Committee on Oversight and Government Reform, Memorandum re: Supplemental Information on Iraq Reconstruction Contracts, February 15, 2007.
42. Calculations based on Yahoo! Finance, prices at close on November 15, 2007, adjusted for dividends and splits.
43. Amy Belasco testified that "In recent years DOD's annual war costs have more than doubled from $72 billion in FY 2004 to about $165 billion in FY 2007, an increase of $93 billion. Little of this increase reflects changes in the number of deployed personnel. Rather the increase is attributable to several factors: 1) certain unanticipated requirements for force protection and gear and equipment; 2) the cost of training and equipping Afghan and Iraqi security forces; and 3) even more, a broadened definition of the types of expenses that would be considered part of war reconstitution or reset—funds to repair and replace war-torn equipment."—Belasco, Statement before the House Budget Committee Hearing on "The Growing Budgetary Cost of the Iraq War."
44. CBO director Peter Orzsag, Testimony to the House Budget Committee Hearing on "The Growing Cost of the Iraq War," October 24, 2007.
45. Jim Michaels, "19,000 Insurgents Killed in Iraq Since '03," *USA Today,* September 28, 2007, p. A1. In chapter 7, we explain how our strategy helped *increase* the number of insurgents.
46. Active and Reserve duty soldiers pay their life insurance premiums out of their paycheck, based on the face value of the policy. Veterans also pay their premiums for the Veterans Group Life Insurance (VGLI), although they are quite low, and the VA will deduct VGLI premiums from VA disability compensation or pension payments. The veteran may only buy VLGI based on the amount of his (or her) policy at the time of discharge. In other words, if a veteran has only $100,000 in Servicemember Group Life Insurance, he can only buy up to $100,000 in VGLI within one year of discharge. If he doesn't enroll within the first year after discharge, he loses the right forever to get VGLI.

47. 97% of total deaths in Operation Iraqi Freedom have been male—Hannah Fischer, "United States Military Casualty Statistics: Operation Iraqi Freedom and Operation Enduring Freedom," CRS Report for Congress, August 17, 2007, order code RS22452.
48. Cf. Preface, note 1. This includes all combat-related injuries and all non-hostile injuries and illnesses that require medical air transport. It does not include any of the non-hostile injuries, illnesses, or diseases in which the soldier was treated but did not require medical air transport. The discrepancy came into the open in January 2007 when Linda Bilmes published her paper on the costs of returning U.S. soldiers—Linda Bilmes, "Soldiers Returning from Iraq and Afghanistan: The Long-term Costs of Providing Veterans Medical Care and Disability Benefits," Kennedy School of Government Faculty Research Working Paper RWP07-001, Harvard University. Interestingly, in the Gulf War, almost 50% of all deaths were classified as non-combat.
49. Economists often use suicide rates as indicators (admittedly crude) of stress—See Gregg Zoroya, "Suicide Rate Spikes Among Troops Sent to Iraq War," *USA Today,* December 20, 2006. See also Mental Health Advisory Team (MHAT-IV) study, conducted by DOD, involving 1,300 soldiers and 450 Marines, in August and October 2006—U.S. Department of Defense News Release No. 530-07, May 4, 2007.
50. See Charles S. Milliken, Jennifer L. Auchterlonie, and Charles W. Hoge, "Longitudinal Assessment of Mental Health Problems Among Active and Reserve Component Soldiers Returning from the Iraq War," *Journal of the American Medical Association*, vol. 298, no. 18, (November 14 2007), p. 2141, citing Paul Bliese, Kathleen Wright, Amy Adler, Charles Hoge, and Rachel Prayner, "Post-Deployment Psychological Screening: Interpreting and Scoring DD Form 2900," Heidelberg, Germany: U.S. Army Medical Research Unit-Europe; 2005, Research Report 2005-003; and Paul Bliese, Kathleen Wright, Amy Adler, Jeffrey Thomas, and Charles Hoge, "Timing of Postcombat Mental Health Assessments," *Psychological Services*, vol. 4, no. 3 (August 2007), pp. 141–48.
51. The study noted particularly increases in relationship problems and the shortcomings in services for family members.
52. Statement of Thomas F. Gimble, Acting Inspector General, Department of Defense, before the Subcommittee on Federal Financial Management, Government Information and International Security, Senate Committee on Homeland Security and Government Affairs, August 3, 2006.
53. Government Accountability Office, "Global War on Terrorism: Observations on Funding, Costs, and Future Commitments," GAO-06-885T, July 18, 2006.

54. The criteria for emergency funding are that the need be necessary and vital, urgent, sudden, requiring immediate action, unforeseen, unpredictable, and unanticipated—Title IX, Sec. 9011 in PL 108-287. President Bush indicated in his initial request for funds for Afghanistan that he would not request further emergency supplemental funding—Letter from George W. Bush to the Speaker of the House of Representatives, October 17, 2001, reprinted in the Appendix on page 207.
55. Belasco, "The Cost of Iraq, Afghanistan, and Other Global War on Terror Operations Since 9/11."
56. James A. Baker III and Lee Hamilton, Co-Chairs, Iraq Study Group Report, December 6, 2006, http://www.usip.org/isg/iraq_study_group_report/report/1206/iraq_study_group_report.pdf.
57. Belasco, "The Cost of Iraq, Afghanistan, and Other Global War on Terror Operations since 9/11."
58. "Global War on Terrorism: Observations on Funding, Costs, and Future Commitments," Statement by U.S. Comptroller General David M. Walker, Testimony before the Subcommittee on National Security, Emerging Threats, and International Relations, Committee on Government Reform, House of Representatives, July 18, 2006.
59. Disability benefits, which are also administered by the VA, are automatic entitlements and do not require special appropriations.
60. Throughout, in our budgetary analysis we convert all past expenditures to constant 2007 dollars, and discount future cash expenditures at the "real" T-bill rate of 1.5%. If inflation continues at recent levels of around 3%, this means discounting cash outlays by 4.5%. When assessing the long-run economic impacts (chapters 4–6), there is some controversy over the appropriate discount rate, which we discuss at length later.
61. Interestingly, our estimates turn out in line with forecasts made by William Nordhaus *before the war* for what a protracted unfavorable war would cost. He estimated, for instance, that the impact on oil markets would cost $778 billion; our moderate scenario puts the oil costs at $800 billion. He estimated the adverse macroeconomic impacts at $391 billion. He slightly underestimated the costs of military spending (including occupation/peacekeeping) at $640 billion—but who could have anticipated that matters would be handled so badly—and ignored all of the other hidden budgetary and non-budgetary costs upon which we focus in this book—Nordhaus, *War With Iraq*, p. 77.

Chapter 2: The Costs to the Nation's Budget

1. This money has been appropriated to Iraq and Afghanistan in twenty-five separate appropriations bills since 2001—Testimony of Robert A Sunshine, Assistant Director for Budget Analysis, CBO, "Estimated Costs of U.S. Operations in Iraq and Afghanistan and of Other Activities Related to the War on Terrorism" before the House Budget Committee, July 31, 2007.
2. Approximately 36% of the U.S. troops who have served in Iraq and Afghanistan have been drawn from the National Guard and the Reserves, particularly the Army Reserves. Between 2001 and 2006, 531,000 were mobilized and 378,000 deployed—Government Accountability Office, "DOD and the Services Need to Take Additional Steps to Improve Mobilization Data for the Reserve Components," GAO-06-1068, September 2006. Additionally, over 60,000 people have been recruited to "backfill" domestic positions in the Guard and Reserves that are vacant because the others are in Iraq. The direct additional cost of mobilizing these individuals is $3 billion per year.
3. This includes only the costs of treating veterans through 2007.
4. Congress appropriated $18.4 billion—an unprecedented sum—for Iraqi reconstruction in September 2003. This funding was specified for purposes including school construction, sewerage, sanitation, repair of the electrical grid, and other civilian projects. To date, most of the money spent has been diverted to military projects, including training bomb squads, training Iraqi security forces, constructing prisons, purchasing armored cars; and for the 3,600 projects completed, some 25% of funds were spent on security. Money has also been diverted to pay for the elections—Special Inspector General for Iraqi Reconstruction. At the end of 2007, the administration announced that it would rescind its request for the remaining reconstruction money.
5. In 2007, the federal budget included $394 billion for Medicare and $276 billion for Medicaid and related payments—Budget of the U.S. Government, 2007.
6. The CBO provides a range of scenarios for military engagement. Our analysis focuses on two of these, the first one reflecting a relatively quick disengagement that would leave only a non-combat force such as that currently stationed in Korea, and a second in which the U.S. would withdraw more slowly and continue to engage in combat operations. In comparing our estimates with the CBO, we reached similar projections for the future costs of operating the war and the military "reset" costs. Our estimates for veterans' health care and disability compensation are higher than the CBO projections, in large part because we project costs for the entire lifetime of the veteran whereas

CBO uses a ten-year timeframe or less. Additionally, we include a number of costs not covered in the CBO's projections.

7. As noted in chapter 1, all dollars have been converted into 2007 dollars, adjusting for inflation and the "time value" of money. This chapter focuses on the budgetary implications for the federal government, so there should be little controversy on the use of the real rate (1.5%) at which government can borrow *for evaluating budgetary implications of the war.* (Corporations cannot typically borrow at the same rate, and often raise money by issuing new equity, which raises difficult issues in evaluating the appropriate discount rate for corporations. More controversial still is the right discount rate to use for the evaluation of the broader social costs of the war, to which we turn in the Appendix on page 216).
8. Some forty countries, led by the United States, Britain, Australia, and Poland were in the coalition during 2003. Since then, in response to voters' public opinion, eighteen countries have pulled out completely, with another eight keeping fewer than fifty troops in the region. In 2007, the only countries that still maintained more than 1,000 troops in Iraq were the U.K., South Korea, and Georgia. As with so many other aspects of this war, finding out how many countries were in the coalition is more difficult than it should be (cf. chapter 6).
9. "The Possible Costs to the United States of Maintaining a Long-Term Military Presence in Iraq," Letter from Peter Orzsag (director of the CBO) to Congressman Kent Conrad regarding the costs of maintaining a presence in Iraq similar to that of U.S. forces in the Republic of Korea and the Northeast Asia region—September 20, 2007, Congressional Budget Office.
10. As this book goes to press, some of this money has already been spent, so it should really be included in "past" rather than "future" expenditures. For simplicity, however, we have taken as our dividing line the beginning of the fiscal year, October 1, 2007.
11. According to the DOD Contingency Tracking System Deployment File, as of October 31, 2007, about 1.64 million U.S. service members had been deployed in the Global War on Terror. This includes the Army (800,681), Navy (304,382), Air Force (325,023), Marines (208,731), and Coast Guard (3,077). It is difficult to estimate the numbers through the year 2017, given the uncertainties about enlistment and retention and casualties. In this scenario, we estimate that a total of 200,000 additional troops will serve in Operation Iraqi Freedom and Operation Enduring Freedom (Afghanistan). In our realistic-moderate scenario, we have estimated that 400,000 additional troops will be deployed by 2017.
12. For example, in the U.K., projected personnel costs for Iraq in FY 2008 are only 5% lower than in FY 2007, despite the fact that Britain has cut its troop levels in half—House of Commons Defence Committee, "Cost of Operations

in Iraq and Afghanistan: Winter Supplementary Estimate 2007–08," November 27, 2007.

13. Veterans Benefits Administration, Annual Benefits Report, Fiscal Year 2005, released September 2006, http://www.vba.va.gov/2005_abr.pdf; and Gulf War Veterans Information System. This amounts to $6,927 in 2007 dollars.
14. Of the nearly 700,000 who served, 620,266 are estimated to be still living. Of these, 280,623 have filed claims, of which 212,867 had been granted (161,313 with 10% or more service-connected disabilities), 30,679 denied, and 38,398 were still pending at the time of the most recent report. Many of these veterans suffer from symptoms that are not fully diagnosed, often termed "Gulf War syndrome." The Department of Veterans Affairs publishes frequent updated reports—Department of Veterans Affairs, "Gulf War Veterans Information System, May 2007," released June 30, 2007, at http://www1.va.gov/rac-gwvi/docs/GWVIS_May2007.pdf. See also Veterans Benefits Administration, "Annual Benefits Report Fiscal Year 2005," released September 2006, at http://www.vba.va.gov/2005_abr.pdf.
15. Karen H. Seal, et al., "Bringing the War Back Home: Mental Health Disorders Among 103,788 U.S. Veterans Returning from Iraq and Afghanistan Seen at Department of Veterans Affairs Facilities," Archives of Internal Medicine, vol. 167, no. 5 (March 2007), pp. 476–82.
16. The average annual Social Security cost-of-living adjustment during the five years from 2003 to 2007 amounts to 3.3 percent.
17. The VA's medical budget is discretionary (that is, lawmakers appropriate funds on an annual basis), so we cannot definitively predict future medical appropriations, which may be increased or decreased by future acts of the Congress. (By contrast, the VA's disability benefits are mandatory—they are not subject to the annual appropriations process, so the amounts estimated here can be projected with greater accuracy.) Our estimates for the total medical costs for the ten-year period 2007–17 are $17.7 billion under the best case scenario and $32 billion under the moderate scenario. This compares to the CBO's estimate of $7–$9 billion for the same period.
18. These disability adjustments typically increase faster than the cost of living. They are intended to (partially) offset the losses in income suffered by veterans as a result of their disability. Historically, wages have risen faster than prices. Veterans' benefits have been rising at a compound average growth rate of 7%; our estimates are based on an average increase of 3.3%, because of current congressional proposals to link increases in veterans' benefits to those in Social Security. (Social Security payments are linked not just to increases in prices but also to wages. This is important if there is not to be a growing gap between the incomes of retirees and those who are working.)

19. Veterans Disability Benefits Commission, "Honoring the Call to Duty: Veterans' Disability Benefits in the 21st Century," October 2007 (http://www.vetscommission.org/pdf/FinalReport10-11-07-compressed.pdf).
20. Lawrence Korb, Loren Thompson, and Caroline Wadhams, "Army Equipment After Iraq," Center for American Progress and the Lexington Institute, Washington, DC, April 25, 2006 (http://www.americanprogress.org/kf/equipment_shortage.pdf).
21. William M. Solis, Director, Defense Capabilities and Management, GAO, "Preliminary Observations on Equipment Reset Challenges and Issues for the Army and Marine Corps," Testimony before the Subcommittee on Readiness and Subcommittee on Tactical Air and Land Forces, Committee on Armed Services, House of Representatives, GAO-06-604T.
22. GAO Report to Congressional Committees, "Military Readiness: DOD Needs to Identify and Address Gaps and Potential Risks in Program Strategies and Funding Priorities for Selected Equipment," GAO-06-141, October 2005.
23. Andrew Feickert, Specialist in National Defense, "U.S. Army and Marine Corps Equipment Requirements: Background and Issues for Congress," Congressional Research Service report, June 15, 2007, order code RL33757.
24. Carl Connetta, "Fighting on Borrowed Time: The Effect on U.S. Military Readiness of America's Post–9/11 Wars," Project on Defense Alternatives, Briefing Report no. 19, September 11, 2006, p. 5 (http://www.comw.org/pda/fulltext/0609br19.pdf).
25. On June 27, 2006, Army Chief of Staff General Peter Schoomaker told lawmakers that the Army alone will require $12–$13 billion "for a minimum of two to three years beyond" the end of the conflict—Statement of Peter J. Schoomaker before the House Armed Services Committee, "On the Army's Reset Strategy and Plan for Funding Reset Requirements," Washington, DC.
26. The $250 billion number is almost certainly "best case." The new chairman of the Joint Chiefs of Staff, Admiral Mike Mullen, told the *New York Times* that he will "press Congress to sustain current military spending levels even after the Iraq War ends so the Pentagon can repair and replace worn-out weapons and rebuild ground forces"—*New York Times* editorial, October 25, 2007, p. A24. Just one year's extension of current levels would be $200 billion.
27. General Ronald Keys, head of Air Combat Command, quoted in Tom Vanden Brook, "General: Air Fleet Wearing Down," *USA Today*, May 8, 2007, p. 1A.
28. Note that we have already taken into account increased expenditures because of inflation. There were some increases in expenditure scheduled before the war (such as increased compensation for troops), but actual increases were far higher than these prescheduled increases. We found an increased DOD

expenditure of $605 billion over and above what would be *predicted* based on the forty-year rate of increase.

29. CRS, for instance, found $14 billion in DOD war funding that could not be tied to any specific item, and therefore might be related to DOD regular operations instead of the war. We explain below, moreover, how the war has led to increased costs, e.g., for recruiting and retaining troops—Belasco, Statement before the House Budget Committee Hearing on "The Growing Budgetary Costs of the Iraq War."
30. Material weaknesses in a company or government agency's accounting system are deficiencies that are so grave that they make it highly likely that significant misstatements in financial systems (say, an underreporting of expenditures) will not routinely be detected on a timely basis.
31. Inspector General, Department of Defense, "Independent Auditors' Report on the Principal Statements," DOD Performance and Accountability Report, Fiscal Year 2006, November 12, 2006.
32. For example, the May 2005 recruiting target was originally 8,050, but it was later lowered to 6,700; similar adjustments were made throughout the year—Eric Schmitt, "After Lowering Goal, Army Falls Short on May Recruits," *New York Times*, June 8, 2005, p. A9.
33. Lizette Alvarez, "Army Giving More Waivers in Recruiting," *New York Times*, February 14, 2007, p. A1.
34. National Priorities Project, "Military Recruiting 2006," December 22, 2006, http://www.nationalpriorities.org/Publications/Military-Recruiting-2006.html.
35. Joseph Galloway, "Asking Too Much of Too Few," McClatchy Newspapers, October 24, 2007.
36. Andrew Tilghman, "The Army's Other Crisis, Why the Best and Brightest Young Officers Are Leaving," *Washington Monthly*, December 21, 2007.
37. Gordon Lubold, "To Keep Recruiting Up, U.S. Military Spends More," *Christian Science Monitor*, April 12, 2007, p. 2.
38. Michael O'Hanlon, "The Need to Increase the Size of the Deployable Army," *Parameters* (U.S. Army War College Quarterly) (Autumn 2004), pp. 4–17.
39. The administration has announced plans to increase the size of the active duty Army to 547,000 personnel, the Marine Corps to 202,000 personnel, and the Army Reserve and National Guard to 564,200 personnel over the next five years. The goal is to add a total of 74,000 by 2010.
40. $16 billion per year, increasing by 2% per annum due to inflation.
41. In their more recent tallies of the war, the Congressional Research Service has added on these prewar costs—Belasco, "The Cost of Iraq, Afghanistan, and Other Global War on Terror Operations Since 9/11."

42. Estimates of the cost of enforcing the no-fly zones vary. Wallsten and Kosec estimated the cost at $13 billion a year. But clearly, the savings were not manifested in overall lower expenditures by the Defense Department; moreover, since we have already accounted for other uses of funds, e.g., funding the war on terror and increased armaments, it suggests that the savings were in effect diverted to the war. In this view, by ignoring these savings, we have underestimated the cost of the war. We need to add $10 to $15 billion a year, offset then by the savings—Scott Wallsten and Katrina Kosec, "The Economic Costs of the War in Iraq," AEI-Brookings Joint Center Working Paper 05-19, September 2005, and Sarah Graham-Brown, "No Fly Zones: Rhetoric and Real Intentions," Global Policy Forum, February 20, 2001.
43. Two World War II–era laws are involved here: the 1941 Defense Base Act requires contractors to be insured; and the 1942 War Hazards Compensation Act allows the insurers to apply to the U.S. government to cover the payments for contractors killed or injured.
44. Compensation for total disability is two thirds of the employee's average weekly earnings, up to a current maximum of $1,030.78 per week (this figure rises to three fourths with dependents). Compensation also is payable for partial loss of earnings. Death benefits are half of the employee's average weekly earnings to the surviving spouse with no children, or 45% to the spouse with dependents and an additional 15% per dependent, up to a maximum of 75%. Permanent total disability and death benefits may be payable for life and are subject to annual cost of living adjustments—U.S. Department of Labor, Employment Standards Administration, "Injury Compensation for Federal Employees," Publication CA-810, January 1999.
45. John M. Broder and James Risen, "Death Toll for Contractors Reaches New High in Iraq," *New York Times*, May 19, 2007, p. A1.
46. The numerous claims from major contractors include: 346 from Halliburton; 309—CSC Dyncorp; 307—Raytheon; 157—Titan; 142—CSA Ltd.; 118—ITT Industries; 99—L-3 Communications; 96—General Dynamics; 89—Northrop Grumman; and 54—Washington Group International—James Cox, "Contractors Pay Rising Toll in Iraq," *USA Today*, June 16, 2004, p. 1B.
47. There also is reason to believe that their life expectancy will be shorter. This is an example where budgetary and economic costs move in opposite directions: the fact that they die earlier will save Social Security money; but there is a real societal cost to their earlier death. Our estimates do not include adjustments for any of these factors.
48. U.S. Department of Transportation Research and Innovative Technology Administration, Bureau of Transportation Statistics; and Al Shaffer, Executive

Director, Office of Defense Research and Engineering, DOD Energy Secretary Task Force, presentation on May 22, 2007.

49. Even a tripling of energy prices would add $12 billion a year to the deficit. In our realistic-moderate scenario, we have attributed to the Iraq war only a small fraction of the increase in energy prices.
50. An *economic analysis* is somewhat more complicated, as the discussion later makes clear.
51. In March 2003, the U.S. debt was $6.5 trillion. The $1 trillion number can be thought of as approximately the present value (in 2007 dollars) of the expenditures on the war up through 2008. It is calculated by adding the total estimated *current* cost of the war (direct expenditures totaling 75.4% of the $645 billion, plus the implied expenditures hidden in the defense budget, $151 billion) in each year, and compounding the debt through March 2008.

Chapter 3: The True Cost of Caring for Our Veterans

1. According to the CBO report, "The All-Volunteer Military: Issues and Performance," July 2007, the typical recruit is eighteen years old; half the active duty force is between seventeen and twenty-four; women comprise 14% of the enlisted force. The percentage drawn from the Reserves and Guard has dropped to under 25% as these have bumped up against two-year deployment limits.
2. We use the term "soldiers" generically here, to include all soldiers, Marines, airmen and women, sailors, Coast Guard, Reservists, and National Guard.
3. See the DOD Web site at http://siadapp.dior.whs.mil/personnel/CASUALTY/castop.htm.
4. John Horton, in his "Army Accident Fatalities Attributable to the Iraq War," Unpublished paper by Ph.D. candidate at the National Bureau of Economic Research and Kennedy School of Government, September 2007, shows that the Iraq and Afghanistan conflicts caused approximately 190 additional accidental fatalities compared with what would have occurred during peacetime deployments—comparing the rate of accidental casualties in the five years to the invasion of Iraq and five years after. Extrapolating this to accidental injuries suggests that the rate of injuries during the current conflict is 50% higher than during peacetime (this is discussed at greater length in chapter 4).
5. Fischer, "United States Military Casualty Statistics: Operation Iraqi Freedom and Operation Enduring Freedom," CRS Report for Congress, August 17, 2007, order code RS22452.

6. This information comes from several sources, including published scientific literature. See Kenneth C. Hyams, et al., "Endemic Infectious Diseases and Biological Warfare During the Gulf War: A Decade of Analysis and Final Concerns," *American Journal of Tropical Medicine and Hygiene,* vol. 65, no. 5 (2001), pp. 664–70; Scott F. Paparello, et al., "Diarrheal and Respiratory Disease Aboard the Hospital Ship, USNS-Mercy T-AH 19, During Operation Desert Shield," *Military Medicine,* vol. 158, no. 6 (June 1993), pp. 392–95; A. L. Richards, et al., "Medical Aspects of Operation Desert Storm," *New England Journal of Medicine*, vol. 325, no. 13 (September 1991), pp. 970–71; Scott Thornton, et al., "Gastroenteritis in U.S. Marines During Operation Iraqi Freedom," *Clinical Infectious Diseases*, 2005, vol. 40, no. 4 (February 2005), pp. 519–25; and Glenn M. Wasserman, et al., "A Survey of Outpatient Visits in a United States Army Forward Unit During Operation Desert Shield," *Military Medicine*, vol. 162, no. 6 (June 1997), pp. 374–79. See also medical surveillance monthly reports published by the Army Medical Surveillance Activity, the U.S. Centers for Disease Control and Prevention, and infectious disease experts at the Department of Defense and the Department of Veterans Affairs.
7. We originally found these statistics published by the Department of Veterans Affairs, Office of Public and Intergovernmental Affairs. The "Fact Sheet: America's Wars," available on September 30, 2006, showed that the number of non-mortal woundings in the global war on terror (combining Iraq and Afghanistan) as of September 30, 2006, was 50,508, as well as 2,333 deaths in battle plus 707 other deaths in theater. This Fact Sheet was linked to the DOD Web site (http://siadapp.dior.whs.mil/personnel/CASUALTY/castop.htm), which at that time reported the same number of total "non-mortal casualties." In January 2007, Linda Bilmes published "Soldiers Returning from Iraq and Afghanistan: The Long-Term Costs of Providing Veterans Medical Care and Disability Benefits" (Kennedy School of Government Working Paper No. RWP07-001), in which she cited these statistics. She subsequently received a phone call from then DOD Under Secretary William Winkenwerder, Jr., asking for the source of her data. She pointed him to the VA Web site and to his own DOD site. Following this phone call, the number of casualties reported on the VA site was lowered from 50,508 to fewer than 25,000 and the DOD site was made inaccessible. This was the subject of two articles by Denise Grady in the *New York Times*—"U.S. Reconfigures the Way Casualty Totals Are Given," *New York Times*, February 2, 2007, p. A17; "Agency Says Higher Casualty Total Was Posted in Error," *New York Times*, January 30, 2007, p. A17)—which reprinted the "before" and "after" charts. These charts are shown in the Appendix on page 210. The full

story was reported in Scott Jaschik, "Shooting the Messenger," *Inside Higher Ed*, January 30, 2007.

8. "The Plight of American Veterans," *New York Times*, November 12, 2007, p. A20.
9. By October 2007, some 564,769 (34%) of 1,641,894 service members had been deployed twice or more to the wars in Iraq and Afghanistan—Defense Manpower Data Center, Contingency Tracking System, October 2007.
10. In mid-December 2007, the DOD Web site listed 28,711 wounded in Operation Iraqi Freedom and 1,840 wounded in Operating Enduring Freedom (Afghanistan)—DOD, U.S. Casualty Status, www.defenselink.mil/news/casualty.pdf. (As noted earlier, this site uses a narrower definition of injuries than the one that includes non-battle injuries and diseases.)
11. Testimony of Dr. Ira Katz, Deputy Chief Patient Care Services Officer for Mental Health, VHA, U.S. Department of Veterans Affairs, before House Committee on Veterans Affairs, July 25, 2007, and Statement by the Honorable Gordon England, Deputy Secretary of Defense, before the Senate Armed Services Committee and the Senate Veterans Affairs Committee, April 12, 2007.
12. The Dole-Shalala Commission (formally titled the President's Commission on Care for America's Returning Wounded Warriors) was created in the aftermath of the Walter Reed scandal and headed by former Senate Republican leader Robert Dole and former Secretary of Health under President Clinton Donna Shalala—President's Commission on Care for America's Returning Wounded Warriors, "Serve, Support, Simplify," July 2007, p. 15, at http://www.pccww.gov.
13. Daniel Cooper, Under Secretary for Health, Disability Claims Roundtable, House Veterans Affairs Committee, May 23, 2007, and Michael McGeary, et al., *A 21st Century System for Evaluating Veterans for Disability Benefits* (Washington, DC: National Academies Press, 2007).
14. Physicians for Social Responsibility, "Fact Sheet on U.S. Military Casualties," http://www.psrla.org/emails/medical-consequences/documents/MilitaryCasualtiesFactSheet.pdf, October 2006 (accessed October 14, 2007). Other causes include vehicle accidents, shrapnel, gunshot wounds, and falls.
15. TBI accounts for a larger proportion of casualties than it has in other recent U.S. wars. The Joint Theater Trauma Registry, compiled by the U.S. Army Institute of Surgical Research, noted that 22% of the wounded troops from Iraq and Afghanistan who have passed through the military's Landstuhl Regional Medical Center in Germany had injuries to the head, face, or neck. This percentage can serve as a rough estimate of the fraction that have TBI, according to Deborah L. Warden, a neurologist and psychiatrist at Walter Reed

Army Medical Center who is the national director of the Defense and Veterans Brain Injury Center. Warden said the true proportion is probably higher, "since some cases of closed brain injury are not diagnosed promptly"—Susan Okie, M.D., "Traumatic Brain Injury in the War Zone," *New England Journal of Medicine*, 352 (May 2005) pp. 2043–47.

16. Ibolja Cernak, Johns Hopkins University Applied Physics Laboratory, who has studied blast-related brain injuries since the conflict in the Balkans, at a presentation before the National Academy of Sciences in August 2007; see also Geoff Ling, DOD, and Maria Mouratidis, head of brain injury treatment at the National Naval Medical Center in Bethesda, MD, in Gregg Zoroya, "Brain Injuries from War Worse Than Thought," *USA Today*, September 24, 2007, p. 8A.
17. Ibid.
18. Dr. Gene Bolles, interviewed on *The NewsHour with Jim Lehrer*, February 15, 2005.
19. Walter Reed is a 260-bed hospital that admits more than 13,000 patients every year; the outpatient care facility holds 700 patients, who stay 10 months on average. The hospital was supposed to be shut down by 2011 under the terms of the Defense Base Closure and Realignment Commission.
20. Co-chairman Togo West, former Secretary of the Army, in Steve Vogel, "Panel Calls for Closing Walter Reed Sooner," *The Washington Post*, April 12, 2007, p.A1.
21. Statement by the Honorable Gordon England, April 12, 2007 (italics added).
22. Quoted in Dana Milbank, "Painting Over the Problems at Walter Reed's Building 18," *The Washington Post*, February 23,2007, p. A2.
23. Sullivan, a former VA employee, and Robinson, both Gulf War veterans, were at that time working for Veterans for America, an organization led by the Nobel Peace Prize winner Bobby Muller. Sullivan now is president of Veterans for Common Sense.
24. Government Accountability Office, "GAO Findings and Recommendations Regarding DOD and VA Disability," GAO-07-906R, May 25, 2007.
25. See Veterans Benefits Administration, Annual Benefits Report, Fiscal Year 2005, p. 17, for a definition of disability compensation; and see Department of Veterans Affairs, Disability Compensation Program, *Legislative History*, VA Office of Policy, "Planning and Preparedness 2004," for the principles behind the program.
26. However, conditions are not scaled continuously from 0 to 100. Some mental conditions, for example, are rated: 0, 10, 30, 70, or 100; coronary artery disease ratings are rated: 10, 30, 60, and 100; spinal conditions are rated: 10,

20, 30, 40, 50, or 100. A huge amount of time is devoted to making these determinations.

27. The VA 2007 *Federal Benefits* manual lists $1,380 for 10% and $30,000 for 100%, but those with 30% or more service-connected disability may also receive additional payments; those who are 100% service-connected will receive an annual payment of about $45,000—Department of Veterans Affairs, *Federal Benefits for Veterans and Dependents, 2007 edition*, available at www1.va.gov/OPA/vadocs/fedben.pdf.
28. Veterans Benefits Administration, Annual Benefits Report, Fiscal Year 2005, p.33.
29. The 30% "service-connected" qualification varies according to the condition, but typically refers to a moderately disabled veteran.
30. Government Accountability Office, "GAO Findings and Recommendations Regarding DOD and VA Disability."
31. Government Accountability Office, "Veterans Benefits Administration: Problems and Challenges Facing Disability Claims Processing," GAO Testimony Before the Subcommittee on Oversight and Investigations, House Committee on Veterans Affairs, May 18, 2000.
32. Ibid.
33. Government Accountability Office, "Veterans Benefits: Further Changes in VBA's Field Office Structure Could Help Improve Disability Claims Processing," GAO-06-149, December 2005.
34. Government Accountability Office, "GAO Findings and Recommendations Regarding DOD and VA Disability Systems."
35. GAO, "Veterans' Disability Benefits: Processing of Claims Continues to Present Challenges," GAO-07-562T, March 13, 2007.
36. The VBA's backlog of pending claims in late December 2007 was 406,065—VBA Monday Morning Workload Report, December 22, 2007 (http://www.vba.va.gov/bln/201/reports/mmrindex.htm).
37. Department of Veterans Affairs, Fiscal Year 2007 Performance and Accountability Report, November 15, 2007 (http://www.va.gov/budget/report/2007/2007FullWeb.pdf).
38. Most claims were submitted by health care providers within thirty days, bringing the total reimbursement period to about sixty days. Claims that were "pending" and required additional attention took a further nine days (Center for Policy and Research, American Health Insurance Plans, 2006). Moreover, forty-nine states and the District of Columbia have enacted "prompt payment" laws that require insurance companies to reimburse health care providers within thirty to sixty days. The penalties for non-compliance are

interest charges of up to 18%. The federal government has a "Prompt Payment" rule that requires it to pay federal contractors within thirty days of receipt of an invoice, or penalties are imposed. Another rule, the Federal Travel Regulation interim rule, requires federal agencies to reimburse an employee within thirty days after the employee submits a travel voucher to the approving official.

39. "Stop-loss" orders allow the military to refuse to allow an enlistee to leave the military, even when his term of contract expires. The military has used these to an unprecedented extent. Even by the end of 2005, some 50,000 troops had been forced to stay beyond their enlistment period—Tom Regan, "Stop-Loss used to Retain 50,000 Troops," *Christian Science Monitor*, January 31, 2006.
40. This may be one of the reasons that denial rates are higher among National Guard and Reservists: the active duty denial rate is 6.6%, compared with a National Guard and Reserve denial rate of 15.5%—Department of Veterans Affairs, "VA Benefits Activity: Veterans Deployed to the Global War on Terrorism," June 2007.
41. Government Accountability Office, Report to Congressional Requesters, "Hundreds of Battle-Injured GWOT Soldiers Have Struggled to Resolve Military Debts," GAO-06-494, April 2006 (http://www.gao.gov/new.items/d06494.pdf).
42. Veterans Benefits Improvement Act of 1994 (Public Law 103-446) and Persian Gulf War Veterans Act of 1998 (PL 105-277). All veterans from 1991 onward are classified together for the purposes of determining eligibility for VA benefits. The VA does not distinguish between the end of the first Gulf War and the present conflict (38 USC Section 101[33] defines the Gulf War as starting on August 2, 1990, and continuing until either the president or the Congress declares an end to it, and 38 CFR 3.317 defines the locations of the conflict).
43. For the first Gulf War, the total claims filed to date are 280,623, of which 212,867 have been approved, 30,679 have been denied, and 38,398 are still pending—Department of Veterans Affairs, "Gulf War Veterans Information System" May 2007 (cf. Preface, note 8), p. 7.
44. VBA, Annual Benefits Report, Fiscal Year 2005, p. 33.
45. By contrast, any disability claims from the first Gulf War also stem from exposure to pollution from oil well fires, low levels of chemical warfare agents, experimental anthrax vaccines, the experimental antichemical warfare agent medication called pyridostigmine bromide, and the antimalaria pill Lariam.
46. Discussion with Dr. Jonathan Shay, October 7, 2007.

47. Department of Veterans Affairs, "VA Benefits Activity: Veterans Deployed to the Global War on Terror." (As of June 2007, 720,000 had been discharged, of whom 202,000 had applied for disability benefits.)
48. In calculating veterans' disability compensation, we have included all the potentially eligible veterans from the 224,000 who have already filed disability claims. We have not adjusted for the incremental cost—that is, the number of veterans who may have claimed disability even during peacetime. This is because the VA does not report which of the 263,000 who have been treated so far in its medical facilities were wounded in combat vs. non-combat. However, it would be possible to estimate very roughly that the VA would have received 25,000 claims even during peacetime (assuming half of the veterans who are evacuated for non-battle-related injuries and 5% of the disease-related make claims). That would lower the total costs attributable purely to the decision to invade Iraq by around 10–15%. (This adjustment is itself much too high, because it assumes the same rate of peacetime injury for National Guard and the Reserves as for full-time servicemen and women.)
49. The average claim for existing veterans in the system in 2005 was $8,890.
50. This projection is based on our best case scenario, using the figure of 1.8 million servicemen and women and the CBO troop deployment figures through 2017.
51. Daniel Cooper, Disability Claims Roundtable, May 23, 2007.
52. Linda Bilmes, Testimony before the House Veterans Affairs Committee, March 13, 2007. See also Cooper, Disability Claims Roundtable, who estimates that additional claims specialists could only reduce the existing backlog by 22%.
53. "Eligibility for Hospital, Nursing Home, and Domiciliary Care," 38 USC Section 1710. This recommendation enjoys strong bipartisan support. The proposal (the Akaka amendment, as it is known) passed the Senate unanimously on July 12, 2007. See http://veterans.senate.gov/public/index.cfm?pageid=12&release_id=11183 (accessed on December 4, 2007).
54. Lisa Sprague, "Veterans' Health Care: Balancing Resources and Responsibilities," Issue Brief No. 796, April 1, 2004, National Health Policy Forum, George Washington University.
55. Veterans Health Administration, Office of Public Health and Environmental Hazards, "Analysis of VA Health Care Utilization Among U.S. Southwest Asian War Veterans," November 2006, p. 14.
56. See the testimony of Ira Katz, M.D., Ph.D., Deputy Chief Patient Care Services Officer for Mental Health, Veterans Health Administration, U.S. Department of Veterans Affairs, before the House Committee on Veterans Affairs, July 25, 2007; Hoge, Auchterlonie, and Milliken, "Mental Health Problems, Use of

Mental Health Services, and Attrition from Military Service After Returning from Deployment to Iraq or Afghanistan," pp.1023–32; and Charles Hoge, Carl Castro, Stephen Messer, et al., "Combat Duty in Iraq and Afghanistan: Mental Health Problems and Barriers to Care," *New England Medical Journal*, vol. 351, no.1 (July 2004), pp. 13–22. These studies estimated that 19–30% of all veterans returning from Iraq will meet criteria for serious mental health disorders.

57. Linda Bilmes, interview with Paul Sullivan, Program Director of Veterans for America, December 23, 2006.
58. Veterans Disability Benefits Commission, Final Report, August 2007, pp. 470–7.
59. See Douglas Zatzick, et al., "Posttraumatic Stress Disorder and Functioning and Quality of Life Outcomes in a Nationally Representative Sample of Male Vietnam Veterans," *American Journal of Psychiatry,* 154 (December 1997), pp. 1690–95.
60. Seal, et al., "Bringing the War Back Home: Mental Health Disorders Among 103,788 U.S. Veterans Returning from Iraq and Afghanistan Seen at Department of Veterans Affairs Facilities," pp. 476–82.
61. Quoted in Rich Daly, "New Freedom Commission Members Assess Report's Impact," *Psychiatric News*, vol. 41, no. 9 (May 2006), p. 1.
62. Statement by Gordon Espamer, litigation partner at Morrison & Foerster LLP, August 7, 2007. The complaint was filed in the U.S. District Court, Northern California.
63. Government Accountability Office, "VA Health Care Budget Formulation," GAO-06-430R, September 2006, pp. 18–20.
64. Cooper, Disability Claims Roundtable.
65. We also assume that some 83% of veterans who are severely disabled will rely on the VA to provide all of their medical care. This percentage declines to 58% for moderately disabled veterans and 42% for veterans who are rated least disabled. Sixty percent will seek short-term treatment (less than five years), and 40% will continue to use the VA as their health care provider for the rest of their lives.
66. The CBO has lower estimates. See the testimony of Matthew S. Goldberg, Deputy Assistant Director for the National Security Congressional Budget Office, before the House Veterans Affairs Committee, October 17, 2007. He estimated the 2006 annual average cost per Iraqi and Afghanistan veteran who used VA health care at $2,610 versus an overall average of $5,765 in 2006. Our two scenarios reflect this range. We adjusted the minimum range to $3,500 after consulting with physicians in the VA treating new veterans.

67. The size of the administrative costs will depend on the nature of the bureaucratic processes. If the reforms we advocate in chapter 8 are adopted, not only will veterans get the benefits to which they are entitled without the hassles they currently face, but the administrative costs will be lower.

Chapter 4: Costs of War That the Government Doesn't Pay

1. Stella M. Hopkins, "Veterans with Severe Ailments Face Long Waits for Care," *Charlotte Observer*, October 21, 2007, revealed that some of the most severely injured veterans have to wait more than thirty days to see a doctor in the VA system; waiting times were longest for problems such as TBI and related diagnostic services. The Inspector General of the VA also reported that only 75% of veterans were able to schedule appointments with doctors within thirty days, in a contradiction of the testimony of Under Secretary Michael Kussman, who stated that 95% of soldiers were seen by the VA within thirty days—Statement of Michael Kussman before the Subcommittee on Health of the Committee on Veterans Affairs, U.S. House of Representatives, February 14, 2007.
2. The commission was established in the National Defense Authorization Act of 2004 to study the adequacy of the benefits provided to compensate and assist veterans and their survivors for disabilities and deaths attributable to military service. The commission is independent of government agencies, such as the Department of Veterans Affairs and the Department of Defense, and its thirteen members are appointed by the president and leaders of Congress. Its final report, "Honoring the Call to Duty: Veterans' Disability Benefits in the 21st Century," dated October 2007, is available at http://www.vetscommission.org/reports.asp.
3. Joyce McMahon Christensen, et al., "Final Report for the Veterans Disability Benefits Commission: Compensation, Survey Results, and Selected Topics," CNA Corporation, Alexandria, VA, August 2007, at https://www.1888932-2946.ws/vetscommission/e-documentmanager/gallery/Documents/Reference_Materials/CNA_FinalReport_August2007.pdf.
4. Hundreds of large jury awards (ranging from $2m–$269m) have been awarded in wrongful death suits over the past five years. They include $112 million to Elizabeth and John Reden of New York for a malpractice case in which their daughter suffered brain damage (2004) and $43 million in Louisiana in 2001 for Seth Becker, a twenty-four-year old who needed both legs amputated after sustaining an injury while working for Baker Oil Tools. In these and many other cases the amount awarded was determined primarily on the basis of the

cost of round-the-clock medical care (not on the basis of economic opportunity costs). The $269m award was for Rachel Martin, a fifteen-year-old Texas girl who died in 1998. In most of these cases with multi-million-dollar settlements, the plaintiffs receive less than the total award, typically about 10%. But even these reduced awards are far greater than the amounts provided to veterans.

5. Michael Kaplen, "Behavior Changes Following Train Accident Leads to 8.5 Million Dollar Brain Damage Settlement," Brain Injury News and Information Blog, April 2005 (http://www.braininjury.blogs.com/).
6. Stephen Vangel, et al., "Long-Term Medical Care Utilization and Costs Among Traumatic Brain Injury Survivors," *American Journal of Physical Medicine and Rehabilitation*, vol. 84, no. 3 (March 2005), pp. 153–60.
7. "Fact Sheet: Traumatic Brain Injury: Selected Statistics," Brain Injury Association of Missouri, http://www.biamo.org/BrainInjuryFacts.asp (accessed on November 26, 2007).
8. As of April 21, 2004, the EPA estimate is $6.2 million in 2002 dollars—Chris Dockins, et al., "Value of Statistical Life Analysis and Environmental Policy: A White Paper," Environmental Protection Agency, National Center for Environmental Economics, April 21, 2004 (http://yosemite.epa.gov/ee/epa/eermfile.nsf/vwAN/EE-0483-01.pdf/$File/EE-0483-01.pdf). This is $7.2 million in 2007 dollars, using changes in CPI from 2002 until August 2007.
9. The "peak" age for VSL, in terms of lost earnings potential, may be twenty-nine, with a VSL in 2002 dollars of between $6 and $7.5 ($6.8 to $8.5 million in 2007 dollars)—W. Kip Viscusi and Joseph E. Aldy, "The Value of Statistical Life: A Critical Review of Market Estimates Throughout the World," National Bureau of Economic Record [hereafter NBER] Working Paper W9487, February 2003.
10. Scott Wallsten and Katrina Kosec estimated the value of a statistical life as $6.5 million in 2000 dollars in their 2005 study of the economic costs of the war, based on an analysis of VSL values ranging from $4 to $9 million in 2000 dollars; converting to 2007 dollars, this gives a range of $4.72 to $10.62 million—Wallsten and Kosec, "The Economic Costs of the War in Iraq."
11. Some argue that the fact that they volunteered means that the person would be willing to pay less not to die or be wounded than an ordinary civilian, and therefore they ought to be compensated less when they die or are injured. In this view, from an economic perspective, the loss if they are injured or killed is less.
12. That is, the economic cost of a person assigned a 50% disability is 0.5 × $7.2 million, or $3.6 million. This methodology is similar to that used by a variety

of government agencies, and by courts in determining appropriate compensation for "wrongful injury." They assess impairments as a fraction of total disability. Similarly, in an 2002 EPA report on averting boating accidents, the EPA stipulates fractions of a life at certain levels of injuries: minor injuries are 0.0020; moderate are 0.0155; serious are 0.0575; severe are 0.1875; and critical are 0.7625—Department of Transportation, "Wearing of Personal Flotation Devices (PFDs) by Certain Children Aboard Recreational Vessels," *Federal Register*, vol. 67, no. 121, June 24, 2002, at http://www.epa.gov/fedrgstr/EPA-IMPACT/2002/June/Day-24/i15793.htm.

13. Horton, "Army Accident Fatalities Attributable to the Iraq War." Unpublished paper.
14. Peter Katel, "Wounded Veterans: Is America Shortchanging Vets on Health Care?" *Congressional Quarterly Researcher*, vol. 17, no. 30 (August 31, 2007), pp. 697–720.
15. CBS News interview with Paul Sullivan, Director of Veterans for Common Sense, November 13, 2007.
16. Mental Health Advisory Team (MHAT-IV) study, Final Report.
17. Seal, et al., "Bringing the War Back Home: Mental Health Disorders Among 103,788 U.S. Veterans Returning from Iraq and Afghanistan Seen at Department of Veterans Affairs Facilities," pp. 476–82.
18. Mental Health Advisory Team (MHAT-IV) study, Final Report.
19. Veterans Disability Benefits Commission, "Honoring the Call to Duty: Veterans' Disability Benefits in the 21st Century," October 2007.
20. Ibid., p. 15.
21. Zatzick, et al., "Posttraumatic Stress Disorder and Function and Quality of Life Outcomes in a Nationally Representative Sample of Male Vietnam Veterans," RAND Corporation, 1997.
22. Eric Christensen, et al., "Final Report for the Veterans' Disability Benefits Commission: Survey Results and Selected Topics," August 2007, p. 269.
23. Veterans' Disability Benefits Commission, "Honoring the Call to Duty: Veterans' Disability Benefits in the 21st Century," p. 155.
24. The maximum lump-sum payment in the U.K. for impairment to quality of life is £285,000 (about $570,000). This is paid in addition to a guaranteed income supplement.
25. President's Commission on Care for America's Returning Wounded Warriors (described in chapter 3), "Serve, Support, Simplify," p. 9.
26. The Brain Injury Association of Missouri estimates that medical and non-medical (e.g., home modifications, vocational rehabilitation, health insurance) expenditures per TBI survivor average $151,587.
27. TRICARE is the health care program serving active duty service members,

retirees, their families, survivors, and certain former spouses worldwide. As a major component of the Military Health System, TRICARE brings together the resources of the uniformed services and supplements them with a network of civilian health care professionals, institutions, pharmacies, and suppliers. These provide access to high-quality health care services while maintaining the capability to support military operations.

28. Uwe Reinhardt, Senate Veterans Affairs Committee Hearing on Veterans' Health Care Funding, Congressional Transcripts, March 8, 2007, reported in Katel, "Wounded Veterans," *Congressional Quarterly Researcher.*
29. The social cost encompasses the entire economic value of the impairment from the injury to the serviceman. Therefore, to calculate the social costs *in excess of the budgetary costs,* we need to adjust this total by subtracting out the amount that the VA pays in disability benefits, which is in fact a partial payment toward the overall economic loss. We have accordingly subtracted $11 billion (best case) and $15 billion (realistic-moderate). We subtracted out $500,000 per soldier in death benefits from the VSL for fatalities.
30. Of the 67,000 soldiers who have been wounded, injured, or suffered illnesses requiring medical evacuation as of late 2007, about 60% have been classified as seriously ill, reflecting the harsh conditions in Iraq. In a peacetime army, stateside, the number of serious illnesses and disease among young men and women in their prime would have been very small. We have thus treated 95% of these as incremental.
31. The "serious" PTSD sufferers are the one third of those affected with PTSD that are unemployable, that is, cannot hold down a job—Veterans Disability Benefits Commission, "Honoring the Call to Duty: Veterans' Disability Benefits in the 21st Century."
32. Government Accountability Office, "RESERVE FORCES: Actions Needed to Identify National Guard Domestic Equipment Requirements and Readiness," Report to the Ranking Minority Member, Committee on Oversight and Government Reform, and to the Ranking Minority Member, Subcommittee on National Security and International Relations, House of Representatives, GAO-07-60, January 2007.
33. Government Accountability Office, "Army and Marine Corps Cannot Be Assured That Equipment Reset Strategies Will Sustain Equipment Availability While Meeting Ongoing Operational Requirements," GAO-07-814, September 2007.
34. David S. Loughran, Jacob A. Klerman, and Craig Martin, *Activation and the Earnings of Reservists*, RAND National Defense Research Institute, Santa Monica, CA, 2006. The study was based on Social Security records, rather than on surveys of soldiers or their spouses. Each methodology has its own

advantages. Surveys depend for their accuracy on the ability to recall accurately incomes. But there are fundamental flaws in relying on Social Security records: (1) reported Social Security earnings do not include fringe benefits, which typically are both untaxed and significant, often comprising 25% or more of income, even more for those with lower-income jobs. (2) The study assumes that self-employment income is accurately reported (and even those with regular jobs often have some self-employment). But underreporting is common. It is therefore all the more striking that the study maintains that 62% of the self-employed called to active duty for less than thirty days show an income loss, some 55% lost more than 10%. (3) The study does not include the loss of income for spouses who cannot rely on a husband (or wife) for babysitting services. (4) It does not take into account the additional expenses (e.g., housing and subsistence) as a result of being called to active duty—which means that "take-home family pay" has not been changed in the way indicated. There is some question too about the appropriate comparison of tax advantages. The largest single item in the RAND study is a housing allowance, intended to offset incremental housing costs, which is tax-exempt. An appropriate comparison, one could argue, would not have included either the allowance or the tax benefit. Moreover, if the soldier had owned a home, he (or she) would have enjoyed a tax benefit on his housing expenditures, a tax benefit he gives up if he has to give up his home.

The study unfortunately does not distinguish between impacts on different groups, e.g., those who have regular full-time jobs and those who do not. For an unemployed individual, being called to active duty *raises* incomes. There is no opportunity cost. For others, the costs may be high.

Finally, the RAND study does not include the value of work for which they are not directly paid, like home repairs, which can increase the value of their house. Troops serving in Iraq lose these opportunities. More generally, even if the pay were higher, the pay per hour is not: the troops are on duty, at risk, twenty-four hours a day, seven days a week.

In short, even apart from the failure not to compensate fully for the risks associated with fighting, there is good reason that Reservists and National Guard troops are not volunteering by the droves for service in Iraq. They may well be economically worse off.

In our earlier analysis, we had borrowed Wallsten and Kosec's estimate that Reserve soldiers earn about $33,000 per year as civilians. They estimated that even by that earlier date, the *opportunity cost* of using Reserve troops at current levels (what these individuals would have earned in their civilian jobs) was $3.9 billion. Take-home pay is, of course, less than worker's full compensation, and it is the full compensation which is the better measure of what workers would have produced had they not been deployed in Iraq—Wallsten and Kosec, "The Economic Costs of the War in Iraq," p. 8. In our earlier study, accordingly, we increased the pay per Reservist slightly, to $46,000, taking into account the fully loaded cost of benefits, particularly for those Reservists who are in police and fire departments, receiving benefits that are some 60% to 100% of their take-home pay. Of course, as the war has continued, these costs have risen. Our current overall tally of the war costs, however, does not include any estimate of these opportunity costs in either scenario.

35. It is apparent (from the increased difficulties in recruiting) that individuals did not fully appreciate the risks they faced when joining the Reserves, so that the wage received does not reflect adequate compensation for those risks.
36. The RAND study raises the issue of the impact on incomes *after deactivation*. The study did not incorporate the effects on returning Reservists and National Guard troops after one, two, or three tours of duty, and especially the evidence of the high incidence of disability. Even apart from these disability effects, there are potential adverse effects of extended tours of duty on those who, at the time they are called up, are in long-term employment. Whatever the value of the experience, it is likely that it was not directly job-related, and hence will not serve to advance the individual in his/her career.

    For those whose jobs are not there upon their return, the costs are likely to be even greater. Extensive studies of the consequences of involuntary job displacement suggest that they are associated with marked declines in income.
37. Government Accountability Office, "Military Pay: Army Reserve Soldiers Mobilized to Active Duty Experienced Significant Pay Problems," GAO-04-911, August 2004, p. 1.
38. Department of Veterans Affairs, Veterans Benefit Administration Office of Performance Analysis and Integrity, "VA Benefits Activity: Veterans Deployed to the Global War on Terrorism," June 25, 2007. (http://www.veteransforcommonsense.org/files/VFCS/VBA_GWOT_Claims_June_2007.pdf).
39. In chapter 8, we discuss these and other reforms more extensively.
40. See Vali Nasr's work on Iraqi regional hegemony in *The Shia Revival: How Conflicts Within Islam Will Shape the Future* (New York: W. W. Norton, 2006).
41. We should emphasize that our discussion of hard-to-quantify costs is far from complete. While chapter 2 focused on the budgetary costs to the federal government, the war has also had budgetary implications for states and localities: for instance, they pick up part of the tab for health care costs, especially under the Medicaid program.

    At the same time, some of the costs that we have identified as budgetary are *transfer payments*, payments from one part of our society to another. For instance, any excess costs from corruption (associated, e.g., with Halliburton and Blackwater) means that the amount paid exceeded the value of the resources used. These were simply transfers from ordinary taxpayers to the coffers of the owners of Halliburton's shares and its management. Similarly, some of the higher energy prices that the government paid (part of the budgetary impact of the war that we did not quantify and that thus is not part of our overall tally) are simply transfers from ordinary American taxpayers to oil and other energy companies in the United States.

Chapter 5: The Macroeconomic Effects of the Conflicts

1. The oil price averaged $23.71/barrel in 2002; in the month before the war, it reached $32.23. Part of this was the result of stockpiling because of worries about supply interruptions. The price averaged $27.71 in 2003, $35.90 in 2004, and rose to $49.28 by June 2005. Hurricane Katrina led to another increase. Since Katrina, prices have stayed relatively high.
2. The fact that war may be bad for the economy was made clear by the Gulf War of 1991, which at the very least contributed to the recession that began in that year—and for some of the reasons outlined in this chapter.
3. For a broader discussion of whether oil played a role, see the Appendix on page 216.
4. In 2007, five of the ten most profitable corporations in the world are oil and gas companies—Exxon-Mobil, Royal Dutch Shell, BP, Chevron, and PetroChina. In 2002, only one of the top ten most profitable corporations was from the oil and gas industry—*Forbes* magazine online, The Forbes Global 2000, March 29, 2007 http://www.forbes.com/lists/2007/18/biz_07forbes2000_The-Global-2000_Prof.html). As we noted in chapter 1, the price of oil company shares has soared since the beginning of the war.
5. Such questions are called *counterfactuals*, and involve an analysis of a "but for" world—what oil prices would have been, but for the war in Iraq. There is no way of answering these questions with certainty, but modern social sciences enable us to provide reasonably reliable estimates.
6. For instance, on January 2, 2003 (when war rumblings already were having some impact on prices), markets still expected the price to be under $25 in December 2003, and the December 2009 contract for Light Sweet Crude settled at $22.57 a barrel—from tables in the Money & Investing section of the eastern edition of the *Wall Street Journal*, January 2, 2003.
7. On November 1, 2007, the futures market predicted the price to remain at

around $94 through the end of 2007, declining to $85 toward the end of 2008, and then gradually lowering to $81 by 2011, where they will remain through 2015—Prices of Light Sweet Crude on the New York Mercantile Exchange.

8. In 2004, imports were slightly over 4.8 million barrels; in 2005 and 2006, slightly more than 5 million barrels. As this book goes to press, imports for 2007 have been running slightly lower than in 2006.
9. We emphasize that these are approximations. We have not adjusted the numbers either for inflation, for the time value of money, or for the changing levels of imports over the period. Fine-tuning the calculations would lead to slightly larger numbers than those used in our estimate ($195.4 billion and $446.4 billion, compared to $175 billion and $400 billion in the conservative and realistic-moderate scenarios, respectively). We use the lower numbers because we think it inappropriate to give the false sense of precision that the higher figures might suggest; there is, in particular, still uncertainty about the level of imports for 2008 and 2009. We prefer to err on the conservative side.
10. This is almost precisely the estimate arrived at by the Joint Economic Committee of the House of Representatives in their report *War at Any Price?"* (November 2007). They cite a figure of $174 billion, but argue that the true number is likely to be much larger.
11. In theory, households could dip into their savings to maintain other expenditures. In practice, given the fact that America's savings rate was already close to zero or negative (cf. note 35 below), the scope for doing so was limited.
12. The effects are felt not just in the year that the oil price increases but in the years thereafter. The multiplier refers to the ratio of the total reduction in consumption to the initial increase in cost of oil. One-year multipliers are typically smaller, but our concern is with the total impact, not the timing of the impact (the focus of most short-run GDP forecasting models).
13. The Joint Economic Committee estimates the multiplier to be just in excess of 2, so that the (conservatively) estimated increased expenditure on oil imports of $124 billion has a further GDP effect of $150 billion. This is consistent with (though slightly higher than) the multiplier we use in our realistic-moderate scenario.

    The committee's result is consistent with the Global Insight simulation—cf. Hillard G. Huntington, "The Economic Consequences of Higher Crude Oil Prices," Stanford Energy Modeling Forum, report for the U.S. Department of Energy, 2005—and is smaller than estimates provided by other studies—cf. the survey article by Donald W. Jones, Paul N. Leiby, and Inja K. Paik, "Oil Price Shocks and the Macroeconomy: What Has Been Learned Since 1996," *The Energy Journal*, vol. 25, no. 2 (2004), and James Hamilton and Ana Herrera, "Oil Shocks and Aggregate Macroeconomic Behavior: The

Role of Monetary Policy," *Journal of Money, Credit, and Banking,* 36 (2004), pp. 265–85; and additional studies cited in the Appendix on Methodologies), in some cases markedly so. It is larger than the multiplier used by the CBO in their report, "The Economic Effects of Recent Increases in Energy Prices" (2006), but as we explain at greater length in our appendix we believe that even the multiplier of 2 used in our realistic-moderate scenario is extremely conservative.

14. We describe these empirical and theoretical analyses in more depth. See the Appendix on p. 216.
15. Again, see the Appendix for some of the reasoning behind this conclusion.
16. Earlier, we were dealing with discussed the *oil multiplier,* the effect on GDP of increased spending on oil.
17. For some of the long-run costs referred to in chapter 3, such as increased disability and health care costs for veterans, there are not likely to be large differences in multipliers. That is why we have focused on the impact of switching only $800 billion, which is just half of the total (present discounted value) of direct military expenditures. Recall that the realistic-moderate estimate, based on standard DOD scenarios, envisions a significant American presence in Iraq at least through 2017.
18. Assume, for instance, that in the case of normal investment expenditures (such as university-based research), two thirds of the money is *not* spent on domestic goods and services—we say that the first-round "leakage" (the amount not respent back in the United States) is two thirds, then this will generate an overall multiplier of 1.5, consistent with our earlier analysis. But in the case of money spent in Iraq, if instead of two thirds of the initial expenditures being for American-made goods, one half of the initial expenditures is spent in that way—but after this first round, money is spent in similar ways (that is, leakages are the same), then the overall Iraq spending multiplier is 1.1, for a difference of 0.4 from the normal multiplier. Small differences in first-round expenditure patterns have large effects on multipliers. In reality, the differences in "leakages" for first round expenditures are greater, and there are significant differences in subsequent patterns of expenditures, so that once again our estimate is almost surely very conservative.
19. The Joint Economic Committee's report *War at Any Price?* estimates the total increase in taxpayer spending at a projected $1.9 trillion; including interest on the cumulative debt brings the number to well over $2 trillion. In our projections, the cost of direct military operations for Iraq alone is $1.4 trillion. Cumulative interest on the increased indebtedness—even ignoring Social Security, veterans' disability, and veterans' health care expenditures—brings the total to $2 trillion. (If Afghanistan is included, all numbers are increased by a third.)

20. These ideas are known as *Ricardian equivalence*, after David Ricardo, the nineteenth-century economist who first proposed them.
21. At most, between one half and one third of the amount of the increased deficit—See William Gale and Peter Orszag, "Budget Deficits, National Savings, and Interest Rates," *Brookings Papers on Economic Activity*, vol. 2004, no. 2 (2004), pp. 101–210.
22. Quoted in Jeremy Grant, "Learn from Fall of Ancient Rome, Official Warns U.S.," *Financial Times*, August 14, 2007, p. 4.
23. See, e.g., Alice Rivlin and Isabel Sawhill, "Growing Deficits and Why they Matter," in Rivlin and Sawhill, eds., *Restoring Fiscal Sanity 2005: Meeting the Long-Run Challenge* (Washington, DC: Brookings Institution, 2005); William Gale and Peter Orszag, "The Budget Outlook: Analysis and Implications," *Tax Notes,* October 6, 2003, pp. 145-57; or Gale and Orszag, "Budget Deficits, National Savings, and Interest Rates." If the United States borrows the full amount abroad, and there are no effects on the interest rates at which it can borrow, then there is no displacement effect, and the only costs *to GDP* are the direct costs already estimated. But *national income* is still lower, as we shall see next. The studies referred to above reflect an attempt to calculate empirically the extent of displacement, taking into account that some of the deficit is, at the margin, financed abroad.
24. Assuming that (over the period) the $2 trillion deficit reduces investment by 60% (cf. the discussion below), private investment is reduced by $1.2 trillion. With a multiplier of 1.5, the reduction in aggregate demand is $1.8 trillion; with a more realistic multiplier of 2, the reduction is $2.4 trillion. If the war expenditures have a multiplier of 1.1, the $1.4 trillion of war expenditures increases aggregate demand (and output) by $1.54. Thus, the net reduction in output is between $240 billion and $840 billion. The midpoint in this range is around $500 billion, somewhat greater than the number we have used in our "expenditure-switching" methodology. A third methodology focuses on *marginally balanced budgets*, where taxes are assumed to increase to cover the additional government expenditures. There is little evidence, however, that the Bush administration ever tried to finance extra expenditures through increased taxes. Even if it had, the short-run effects would be similar, as the increased taxes lead to lower consumption—in this scenario, the Iraq war crowds out consumption, which again has a much higher multiplier than war expenditures. However, the long-run effects would be much less.
25. This is the estimate used by the Joint Economic Committee, based on estimates provided by the Bush administration's Council of Economic Advisers, *Economic Report of the President* (2003), pp. 54–55. It is within the range of the numbers estimated in the studies cited above.

26. For a broader discussion of discount rates, see the Appendix on page 216.
27. For instance, if we assume, as before, that the investments yield a real return of only 7 percent, and the benefits are discounted back at the rate of 1.5%, and if we note that the real payments are only $30 billion, then the value of the loss in future output from one year's taxes is $14 billion, and year after year, this amounts to $933 billion. Furthermore, these estimates do not even include the knock-on effects of the lower tax revenues from the displaced investment. Two trillion dollars is a large number—and it can have large consequences.
28. Investments in government research have been shown to have much higher rates of return. The standard cutoff for government projects is 7%, so that average returns should be considerably in excess of 7%. Because raising taxes is costly, there is a general consensus among economists that in the public sector, investment is constrained, and so the value of the lost output is in fact greater than the value of the investment itself. A relatively modest investment in levees in New Orleans would have saved hundreds of billions of dollars.
29. In 2007, there were 116 million households—*Selected Characteristics of Households*, U.S. Census Bureau, Current Population Survey, 2007, *Annual Social and Economic Supplement*, Table HINC-01.
30. And the sources of the cost may differ; that is, in some estimates, there are greater short-run multiplier effects, in others, greater private or public investment displacement effects, and in still others, greater losses from increased foreign indebtedness. The short-run costs are less sensitive to the choice of discount rates than the long-run costs.
31. *War at Any Cost?* But we emphasize that we believe that the committee's number is very low. They reached it using a discount rate of 3%. If our analysis is correct, and the appropriate discount rate is 1.5%, then the value of the lost output (as they project it) is twice that number, or $2.2 trillion. Of the array of numbers, the one that we think constitutes the most realistic estimate of the overall macroeconomic costs is that derived by assuming deficit financing, with 40% financed abroad, with interest payments financed by crowding out public investment, a 7% return of displaced private or public investment, and a 1.5% discount rate, based on a conservatively estimated approximate $1.5 trillion (present value) debt-financed operational budget. The present discounted value of future lost output is then $7 trillion. The results are robust: almost any plausible set of assumptions yields a cost in excess of the $1.1 billion budgetary impact we have used in our estimates.
32. In chapter 2, we noted that many economists believe that the interest costs of the war should not be added to the direct expenditures, but that it is appropriate to calculate the *opportunity costs*, what would have happened to the

economy had we not gone to war and financed it by increased deficits. The calculations reported here are our attempt to provide a conservative estimate of these opportunity costs.

33. Personal correspondence with Robert Westcott. A primary explanation of this poor performance is the heightened uncertainty associated with soaring fiscal and trade deficits and rising oil prices.
34. Mortgages where interest payments vary as market interest rates change. With interest rates at an all-time low in the early years of the decade, this meant that individuals could afford much larger houses than they otherwise would have considered. But almost surely, interest rates would rise from these low levels (real interest rates in this period, taking into account inflation, were negative); and, with variable rate mortgages, as they rose, many households would predictably face problems. What was predicted has now happened. Yet on February 23, 2004, Alan Greenspan pointed out that "many homeowners might have saved tens of thousands of dollars had they held adjustable-rate mortgages rather than fixed-rate mortgages during the past decade"—"Understanding Household Debt Obligations," Remarks by Alan Greenspan at the Credit Union National Association 2004 Governmental Affairs Conference, Washington, DC, February 23 (http://www.federalreserve.gov/boardDocs/speeches/2004/20040223/default.htm).
35. In the third quarter of 2005, the personal savings rate was –0.5%, and from the first quarter of 2005 through the second quarter of 2007, the rate was below 1%—Bureau of Economic Analysis, Department of Commerce, http://www.bea.gov/briefrm/saving.htm.
36. It is estimated that more than 2.2 million Americans will lose their homes—and all of the money they have put into them—to foreclosure—Ellen Schloemer, et al., "Losing Ground: Foreclosures in the Subprime Market and Their Cost to Homeowners," Center for Responsible Lending, December 2006. In the United States, there were 635,159 filings for foreclosure in the third quarter of 2007, up 30% from the previous period—Dan Levy, "U.S. Home Foreclosures Doubled in the Third Quarter," Bloomberg News, November 1, 2007.
37. The subprime borrowers, most of whom were financially unsophisticated, may not have fully understood this, especially given the encouragement received from those who were supposedly financially sophisticated. But it is harder to understand the failings of the regulators.
38. Some might argue that these problems are not the result of the Iraq war as such, but of the way the war was financed, and of accompanying monetary and fiscal policies. Earlier, we encountered a similar argument in discussing

the deficits, and said that similar points could be raised about many other aspects of the war: they are not the inevitable result of the war but of the particular way in which it was conducted. But the analysis of this chapter shows that any way the war was financed would have had adverse macroeconomic consequences. Different ways of financing the war affect the timing of the impact. The monetary policies may have hidden the impacts in the short run and shifted the burden to later years. Had the United States not confronted, for instance, the dampening effects of higher oil prices, the Fed would not have been able or willing to lower interest rates as much as they did, and there would have been less profligate borrowing.

39. The magnitude of the boost that this borrowing gave to the economy is highlighted by the size of the refinancing of mortgages and the amount of money taken out to finance consumption. Net mortgage equity withdrawals are estimated to have ranged between $500 bn–$750 bn in the years 2003–06, with a significant fraction (around one half) of these amounts going into consumption—See Alan Greenspan and James Kennedy, "Sources and Uses of Equity Extracted from Homes," Federal Reserve Finance and Economics Discussions Series (FEDS) No. 2007-20, March 2007. The positive stimulus from this increased consumption more than offsets the effects we have depicted here—but, as we have emphasized, the increased indebtedness will lead (or is already leading) to problems down the line.
40. Of course, just as Johnson and Nixon could have pursued alternative policies for financing the Vietnam War, the Bush administration could have pursued other policies that would not have left the legacy of debt: e.g., it could have shifted the burden of taxation more to upper-income individuals. While the adverse long-run effects would have been less, it would have been hard to avoid them totally, as we have emphasized.
41. And our conservative scenario does not even include any estimate of the costs of the legacy of debt of the federal government.
42. This is another example in which the Bush administration tried to misuse data to shape public opinion. In 2003, it put out statistics purporting to show a decline in terrorism—presumably as a result of the war against terrorism. In fact, a closer look at the correct numbers showed exactly the opposite, as Professor Alan Krueger of Princeton University pointed out, much to their chagrin. Alan Krueger and David Laitin, " 'Misunderestimating' Terrorism," *Foreign Affairs* (September–October 2004).
43. The higher oil prices resulting from the war have substantially increased these transportation costs.

Chapter 6: Global Consequences

1. Office of the UN High Commissioner on Refugees, "UNHCR Doubles Budget for Iraq Operations," news release, July 12, 2007, http://www.unhcr.org/cgi-bin/texis/vtx/media?page=home&id=469630434 (accessed on December 2, 2007).
2. A survey conducted by UNHCR in Damascus showed that 76% of Iraqi refugee children were not in school, many of them for two or three years—Ibid.
3. Ibid.
4. Jennifer Pagonis, spokeswoman for UNHCR, news release "The Iraq Situation: UNHCR Cautious About Returns," November 23, 2007. The report noted that some Iraqis were returning from Syria, but for reasons not related to security conditions. The majority said they were returning because they are running out of money, or because their visas have expired. However, on a positive note, the report noted that this was the first time in several years that Iraqis were even discussing the possibility of returning.
5. Dale Gavlak, "Jordan Appeals for Help in Dealing with Iraqi Refugees," *The Washington Post*, July 27, 2007, p. A16.
6. About $70 million of the $123 million 2007 budget is supposed to be paid by the United States—"UNHCR's Annual Programme Budget 2007," UN General Assembly, A/AC.96/1026, September 1, 2006, at http://www.unhcr.org/excom/EXCOM/44fe8cb52.pdf; and UNHCR, "UNHCR Doubles Budget for Iraq Operations."
7. Martin A. Weiss, "Iraq's Debt Relief," CRS report for Congress, April 21, 2006. Because the United States had already written off most of the debt, the budgetary cost to the United States of its debt forgiveness was only $360 million. Other countries that forgave Iraq's debt included: Japan, $4.1 billion; Russia, $3.45 billion; France, $3 billion; and Germany, $2.3 billion (all excluding interest). Under traditional rules, Iraq would not have been eligible for debt relief because of its large oil reserves, but the Bush administration pushed for a revision of the rules. (The debt forgiveness was conducted through the "Paris Club," an informal group of eighteen major creditor countries that from time to time reschedule or forgive debts owed to them by developing countries.)
8. O'Hanlon and Campbell, *Iraq Index,* December 3, 2007.
9. The Economist Intelligence Unit estimates 2003 GDP per capita at $2,469, about 7% of that of the United States—"Country Report: Iraq," November 2007.
10. O'Hanlon and Campbell, *Iraq Index,* December 3, 2007, p. 20.
11. We focus here on the numbers killed or injured. But large numbers have

been "injured" in other ways, such as extended periods of imprisonment. For instance, in August 2007, 23,000 Iraqis were in U.S. custody (up more than 25% from a year earlier, and more than 50% from June 2006) and another 37,000 in Iraqi custody (almost double the number a year earlier). In July 2007, U.S. and Iraqi government officials reported that since March 2003, an estimated 44,000 suspected Iraqi insurgents or sectarian killers previously detained had been released—O'Hanlon and Campbell, *Iraq Index*, p. 22. Another 19,000 insurgents had been killed—Jim Michaels, "Thousands of Enemy Fighters Reported Killed," *USA Today*, September 27, 2007, p. A1. But these numbers raise many questions. The International Crisis Group (ICG) estimates that there are approximately 5,000 to 15,000 insurgents in Iraq—*In Their Own Words: Reading the Iraqi Insurgency,* Middle East Report No. 50, February 15, 2006. The *Iraq Index* estimates have hovered in the 15,000–20,000 range, far less than the total numbers in prison/killed. If these numbers are correct, it is clear that many of those in prison are almost surely not part of the insurgency. More recent numbers for the insurgency size suggest that the numbers have increased substantially—the *Iraq Index* now puts the number of Sunni insurgents alone at around 70,000, though the number may include non-operational supporters. This means that the insurgency has recruited more than we have killed—O'Hanlon and Campbell, *Iraq Index*, October 29, 2007, p. 26.

12. Iraq Coalition Casualty Count, http://icasualties.org/oif/IraqiDeaths.aspx (accessed November 14, 2007). Other sources give slightly different numbers.
13. O'Hanlon and Campbell, *Iraq Index*, October 1, 2007, p. 11. There is some good news: the number of recorded deaths declined beginning in August 2007.
14. In October 2006, they reached 3,709.
15. Of the 34,000 physicians at the beginning of the war, 17,000 have left, 2,000 have been killed, and 250 have been kidnapped—O'Hanlon and Campbell, *Iraq Index,* December 3, 2007, p. 43.
16. In 2000, some 140,000 cases of cholera worldwide, resulting in approximately 5000 deaths, were reported to WHO; Africa accounted for 87% of these cases—World Health Organization Statistical Information System (WHOSIS). In 2006, there were 234,349 cases and 6,303 deaths in Africa, of which 70% were in Angola, Sudan, and Djibouti. In 2006, there were 2,472 reported cases in Asia, including 161 cases in China (two deaths), 1939 in India (three deaths), and three other deaths reported in Malaysia and the Philippines—WHO, 2006 Cholera Annual Report, Weekly Epidemiological Record No. 31, August 3, 2007.
17. In 2003, there were 73 cases were reported—WHO statistics, 2003.

18. WHO, Epidemic and Pandemic Alert and Response Report, "Cholera in Iraq" Update 3, October 3, 2007 (http://www.who.int/csr/don/2007_10_03/en/index.html).
19. Ibid.
20. Gilbert Burnham, et al., "Mortality After the 2003 Invasion of Iraq: A Cross-Sectional Cluster Sample Survey," *The Lancet*, vol. 368, no. 9545 (October 21, 2006), pp. 1421–28.
21. The study compared the number of deaths that one would have expected—on the basis of prewar mortality data—with the number of deaths on the basis of the higher after-war mortality data. The difference was 654,965, with a range of 392,979 to 942,636 (the 95% confidence interval). A more recent study, based on survey data, estimated the number of violent deaths in the first three years and three months of the war at 151,000—a tenfold increase in the prewar rate. The study also found that the war led to an almost doubling in overall death rates. Iraq Family Health Survey Study Group, "Violence-Related Mortality in Iraq from 2002 to 2006." *New England Journal of Medicine*, January 31, 2008, pp. 484–93.

    The fact that even after only four years of conflict, some 26% of Iraqis reported experiencing the murder of a family member or relative, and, outside of the Kurdish areas, far fewer than half had experienced neither a murder nor a kidnapping of a family member, relative, or friend lends credence to these high numbers—"Public Attitudes in Iraq; Four Year Anniversary of Invasion," survey conducted by Opinion Research Business, March 2007 (www.opinion.co.uk).
22. The pace of killing accelerated in the months following the survey, but there is some evidence that since the summer of 2007, it has been somewhat reduced. It is hard, accordingly, to predict what will happen in 2008 and 2009. But note that the "excess deaths" include not only those dying from violence but also from malnutrition, disease, lack of access to medical care, etc. Moreover, we have arbitrarily used a cutoff date of March 2010; more realistically, the problems are likely to persist for years beyond. In short, while one cannot predict with certainty whether the eventual numbers will exceed, or be less than, the 1.2 million estimated, the likelihood is that over the entire period of this study, from the beginning of the war to 2017, the numbers will very probably exceed our estimate of 1.2 million.
23. That so much of Iraq's middle class has also departed does not bode well for its future. Cf. chapter 1.
24. Comprehensive Report of the Special Advisor to the Director of Central Intelligence on Iraq's WMD, September 30, 2004, p. 207 (https://www.cia.gov/library/reports/general-reports-1/iraq_wmd_2004/index.html).
25. O'Hanlon and Campbell, *Iraq Index*, December 3, 2007, p. 40.
26. Nationwide, matters are somewhat better: prewar, there were only 4–8 hours

of electricity; by November 2007, it was up to 12.9 hours—Ibid., p. 36. The most current data on unemployment are from the *Iraq Index*, which continues to show unemployment rates between 25% and 40% (that is, as many as two out of five Iraqis may be unemployed—in spite of the fact that more than 2 million have already left the country). Different data sources suggest different magnitudes of decline of GDP. Based on Economist Intelligence Unit data, we estimate a decline of 13% between 2002 and 2006; based on IMF estimates, there is a smaller, 8.3% decline. There is continuing controversy over 2007 growth. The World Bank and IMF suggest that 2007 growth may be sufficiently great to bring Iraq to where it was before the war. The estimates in the *Iraq Index* for 2007 growth suggest that even by the end of 2007, GDP was lower—by 5–10%—than its prewar level. But it should be clear that this is *not* because the economy is performing well; rather, it is because the price of oil—the country's main product—has been booming. Even though crude oil exports are down by some 25% from prewar levels (with a great deal of variability month to month), revenues are up. And even though exports from September 2004 to October 2007 increased by only 10%, revenues increased two and a half times—O'Hanlon and Campbell, *Iraq Index*, November 29, 2007, pp. 34–35.

27. Ibid, p. 34.
28. Ibid, p. 53
29. Alan Beattie and Charles Clover, " 'Surprise' Revamp for Iraq's Economy," *Financial Times*, September 22, 2003, p. 1. Other goods faced a nominal 5% tariff. These policies—the sudden privatization and liberalization of an economy—are referred to as "shock therapy." In the early nineties, the IMF encouraged the countries in transition to engage in "shock therapy." Today, there is broad consensus that shock therapy failed, and that countries such as Hungary, Poland, and Slovenia, countries that took the gradualist approach to privatization and the reconstruction (or, in many cases, the construction for the first time) of their institutional infrastructure, managed their transitions far better than those that tried to leapfrog into a laissez-faire economy. The shock therapy countries saw incomes plunge and poverty soar. Social indicators, such as life expectancy, mirrored the dismal GDP numbers.

    More than a decade after the beginning of the transition, many of the shock therapy post-Communist countries haven't even returned to pretransition income levels. Worse, the prognosis for establishing stable democracies and the rule of law in most of shock therapy countries looks bleak. If Bush or his advisers had paid attention to these historical experiences, they would have been more cautious in urging this failed strategy upon Iraq.
30. For instance, the Iraqi constitution placed restrictions on foreign ownership of certain parts of the Iraqi economy and deemed essential services protected

and not able to be privatized. However, Bremer's new law permitted complete foreign ownership of Iraqi companies and assets that have been publicly owned. Article 43 of the 1907 Hague Convention "Regulations" states that the occupying power must "take all the measures in his power to restore, and ensure, as far as possible, public order and safety, while respecting, unless absolutely prevented, the laws in force in the country." See also Shirley Williams—"The Seeds of Iraq's Future Terror," *The Guardian* (London), October 28, 2003, p. 22.

31. Rajiv Chandrasekaran, *Imperial Life in the Emerald City: Inside Iraq's Green Zone*, (New York: Alfred A. Knopf, 2006), p. 126.
32. Linda Bilmes, "Civil Service Has Morphed into U.S. Inc.," *Los Angeles Times*, July 18, 2004, p. M1.
33. U.S. contractors with cost-plus contracts did not, of course, have to worry about their costs. But not all contractors had these contracts. And interestingly, even many contractors with cost-plus contracts preferred to import workers into Iraq. Perhaps they realized that their overall costs were being scrutinized: if they were going to be lax on their costs, it was better to do so with the pay of U.S. employees, including their executives, or in some of their other subcontracts. Worries about which Iraqis could be trusted also played a role, increasingly so as the insurgency grew.
34. Of course, given the high price of oil, there is considerable interest in investing in Iraq's oil fields; but oil companies have demonstrated a willingness to go almost anywhere in the world so long as they can get the oil at a low enough price. They are willing to bear the risk. This should not be viewed as indicative of economic success.
35. There are scenarios in which one could have seen their economy expand markedly. Assume, for instance, that one takes seriously our conservative calculation that at least $35 of the $90 or more per barrel price of oil is a result of the increase in demand from China and elsewhere in the world. Clearly, the world might have responded by a "deal" in which Iraq could have expanded its production considerably, with some of the money used to pay back its debts and some of the money going to food and medicine for Iraq. Higher oil prices and increased output would have led to a boom in the Iraqi economy—instead of the disaster that emerged. With a GDP as low as it was at the beginning of the war, even Iraq's complete destruction would have added only a limited number to our tally—highlighting in a way the magnitude of these losses from the Iraqi perspective.
36. Samuel P. Huntington, *The Clash of Civilizations and the Remaking of World Order* (New York: Simon & Schuster, 2006).
37. "Operation Iraqi Freedom," White House news release, March 27, 2003. There seems to have been some disingenuousness in the statistics describing the "coalition of the willing" (as in other areas of the Iraq war). The exact number

of countries contributing troops is certainly markedly less than forty-nine—only four countries participated in the invasion, and of the forty countries that seem to have contributed support (in the widest sense, including logistical support), eighteen have now withdrawn, including Tonga's forty-five troops and Iceland's two. Moldova's support has dropped from a peak of twenty-four to eleven and Latvia's from a peak of one hundred thirty-six to three.

At President Bush's request, in May 2005, Congress created a $200 million Coalition Solidarity Fund that supports coalition partners in Afghanistan and Iraq. For example, Estonia received $2.5 million in Coalition Solidarity Fund money to support its troops—about forty in Iraq and eighty in Afghanistan. Albania, with its 120 or so troops in Iraq and 35 or so in Afghanistan, received $6 million, as did the Czech Republic, which has roughly 100 troops in Iraq and 60 in Afghanistan—Patricia Weitsman, "The High Price of Friendship," *New York Times*, August 31, 2006, p. A1.

38. A total of 173 U.K. troops through November 11, 2007, and 133 troops of other nationalities—Hanlon and Campbell, *Iraq Index*, December 3, 2007, p. 18.
39. Since the bulk of the Coalition forces are from the U.K, and since, at current exchange rates, differences in incomes are relatively small, the adjustments to take into account differences in living standards is relatively small, under 20%. We have conservatively assumed that the cost of a serious injury is, on average, 20% of a VSL, and that there are twice as many serious injuries as fatalities.
40. Some of the costs may be lower because of differences in per capita income; on the other hand, many of our allies may provide better disability benefits for their veterans, as well as more extensive public health care.
41. Joe Sestak, "Iraq and the Global War on Terror," 2006, at http://www.sestakforcongress.com/media/pdf/sestak_defense_060309.pdf (accessed December 6, 2007).
42. Providing in some years over 90% of the world's supply—UN Office of Drugs and Crime, "The Opium Economy in Afghanistan: An International Problem," New York, 2005.
43. Total International Security Assistance Force (ISAF) troop strength as of December 2007 was 41,700, with thirty-nine nations contributing. Contingents were led by the United States (15,038), the United Kingdom (7,753), Germany (3,155), Canada (1,730), Italy (2,358), the Netherlands (1,512), Turkey (1,219) and Poland (1,141). Additionally, approximately 7,000 U.S. troops are deployed under Operation Enduring Freedom, bringing the total of foreign troops to above 50,000—International Security Assistance Force, "ISAF Placemat," December 5, 2007, at http://www.nato.int/isaf/docu/epub/pdf/isaf-placemat.pdf.
44. "Afghanistan Army Needs 200,000 Troops to Assure Long-term Stability," Associated Press, December 3, 2007.

45. "Suicide Bomber Attacks Afghan Soldiers in Bus; At Least 13 Killed," Associated Press, December 6, 2007.
46. The British ruled Iraq (then called Mesopotamia) under a League of Nations Class A mandate when the Ottoman Empire was divided in 1919 by the Treaty of Sèvres following World War I. Mesopotamia was granted independence in 1932. During World War II, when Iraq sided with the Axis powers, Britain invaded Iraq again, fought a brief war, then reoccupied the country.
47. The United Kingdom contributed 46,000 troops, including army, navy and air force, out of a total Coalition force of 467,000—U.K. Ministry of Defence, "Operations in Iraq: First Reflections Report," July 2003 (http://www.mod.uk/NR/rdonlyres/0A6289F6-898B-44C5-9C9D-B8040274DC25/0/opsiniraq_first_reflections_dec03.pdf).
48. William Mathew, University of East Anglia, School of History, August 20, 2007, "Parliamentary Rubber-Stamping: The Military Costs of War in Iraq and Afghanistan, 2001–2007." See also Iraq Analysis Group, "The Rising Costs of the Iraq War," March 2007, which estimates that UK £5.4 billion was spent by the Reserves from 2001–02 through 2005–06 plus £1.08 billion from the Ministry of Defence, for a total of £6.27 through 2006. The total to date would be this sum plus the 2006–07 amount.
49. Jane Perlez, "Britain to Halve Its Force in Iraq by Spring of '08," *New York Times*, October 9, 2007, p. A1.
50. Operation Herrick (Afghanistan) Casualty and Fatality Tables, October 7, 2001–October31, 2007, Ministry of Defence, Defence Analytical Services Agency; and Operation Telic (Iraq) U.K. Military and Civilian Casualties, January 1, 2003–October 31, 2007, Ministry of Defence, Defence Analytical and Services Agency.
51. Under Secretary of State Derek Twigg, speech to the Confederation of British Service and Ex-Service Organisations (COBSEO) Annual General Meeting, October 25, 2007. British veterans are entitled to a wide range of benefits, including appliances, convalescence care, home nursing equipment, hospital traveling expenses, housing adaptation grants, prescription refunds, access to private or overseas care in some cases, treatment allowances, and priority treatment. Those receiving a war pension may qualify for clothing, comforts, home attendant, invalidity allowances, funeral expenses, mobility supplements, and other benefits. The amounts vary depending on the particular case.
52. Ned Temko and Mark Townsend, "The Fresh Agonies of Our Returning Soldiers," *The Observer*, March 11, 2007.
53. See, e.g., Matthew Hickley, "British Legion Accuses Defence Chiefs of Hiding True Scale of War Casualties," *Daily Mail* (London), March 17, 2007, p. 6. The article reports on "growing complaints over the treatment of injured

troops on NHS [National Health Service] wards have become a major embarrassment to the MoD"; problems at Selly Oak in Birmingham, the hospital where most casualties arrive; and the shutdown of the extensive network of dedicated military hospitals that once existed across the country.

54. Jonathan Ungoed-Thomas, "Focus: Our Forgotten Victims," *Sunday Times* (London), March 11, 2007.
55. Mr. Caplin reported £3.3 billion in payments to private health care providers in the U.K. in 2002–03—Question 118799 from Mr. Hoban, *Commons Written Answers, Hansard 2003*. (*Hansard* is the traditional name for the printed transcripts of parliamentary debates in Britain.)
56. Chief of the General Staff's Briefing Team Report, 2007, reported by Sean Rayment, "Army Chief: Our Forces Can't Carry On Like This," *Sunday Telegraph* (London), November 18, 2007, p. 1.
57. *Lords Hansard*, November 22, 2007.
58. "Recruitment and Retention in the Armed Forces," Report by the Commons Public Accounts Committee, and survey by the National Audit Office, reported in *The Times* (London), July 3, 2007.
59. The 3rd Battalion Parachute Regiment (routinely shortened to "3 Para") is an elite parachute battalion in the British army.
60. *Lords Hansard*, November 22, 2007.
61. Gordon Brown, Statement of October 8, 2007. General Peter Wall, deputy chief of defense, reportedly told the House of Commons Defence Committee afterwards that military planners did not think it was possible to draw down numbers below the 2,500 mark, and that additional numbers could even be sent in as reinforcements if the security situation deteriorates—See Kim Sengupta, "Military Planners Doubtful of Early Iraq Withdrawal," *The Independent* (London), October 24, 2007, p. 8.
62. Keith Hartley, "The Economics of the Iraq Conflict," *VOX: The Periodical of Politics, Economics, and Philosophy*, vol. 1, no. 2 (May 2006).
63. House of Commons Defence Committee, "Cost of Operations in Iraq and Afghanistan," Winter Supplementary Estimate, 2007–2008, November 27, 2007.
64. Although some U.K. estimates of VSL are much larger, in the range of £8.8 million, 1990 prices—W. S. Siebert and X. Wei, "Compensating Wage Differentials for Workplace Accidents: Evidence for Union and Nonunion Workers in the U.K.," *Journal of Risk and Uncertainty*, vol. 9, no. 1 (July 1994), pp. 61–76.
65. Energy Information Administration (EIA), "International Petroleum Monthly," September 20, 2007. OECD Europe includes the EU-15, which comprises Austria, Belgium, Denmark, Finland, France, Germany, Greece, Ireland, Italy, Luxembourg, the Netherlands, Portugal, Spain, Sweden, and the United King-

dom, plus the Czech Republic, Hungary, Iceland, Norway, Poland, Slovakia, Switzerland, and Turkey.

66. Ibid.
67. As we noted in chapter 5, the effects are expected to last much longer, at least through 2015, but we have only included cost increases through 2010 in our realistic-moderate scenario. Of course, the high prices will have some effect on oil demand, moderating its growth or even leading to reduced consumption. Still, by leaving out any impact going forward and including only $10/ barrel, we have vastly understated the oil impacts.
68. In contrast to the U.S. Federal Reserve Board, which focuses on growth and employment as well as inflation. And unlike the United States, where attention is centered on a measure of "core inflation," i.e., inflation exclusive of the highly volatile agriculture and energy sectors, Europe focuses on the overall inflation rate, to which rising oil prices have contributed.
69. Total Central Government Debt (percent of GDP), 2005, *OECD Statistics Catalogue*, 2007.
70. Ed Crooks and Matthew Green, "Soaring Oil Bills Put Pressure on Africa's Fragile Economies," *Financial Times,* December 29, p. 3.
71. A point that was emphasized to Stiglitz in meetings with the leaders of several of these countries.
72. "America's Image in the World: Findings from the Pew Global Attitudes Project," Remarks of Andrew Kohut to the U.S. House Committee on Foreign Affairs, hearing on "Global Polling Data on Opinion of American Policies, Values, and People," Subcommittee on International Organizations, Human Rights, and Oversight, March 14, 2007.
73. Pew Research Center, "Global Unease with Major World Powers: Rising Environmental Concern in 47-Nation Survey," Pew Global Attitudes Project, June 27, 2007 (http://pewglobal.org/reports/pdf/256.pdf).
74. Kohut, "America's Image in the World: Findings from the Pew Global Attitudes Project." These results are corroborated by other surveys. A BBC World Service poll (undertaken by the Program on International Policy Attitudes, and commissioned by the *Toronto Star* and *La Presse* in Canada, *The Guardian* in Britain, *Reforma* in Mexico, and *Haaretz* in Israel), surveyed 1,000 people in each country at the end of October 2006. Most striking, a majority of people in Britain, Canada, and Mexico consider President George W. Bush a threat to world peace, along with North Korea's Kim Jong Il and Iran's Mahmoud Ahmadinejad—Associated Press, "International Poll Ranks Bush a Threat to World Peace," *International Herald Tribune*, November 3, 2006 (http://www.iht.com/articles/ap/2006/11/03/america/NA_GEN_World_Views_of_Bush.php).

75. Kohut, "America's Image in the World: Findings from the Pew Global Attitudes Project."
76. This is a point that even conservative commentators have emphasized. Anne Applebaum, for instance, noted that "Countries that would once have supported American foreign policy on principle, simply out of solidarity or friendship, will now have to be cajoled, or paid, to join us. Count that—along with the lives of soldiers and civilians, the dollars and equipment—as another cost of the war"—Anne Applebaum, "Why They Don't Like Us," *The Washington Post*, October 2, 2007, p. A19.

Chapter 7: Exiting Iraq

1. "Corruption Perceptions Index 2007," Transparency International, December 2007.
2. Damien Cave, "Nation Staggered by Extent of Theft and Corruption," *New York Times*, December 2, 2007, p. A1.
3. Tina Susman, "Insurgents Attack Sleeping Villagers in Iraq," *Los Angeles Times*, December 2, 2007, p. A13.
4. Tina Susman, "Solidify the Gains, U.S. Tells Iraqis," *Los Angeles Times*, December 3, 2007, p. A3.
5. www.icasualties.org
6. Ahmed Ali and Dahr Jamail, "Iraq Slashes Food Rations, Putting Lives at Risk," Inter Press Service, December 27, 2007.
7. General Eric Shinseki, among others, had urged a much larger initial force. He was overruled by Secretary Rumsfeld and other civilians. It is widely known that Colin Powell privately advocated a higher number of troops at the outset.
8. Interestingly, the vast majority of Iraqis (80%) believe that the U.S. government plans to have a permanent presence in Iraq—O'Hanlon and Campbell, *Iraq Index,* December 3, 2007, p. 54.
9. A poll conducted by Opinion Research Business, March 2007, showed that 53% believed that it would get a great deal better, more than twice the number who thought it would get worse; and among the Shia, the imbalance was even larger, with 62% believing that it would get better, and only 4% that it would get worse—O'Hanlon and Campbell, *Iraq Index,* December 3, 2007, p. 49.
10. Survey conducted by the U.K.-based polling agency, Opinion Research Business, as reported by the BBC, "Basra Residents Blame UK Troops," December 14, 2007, at http://news.bbc.co.uk/2/hi/middle_east/7144437.stm.

11. Events in the fall of 2007 made it clear that Turkey will do what it chooses, whether we withdraw or not; it is obvious that neither the Iraqi government nor the American occupation forces can control Kurdish attacks against Turkey.
12. House Appropriations Committee Report 109-388 to accompany H.R. 4939, "Making Emergency Supplemental Appropriations for the Fiscal Year Ending September 30, 2006, and for Other Purposes," March 13, 2006.
13. These were among the reasons that President Eisenhower—who knew first-hand the horror of war—was quick to settle the Korean conflict after assuming office.
14. Iraq Study Group Report, p. 27.
15. O'Hanlon and Campbell, *Iraq Index,* October 1, 2007, p. 26.
16. U.S. Department of State, "Iraq Weekly Status Report," September 12, 2007.
17. O'Hanlon and Campbell, *Iraq Index,* December 21, 2007, p 26.
18. Economists often look to financial markets for judgments: they are "putting their money where their mouth is," in contrast to politicians, who are putting at risk other people's money and who typically have a vested interest in persuading others, for instance, that their strategy is working. Financial markets have not been particularly favorable in their judgments on the effectiveness of the surge; in fact, Iraqi state bond prices fell, suggesting an increased probability of default. A study by Michael Greenstone of MIT showed that, correcting for other factors that might have influenced bond prices, the market decline "signaled a 40 percent increase in the market's expectation that Iraq will default"—Michael Greenstone, "Is the 'Surge" Working? Some New Facts," NBER Working Paper 13458, October 2007, p. 1.
19. O'Hanlon and Campbell, *Iraq Index,* December 3, 2007, p. 46, from a poll conducted by D3 Systems for the BBC, ABC News, ARD German TV, and *USA Today*, in March 2007.
20. Recent events show clearly how much what happens in the region is beyond our control. The imposition of emergency powers by General Musharraf in Pakistan has left America isolated in supporting the dictator, as democratic political forces in the country become increasingly critical. The British Commonwealth suspended Pakistan's membership. America, which supposedly went to war to promote democracy, while it has criticized the imposition of the emergency, is left saying almost nothing about suspension of the judiciary. The assasination of Benazir Bhutto in December 2007 has shown even further the extent to which events are beyond our control.

    Similarly, tensions along the Iraq-Turkish border have risen to the boiling point, with Kurdish attacks and Turkish counterattacks. It is not clear that the

United States and the Iraqi government can fully contain the Kurdish attacks or Turkey's response—especially as support for America in Turkey is so low.

21. The *Iraq Index*, October 1, 2007, concludes that "there is . . . little good to report on the political front" (p. 4). Seventy-five percent of Iraqi's rate their security position as "poor," 91% as "fair" or "poor"—Ibid., December 3, 2007, p 53. Divisions within the country are evident in response to opinion polls on Prime Minister Nouri Al-Maliki. Some 96% of Sunni's disapprove of the way he is handling the job, while two thirds of the Shia approve—Ibid., p 47.
22. Economists refer to this problem as that of *time consistency*: it must still be in one's interests to carry out threats made at one date to be executed at a later date, when that later date rolls around. In the 1990s, America threatened to impose trade sanctions on China if it did not comply with a ten-point list of demands. The threat was not *time consistent:* when China did not comply, it was not in the U.S. interest to impose the sanctions. China knew this, and not surprisingly, the threat was ineffective.
23. The downward spiral resulting from initial decisions is well documented in Charles Ferguson's documentary film, *No End in Sight*, which won the Sundance Special Jury Prize in 2007, and numerous other awards.
24. In partial equilibrium economic models, the behavior of others (such as other firms) is taken as given, unaffected by the action of the firm in question.
25. By the beginning of 2006, 88% of Sunnis approved attacks on U.S.-led forces; 47% of all Iraqis did so—O'Hanlon and Campbell, *Iraq Index,* December 3, 2007, p. 54.
26. Even if, as we have seen, it does not fully disclose these numbers.
27. Burnham et al., "Mortality After the 2003 Invasion of Iraq: A Cross-sectional Cluster Sample Survey." This study was discussed extensively in the previous chapter.
28. We mistakenly thought that punishing those who supported the insurgency would *deter* individuals from joining; but as our discussion makes clear, the accuracy with which punishment is meted out matters a great deal.
29. A large number of policies served to increase the number of insurgents and their effectiveness; this increased perceptions of the likelihood of success, again reinforcing the insurgency's actual success.
30. Rational "game theoretic" models underlay the deterrence strategies of the Cold War. It is clear that, for the most part, such models are of little relevance in a world in which one party believes in the virtues of sacrificing their own lives.
31. O'Hanlon and Campbell, *Iraq Index,* December 3, 2007, p. 22.
32. Dr. Salam Ismael appears alongside U.S. chief Landstuhl surgeon Dr. Gene

Bolles in the independent documentary *Healing Iraq: A Tale of Two Doctors*, directed by Kevin Kelley (2006).

Chapter 8:
Learning from Our Mistakes: Reforms for the Future

1. For a broader discussion of the failures of America's system of checks and balances, see Frederick A. O. Schwarz, Jr., and Aziz Huq, *Unchecked and Unbalanced: Presidential Power in a Time of Terror* (New York: The New Press, 2007).
2. Cf. the discussion of Tony Blair's pivotal role in chapter 6.
3. Patrick Moynihan wrote eloquently on the dangers—and abuses—of secrecy. See Daniel Patrick Moynihan, *Secrecy: The American Experience* (New Haven: Yale University Press 1999). America passed its Freedom of Information Act after Nixon's abuses came to light. Sweden recognized its citizens' "right to know" more than two hundred years ago.
4. Greg Jaffe, "Balancing Act: As Benefits for Veterans Climb, Military Spending Feels Squeeze," *Wall Street Journal*, January 25, 2005, p. A1.
5. There has been congressional complicity in the use of emergency supplementals: this meant that congressmen and women also could avoid voting on huge appropriations for the war. They too seemed to believe that they could gain from the reduced accountability.
6. Chief Financial Officers Act, Public Law 101-576, November 15, 1990, and Financial Management Integrity Act, Public Law 97-255, September 8, 1982.
7. Executives in publicly listed private firms have been made personally accountable for the accounts of their firms under Sarbanes-Oxley. It is striking that public officials are not held to the same degree of accountability.
8. Required by the Federal Managers Financial Integrity Act of 1982.
9. Sarbanes-Oxley imposes criminal penalties, but we would not advocate imposing criminal penalties on government officials, because they have less control over financial assets than their private sector counterparts.
10. Congress has, from time to time, faced up to these problems and tried to improve the quality of information, e.g., by creating an independent Congressional Budget Office to provide assessments of costs of administration proposals. Some earlier directors, such as Alice Rivlin and Robert Reischauer, performed their role admirably.
11. VA, "Fact Sheet: America's Wars," and David Segal and Mady Wechsler Segal, "America's Military Population," *Population Bulletin*, vol. 59, no 4 (December 2004).
12. Robert Hormats, in his excellent book *The Price of Liberty: Paying for America's*

Wars (New York: Times Books, 2007), explains the important role that budgetary constraints have historically played in reining in kings with imperial ambitions from waging war.

13. Dividing the $3 trillion war by the number of U.S. households implies a cost to each in excess of $25,000, for this is the burden that the average American family will face as a result of the war.
14. This proposal runs against some technical economics arguments, which contend that the cost of unusual expenditures, like wars, should be spread out over a large number of years (this is called "consumption smoothing"). In the case of a major conflagration like World War II, which was *not* a war of choice, these arguments are compelling. But the political economy argument for forcing those undertaking a war of choice to have to bear *more* of the burden of the war we find even more compelling.
15. Cf. Reform 12 on page 200.
16. Monthly claims amounts could be adjusted downward, but we should not seek to reclaim amounts already paid, even if subsequent audits suggest that lower payments are warranted.
17. National Institute of Medicine, *A 21st Century System for Evaluation Veterans Disability Benefits*, ed. Michael McGeary, et al. (Washington, DC: The National Academies Press, 2007).
18. According to the Homelessness Research Institute, veterans comprise 11% of the total U.S. population but 26% of the homeless population—Mary Cunningham, Meghan Henry, and Webb Lyons, "Vital Mission: Ending Homelessness Among Veterans," Homelessness Research Institute, National Alliance to End Homelessness, November 8, 2007 at http://www/naeh.org/content/article/detail/1839.
19. Tom Philpott, "Bitter Split Over Making VA Care Open to All Veterans," *Military Update*, June 23, 2007.
20. Actual cutoff income levels vary according to the region of the country, but average between $35,000 and $40,000 a year.
21. Department of Veterans Affairs, "Seamless Transition Task Force Year End Report," December 2004, conducted as the "Seamless Transition of Returning Service Members Task Force" under former VA secretary Anthony Principi.
22. A National Priorities Project study shows that the number of recruits from the top quintile has declined since 2003; that in 2004, 13.1% had a high school graduate equivalency degree (not a high school diploma); and that today 26.7% have an equivalence degree (not a high school diploma)—National Priorities Project, "Military Recruiting 2006," December 2006, at http://www.nationalpriorities.org/Publications/Military-Recruiting-2006.html (accessed December 5, 2007).

23. "Declaration of Principles for a Long-Term Relationship of Cooperation and Friendship Between the Republic of Iraq and the United States of America," White House, November 26, 2007, signed by George W. Bush (President of the United States) and Nouri Kamel al-Maliki (Prime Minister of the Republic of Iraq).

Appendices

1. "Saddam's Oil," *Wall Street Journal*, September 16, 2002, p. A14.
2. Bob Woodward, "Greenspan: Ouster of Hussein Crucial for Oil Security," *The Washington Post*, September 17, 2007, p. A3.
3. See Alan Greenspan, *The Age of Turbulence: Adventures in a New World* (New York: Penguin Press, 2007), p. 463.
4. Andrew E. Kramer, "Iraq, with U.S. Support, Voids a Russian Oil Contract," *New York Times*, November 4, 2007, p. A4.
5. Joshua Partlow, "Missteps and Mistrust Mark the Push for Legislation," Washington Post Foreign Service, September 5, 2007; p. A12, at http://www.washingtonpost.com/wp-dyn/content/article/2007/09/04/AR2007090402190.html.
6. China's oil consumption increased by 153 million barrels in 2003, or 8%, after a 5% increase in 2002. Some oil analysts did underestimate not only oil demand in China and India but also in the United States where it increased by some 268 million barrels in 2003, or 6%, after having declined in 2002. But the Energy Information Agency model's *conservative* prediction of crude oil imports in 2001 for 2003 was right on the spot, and actual consumption was markedly lower than its projections for the high growth scenario—http://tonto.eia.doe.gov/dnav/pet/hist/mttimus1A.htm, accessed on October 6, 2007.
7. That is, the costs of extraction in Iraq (apart from the security concerns), Saudi Arabia, and elsewhere in the Middle East are much lower than $20 per barrel. In fact, the extraction ("lifting") costs in Iraq, ignoring security concerns, have been estimated at as low as $1 a barrel, and elsewhere in the Middle East at under $5 a barrel (more like $1–$2.50 per barrel). At $45 to $55, there are many alternative sources (shale, tar sands) that become profitable. (Some estimates put the total costs of "melting" a gallon of oil out of the tar sands of Alberta much lower than that.) But developing these alternatives will require heavy long-term investments, and the worry is that, should some semblance of stability be restored to the Middle East, oil prices would fall, and investors

would incur a loss—See Peter Huber and Mark Mills, "Oil, Oil, Everywhere . . ." *Wall Street Journal,* January 27, 2005, p. A13.

8. As we noted in note 7 of chapter 5, futures markets expect the price of oil to remain above $80 through 2015.
9. The increase in the price immediately after the war can in part be directly attributed to Iraq, as what it had been supplying to the world markets under the oil-for-food program was greatly diminished (by almost 1 million barrels a day). Oil prices had, of course, increased even before the war, in anticipation of these effects, so that the costs of the war began even before the war itself. Iraq produced 3.5 mbd in 1990, prior to the Gulf War, and is said to have one of the world's greatest oil reserves. Prewar, it was exporting 1.7 to 2.5 mbd. Exports have varied greatly—down to 1.05 mbd in January 2006, and up to 1.42 mbd by November 2007—still below the prewar level—O'Hanlon and Campbell, *Iraq Index,* December 3, 2007, p. 34.

   There is a further aspect of oil price dynamics in which the war played a role. High oil prices sometimes induce current oil producers to produce less and even to invest less in expanding production. They realize that the *demand elasticity* is low (so that small reductions in supply can generate large increases in prices), and that means that they have a real incentive to restrict production; but it is often difficult for them to act as collusively as they should (from the perspective of their own interests). When oil prices are high, they have less need for further government revenues; indeed, they often face difficulties spending what they have well. It makes more sense for them to keep their resources below the ground—which may appear as the "investment" with the highest rate of return.
10. See Alan Blinder and Robert Wescott, "Higher Oil Prices Will Hurt the U.S. Economy," Unpublished paper, August 2004, based on model simulations from Global Insight, Inc., simulation results supplied August 9, 2004 (results with a monetary policy reaction function engaged and disengaged were essentially the same); and Macroeconomic Advisers, LLC, simulation results supplied August 2, 2004.
11. See International Monetary Fund, "The Impact of Higher Oil Prices on the Global Economy," December 8, 2000, prepared by Research Department staff under the direction of Michael Mussa.
12. One of the standard studies, that of James D. Hamilton—"What Is an Oil Shock?" *Journal of Econometrics*, 113 (April 2003), pp. 363–98—estimates that *in the past* a 10% increase in the price of oil has been associated with a 1.4% decrease in GDP. A $5 (20%) increase in the price of oil thus implies a lowering of GDP by 2.8%, or approximately $300 billion *per year that oil prices*

remain at that level. A five-year price rise would generate costs of $1.5 trillion. Hamilton's analysis is consistent with an oil price multiplier that is much larger than the earlier studies. Hamilton and Herrera's more recent 2004 study suggests that a 10% increase in oil prices leads to a reduction in GDP of 0.5 to 0.6 percentage points, still much larger than the numbers that we use—James Hamilton and Ana Maria Herrera, "Oil Shock and Aggregate Macroeconomic Behavior: The Role of Monetary Policy," *Journal of Money, Credit, and Banking*, vol. 36, no. 2 (April 2004), pp. 265–86.

A word of caution in using these statistical studies: Many studies of the impact of oil price increases are based on the experiences of the 1970s. The world economy has changed a great deal since then. At the time, monetarism was in fashion, and governments put a lot of emphasis on fighting the inflation caused by oil price rises. As they responded with higher interest rates and tighter monetary conditions, the economy was dampened. Today, when many countries have adopted inflation targeting, monetary policy may still significantly amplify the adverse effects of increase in the oil price (cf. the discussion below). Moreover, in some ways the economy is less dependent on oil than it was at the time of the earlier oil price shock. The result of these changes is that recent oil price increases have had less of an impact than comparable increases in the 1970s—See William Nordhaus, "Who's Afraid of a Big Bad Oil Shock?" Paper prepared for Brookings Institution Panel on Economic Activity, September 2007.

13. Throughout the period, Europe had a high level of employment, and output was clearly below potential. So was Japan's for most of the period.
14. As a matter of theory, policymakers could respond in ways that offset or increase the direct effect of the oil price increase. Monetary policy response is determined by two offsetting factors. The oil price increase generates some inflationary pressures, and especially among central banks focusing on inflation, this leads to higher interest rates, exacerbating the slowdown of the economy. On the other hand, *if* central banks focus on aggregate demand and unemployment, it is conceivable that monetary policy could offset the adverse effects of oil price increases. If they fully offset the effect, then the *only* effect (in the short run) would be the transfer effect described earlier.

    Fiscal policy (such as tax collection) typically does not adjust quickly enough to stabilize the economy, and the effect of built-in automatic stabilizers (the impetus to aggregate demand automatically provided, e.g., by increased unemployment benefits as the economy weakens)—is reflected in the multipliers discussed elsewhere. Again, there are two effects. For countries with fixed government expenditures, the increase in the oil price means that there is less to be spent on domestic goods, and that exerts a downward effect on the economy. On the other hand, for countries running active countercyclical fiscal policies, the slowdown in the economy could be offset by such policies: the government could lower taxes to boost demand.

In the text, we have argued that over much of the period, the Federal Reserve seemed more focused on high unemployment and low growth than on inflation; it kept interest rates low to offset the adverse effects on the economy—with consequences that we are paying for today.

15. By contrast, in Japan, with interest rates close to zero in any case and fiscal policy stretched to its limits, probably little policy response can be attributed to the oil price increase.

    European policy responses contrast with those in the United States, where the aggressive lowering of interest rates meant that the U.S. economy slowed much less than it otherwise would have done. Indeed, some more recent reduced-form econometric estimates for the United States suggest a small multiplier—even as small as 1.0. But this analysis focuses only on the impacts *in the short run*. Aggressive monetary policy responses can offset the adverse effects, and may have done so, *in the short run*. There are, however, significant long-run costs of the monetary policy responses. In effect, the costs have just been postponed—and by being postponed, they may be even larger.

16. These dynamic feedbacks are even present in first-year income: increased savings this year leads to increased wealth next year, and that increased wealth leads to increased output (if output is sensitive to demand). But rational consumers will realize this—See J. Peter Neary and Joseph E. Stiglitz, "Toward a Reconstruction of Keynesian Economics: Expectations and Constrained Equilibria," *Quarterly Journal of Economics*, vol. 98, Supplement 1983, pp. 199–228.

    Consider a simple two-period model in which increased savings this period does lead to increased consumption next period. In standard elementary textbooks, which focus only on a single period, the multiplier is $1/s$, where s is the savings rate; but once taxation is introduced, the multiplier becomes $1/m$, where $m = s(1\text{-}t)$. But the *two-period* ($Y_1 + Y_2$) multiplier, that is the increase in GDP over *both* periods, associated with increased spending (say from investment) in the first period is much larger—$(1 + \alpha(1{+}r))/m$, where α is the marginal propensity to consume out of wealth and r is the interest rate. In a simple life cycle model with no bequests, where the only reason to save is for consumption in future periods, $\alpha = 1$, so the multiplier has more than doubled. The analysis here assumes that the economy is operating below its potential, that is, there is a problem of lack of aggregate demand. Some have argued that the United States was operating at close to its potential even as early as 2005. We have argued against this view; but the macroeconomic effects in a supply constrained model may not be that different.

When supply constraints are binding in some periods but not others, individuals may displace consumption to periods when they are not binding; so the net effect may be not much different from that which would prevail if demand constraints were always prevailing.

17. While these models predict that the effects are not fully felt immediately, they also predict that the effects are felt even after the prices come down. Our calculations ignore the timing of the impacts. Oil price shocks have effects that are different (and presumably greater) than many other shocks, since they adversely affect all the advanced industrial countries simultaneously.
18. We even believe the very large multipliers implicit in Hamilton's study are not implausible, especially when account is taken of potential responses from central banks.
19. 2003—6.0%, 2004—5.5%, 2005—5.1%, 2006—4.6% (average is 5.3%)—Bureau of Labor Statistics, Employment status of the civilian non-institutional population, at www.bls.gov/cps/cpsaat1.pdf.
20. In 2006, the number of workers officially unemployed was 7 million, up from 5.7 million in 2000; but in addition, 381,000 were officially categorized as "discouraged workers" (who had dropped out of the labor force, and therefore were not included), up almost 50% from 2000, and another 1.5 million were sufficiently marginally attached not to be included in the labor force (individuals who have looked for a job sometime in the prior twelve months, or since the end of their last job if they held one within the past twelve months, but were not counted as unemployed because they had not searched for work in the four weeks preceding the survey), up from 1.16 million in 2000. The numbers of those underemployed—working part time because they could not get full-time jobs—had increased almost 25%, to 2.1 million. In addition, increased numbers were on disability—above what one would have expected from the normal increase in the labor force—and many retired earlier than would have normally been expected. Slightly more than 0.5 million were in government training programs (and other government programs) and were thus not classified as unemployed; and an additional 300,000 were in jail and prison (an increase of 15% in just six years). All told, the *effective* unemployment rate had increased by 1.65 percentage points, almost three times the official increase (0.63 points). With a total unemployment rate (actual and disguised) of 2.5 million, it is hard to see how one could claim that the economy was running at its full potential—Computations based on the Center on Budget and Policy Priorities; the 2007 Earned Income Tax Credit Outreach Kit, the Center for Economic and Policy Research, and the Bureau of Labor Statistics.
21. According to the Bureau of Labor Statistics, while worker productivity (out-

put per hour in the non-farm business sector) increased by 18.8% between 2001 and the third quarter of 2007, hourly compensation, adjusted for inflation, increased only around 10.5%. From the end of March 2003 to the end of September 2007, productivity increased by just over 10.7%, while hourly compensation increased by less than 7.2%.

22. This is true even with the very loose monetary policy pursued by the Fed, which, while it may have offset some of the adverse effects in the short run, seems likely to cause significant adverse macroeconomic effects in the medium run.

    If the *official* unemployment rate were reduced to 3.8%, employment would have increased by an average of some 1.5% over the period. Typically, a 1 percentage decrease in the unemployment rate leads to a 2 to 3 percentage increase in output (this relationship is known as Okun's law, after Arthur Okun, chairman of the Council of Economic Advisers under President Johnson, and former professor of economics at Yale, who first enunciated the relationship between changes in the unemployment rate and changes in GDP). Thus, this reduction in unemployment would have resulted in an increase in annual output in the range of $338 to $506 billion, far larger than the amounts under consideration here.

    We have conducted a year-by-year analysis of the GDP gap, the discrepancy between actual and potential GDP, using a conservative estimate that the unemployment rate at which inflation starts to increase is 4.0% (rather than the 3.8% to which unemployment fell in the 1990s), and assuming a conservative estimate of Okun's law (we assume a coefficient of 2, in contrast with Okun's original estimate of 3). In every year, the GDP gap is greater than the amounts included in our analysis of the macro-impacts of the combined effects of increased oil prices and the war's budgetary impacts under our realistic-moderate scenario. For future years (through the period in which we have calculated short-run macroeconomic impacts), we have used EIU projections.

23. See, e.g., Rebecca Rodriguez and Marcelo Sanchez, "Oil Price Shocks and Real GDP Growth: Empirical Evidence for Some OECD Countries," *Applied Economics*, 37 (2005), pp. 201–28.

24. Adjustment costs help explain why sharp unanticipated increases in oil prices have (proportionately) far larger negative effects than those that are smaller and have been anticipated. This would suggest that the oil price shocks associated with the Iraq war may be particularly costly—See Hillard Huntington, "Crude Oil Prices and U.S. Economic Performances: Where Does the Asymmetry Reside?" *Energy Journal*, vol. 19, no. 4 (October 1998), pp. 107–32, and Joint Economic Committee, *War at Any Price?*

25. Much of the non-investment budget of the federal government is non-discretionary. Expenditures such as Social Security and Medicare are automatic and depend simply on the number of individuals eligible for benefits. This means that as Iraq war expenditures put pressure on other aspects of government expenditures, it is investment expenditures which typically are among those most affected.
26. This is true even if there is a gap between potential and actual output. Over the long run, actual output tends to increase as potential output increases, even if there remains a gap between the two.
27. GDP does include the value of wages paid to the soldiers, but there are reasons to believe that at least substantial fractions of Reservists and National Guard soldiers see a decline in their incomes (cf. chapter 3). But even if there were no decline, wages are typically less than the value of their productivity, e.g., because of taxes, including Social Security taxes. Hence, there is a *direct* negative effect on GDP.
28. And we also noted that some spouses may have had to drop out of the labor force, or go into part-time employment, because of the lack of backup support from their partners.
29. This is the thrust of the "new growth economics"—See, e.g. Paul Romer, "Increasing Returns and Long-Run Growth," *Journal of Political Economy,* vol. 94, no. 5 (October 1986), pp. 1002–37, and Robert Lucas, "On the Mechanics of Economic Development," *Journal of Monetary Economics*, vol. 22, no. 1 (July 1988), pp. 3–42.
30. If the economy really were supply constrained, the absence of these workers would contribute to the appearance of bottlenecks.
31. Allen Sinai, "Wars and the Macroeconomy: The Case of Iraq," Paper presented to a meeting of the American Economic Association/Economists for Peace and Security, January 8, 2005.
32. See F. P. Ramsey, "A Mathematical Theory of Saving," *Economic Journal,* 38 (1928), pp. 543–59.
33. The present discounted value of lost income of an investment I yielding a return of g at a discount rate of r is Ig/r. If $g = r$, the value of the lost income is just equal to the investment. But if, more plausibly, the discount rate is less than the opportunity cost—as it will be if there is capital taxation or constraints on investment—then the value of lost income exceeds the value of the investment itself.

    For instance, if $g = 7\%$ and $r = 4\%$ (as is the case for plausible values of capital tax rates), then the value of the lost income is 75% greater than the value of the investment itself, so that \$1 trillion of forgone investment generates a lost income, *in excess of the value of the investment itself,* of \$750 billion; if

g = 8% and r = 4%, then the value of the lost income, in excess of the value of the investment itself, is $1 trillion.

34. For discussions of the appropriate discount rate for long-term investments, see J. E. Stiglitz, "The Rate of Discount for Cost-Benefit Analysis and the Theory of the Second Best," in R. Lind, ed., *Discounting for Time and Risk in Energy Policy* (Baltimore: Resources for the Future, 1982), pp. 151–204; K. J. Arrow, J. E. Stiglitz, et al., "Intertemporal Equity, Discounting, and Economic Efficiency," chap. 4 in *Climate Change 1995: Economic and Social Dimensions of Climate Change,* ed. J. Bruce, H. Lee, and E. Haites (Cambridge: Cambridge University Press, 1996), pp. 21–51, 125–44; and William R. Cline, *The Economics of Global Warming* (Washington, DC: Peterson Institute for International Economics, 1992).

Index

Page numbers from 235 refer to end notes; page numbers in *italics* refer to tables